HOW TO DO just about ANYTHING ON A Computer

Microsoft® Windows®
vista™
edition

HOW TO
ANYTHING

DO just about
ON A
Computer

Microsoft® Windows®
vista™
edition

Published by The Reader's Digest Association (Canada) ULC
MONTREAL • PLEASANTVILLE, NY • SINGAPORE • SYDNEY

Contents

How to use this book   6

PRACTICAL HOME PROJECTS

TROUBLESHOOTING

How to use this book

Find out how this book will help you make the most of your PC

With easy step-by-step instruction, expert advice and inspiring ideas, How to Do Just About Anything on a Computer *will help you put your computer to the best use.*

Unlike most other computer books, *How to Do Just About Anything on a Computer* assumes that you are more interested in, say, creating a letterhead than you are in becoming an expert on electronics. For this reason, the book is organized into projects – all the things you are likely to want to do with your PC. These projects are designed to be of real, practical benefit to you and your family.

Learning to use your computer is more fun when approached in this way. You'll see why the programs work the way they do, and you can then apply these skills to other tasks.

Each project is set out into easy-to-follow, step-by-step procedures. The steps are accompanied by pictures that show you what you'll see on your screen. This means you'll never be left wondering "Where's the menu they are telling me to click?" because you'll see a snapshot that shows exactly where the arrow should be when you click it.

Before you explore the full potential of your PC, you need to set it up, learn some house-keeping and get to know Microsoft® Windows®, the ringmaster of your PC's programs. This is covered in the first part of the book: "You and Your Computer."

Today's computers are increasingly reliable, but the Troubleshooting section will help you solve any glitches. In most cases, you'll find what you need to get your PC running smoothly again.

All the rest is up to you: we hope you enjoy the countless tasks you can achieve on your PC.

Getting around the book

How To Do Just About Anything On A Computer contains four sections, taking you from the initial setup, to connecting to the Internet, applying your skills practically and solving problems. Each follows a similar step-by-step format with snapshots of what should be on your screen at each stage of the process.

You and Your Computer

This section guides you through setting up your PC, understanding the roles of hardware and software, and learning the basics of key programs. Find out how to care for your computer and how to maximize its efficiency.

The Internet

Learn how to connect to the Internet. Find out how to send and receive electronic mail (e-mail), and access information through the World Wide Web quickly and safely. You can even learn how to create your own blog and communicate with the online world.

Practical Home Projects

Choose from 38 practical projects that take you through the steps involved in creating a range of documents, including a recipe database, kitchen plan, address labels, home accounts spreadsheet, greetings cards and posters.

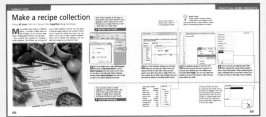

Troubleshooting

Your computer and its related hardware and software can behave unexpectedly at times. If this happens to you, don't panic. This section helps ease your concerns and offers a wide range of easy-to-follow solutions to common problems.

Special features

The book also offers the opportunity to apply your skills to real-life projects.

Make your PC skills work for you

The book contains larger tasks that require you to draw on the skills you have developed as you try your hand at individual projects. Use your word-processing skills, your spreadsheet know-how and your graphics experience to take the stress and drudgery out of moving house, running a club, or organizing a family celebration.

Glossary and Index

Found a word you don't understand? Turn to the back of the book to find clear, concise definitions of the most commonly used terms and phrases. You'll also find a comprehensive index to guide you around the book.

Which software?

This book assumes that readers are operating PCs that run Microsoft® Windows® Vista Home Premium Edition. With the exception of a few projects that use special software, most projects use either Microsoft® Office® (Small Business Edition 2007) or Microsoft® Works® 8.0. Any instructions for Microsoft Word (the Word Processing program within Office) will also apply to Works Word Processor unless otherwise stated. (If you are using Works Suite 2005 (or later), note that this includes Microsoft Word rather than Works Word Processor.)

And which hardware?

You do not need a top-of-the-line computer to get the most out of this book. The minimum specifications for your PC are a 800MHz processor, 512MB of memory, a 20GB hard drive with at least 15GB of available space and a CD-ROM or DVD drive. However, a 1GHz 32-bit (x86) or 64-bit (x64) processor with 1GB of system memory and a 40-60GB hard drive with at least 15GB of available space would make everything work faster.

Finding your way around the page

You are guided through every project in this book by means of a series of illustrated steps and a range of visual features. Here are the key features you should look for on the page.

Before you start
Projects begin with a Before You Start box. This outlines points to consider, documentation to collect, and tasks to do before beginning the project.

Extra help
Above and below the steps you will find hints, tips and warnings of common pitfalls.

Step by step
Projects are set out in easy-to-follow steps, from the first mouse click to the last. You get instructions on what keyboard and mouse commands to give, and what programs and folders you need to access to complete the project.

Other programs
This tells you which other programs can be used to complete the project, and how to access them.

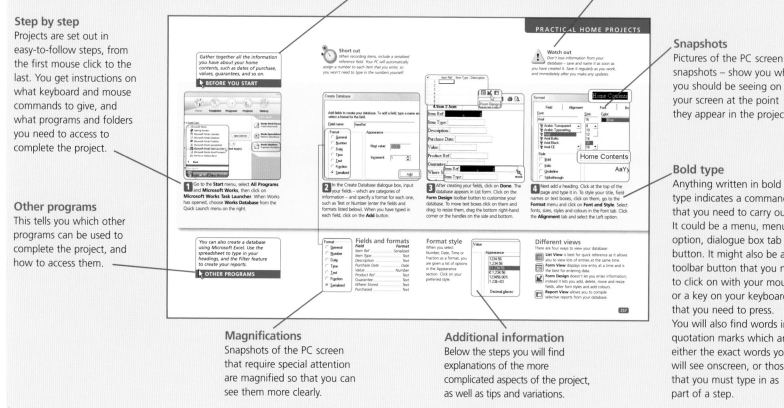

Snapshots
Pictures of the PC screen – snapshots – show you what you should be seeing on your screen at the point they appear in the project.

Bold type
Anything written in bold type indicates a command that you need to carry out. It could be a menu, menu option, dialogue box tab or button. It might also be a toolbar button that you need to click on with your mouse, or a key on your keyboard that you need to press. You will also find words in quotation marks which are either the exact words you will see onscreen, or those that you must type in as part of a step.

Magnifications
Snapshots of the PC screen that require special attention are magnified so that you can see them more clearly.

Additional information
Below the steps you will find explanations of the more complicated aspects of the project, as well as tips and variations.

Hints and tips
You will find additional information to help you complete the task at hand and to improve your understanding of the workings of your PC.

Shortcut
Look for this symbol for guidance on increasing your efficiency by learning quick and easy ways to complete common tasks.

Close-up
These offer an insight into the complicated workings of your computer, allowing you to get an idea of what happens "behind the scenes."

Watch out
These warn you about problems that you may encounter, or mistakes you might easily make, as you use your computer.

Keywords
Important words or phrases are defined in order to increase your understanding of the process being addressed on the page.

Bright idea
These are suggestions for variations or additions you can make to a project which can help you adapt it to your specific needs.

Talking to your computer

Your PC is always ready to carry out your orders. You can communicate with it in any of the following ways.

Menus

Some programs, such as Works, have a menu bar sitting across the top of the program window. Clicking on one of the menu options will reveal an extended menu, with many more tasks or functions available. You can then just click on the command you want your PC to perform.

Ribbon

Microsoft Office 2007 has revised the menu format into a "Ribbon." This runs across the top of the screen of all

Office programs – including Word and Excel – giving access to commands through different "tabs." Clicking on a tab changes the Ribbon to show buttons for a number of associated tasks, collected into "groups." Some drop-down menus will still appear where there are a number of options.

Toolbars

Toolbars feature a series of buttons that can be clicked to access frequently used commands. They offer a quick alternative to using drop-down menus in programs such as Works. The toolbar or toolbars (some programs have several) are located at the top of the program window or on the left-hand side of the screen. To find out what a toolbar button does, place your mouse pointer over it – in most programs a description (called a "tooltip") pops up.

Dialogue boxes

If your computer needs you to make a decision or give it additional information, a box will pop up on your screen asking you to confirm or alter the program's standard settings, or type in some information.

Do so by clicking in the relevant parts of the box, by selecting choices from lists, or by typing in what's required. Some dialogue boxes contain identification tabs, which

you click on to access other, related elements. In Excel's Format Cells dialogue box, there are tabs for Number, Alignment, Font, Border, Fill and Protection. If you click on the Font tab (below) you can select a font, font style, size and colour for your text.

Mouse instructions

You will often be asked to use the buttons on your mouse. These are the terms used:

Click Press and release your left mouse button once.

Double-click Press and release your left mouse button twice in quick succession.

Right-click Press and release your right mouse button once (a pop-up menu will usually appear).

Drag Press your left mouse button and, keeping it pressed down, move your mouse so that your cursor "drags" across the screen (this is used to highlight text or reshape an object).

Keyboard help

Use your keyboard to take shortcuts to commonly used commands (see page 74 for details). If you are advised to use one of the special "hot keys" (shown right), you will

often find a picture of the recommended key, such as the one shown left.

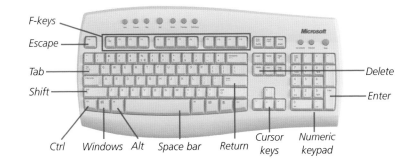

F-keys
Escape
Tab
Shift
Delete
Enter
Ctrl   Windows   Alt   Space bar   Return   Cursor keys   Numeric keypad

YOU AND YOUR

The better you **understand** your PC, the more you will get out of it. Knowing what each element of the PC does, and how to **set it up** properly, will get you up and running. And good **housekeeping** practices will ensure that your PC functions **efficiently**. Once you master the basics, you will have laid the **foundations** for successful computing.

COMPUTER

Setting up your computer

Your new PC has arrived. Start off on the right foot by setting up your work area properly

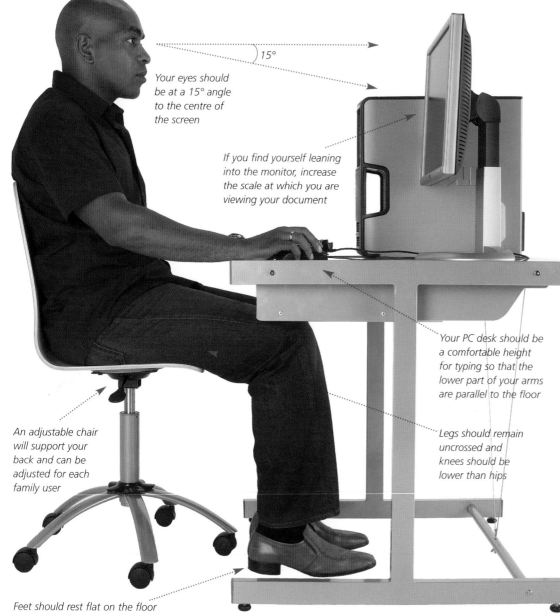

15°

Your eyes should be at a 15° angle to the centre of the screen

If you find yourself leaning into the monitor, increase the scale at which you are viewing your document

Your PC desk should be a comfortable height for typing so that the lower part of your arms are parallel to the floor

An adjustable chair will support your back and can be adjusted for each family user

Legs should remain uncrossed and knees should be lower than hips

Feet should rest flat on the floor

Your computer will be a valuable tool for all the family, so it's worth taking time to plan your workspace and system well, to ensure it is both easy and safe to use.

Ideally, it is best to convert a small room – or a corner of a larger one – into an office so that all the family can use the computer without being disturbed. When selecting an area, check that there is adequate space and several electrical outlets, not just for your PC equipment but for a desk lamp too. Unless you have a wireless modem, you will also need to be near a phone jack so that you can connect to the Internet.

Set aside some time – 3 to 4 hours – to set up your computer properly. Think carefully about how to arrange your area, as a poorly laid out system will be irritating and may even prevent you from using your computer to the fullest.

It's a good idea to spend some time reading those manuals, too. You need to know where to plug in the cables!

- **Invest in a proper computer desk. This allows you to alter the height of the monitor and keyboard, and tuck the keyboard away when not in use.**
- **Buy an adjustable chair, which all the family can adjust for good posture and maximum support.**
- **If your feet don't rest comfortably on the ground, buy a footrest.**

► COMPUTER FURNITURE

Naming and placing the parts of your computer

Your PC's hardware comprises all the parts that you can actually see and handle. Knowing exactly where to place each of these elements will ensure a safe and efficient work area.

Monitor
This houses the computer screen. Position your monitor to avoid reflections. You don't want a window *behind* it, either: that's a good way to develop eye strain.

System unit
The system unit (the actual computer) is where all the action happens, as well as where the peripherals meet via their USB cables. Leave enough space for airflow around the case.

Speakers
Many PCs now have built-in speakers, but if your PC has external speakers you should ensure they are well spaced at desk level or higher, not just pushed under the desk.

Mouse
Place the mouse to the left or right of your keyboard to minimize arm movement. Use a mouse pad to create the correct amount of friction for the mouse, and be sure there is room to move the mouse back and forth.

Keyboard
Make sure the keyboard is on a stable and level surface within easy reach. Leave enough space in front for hands and wrists. Ensure that the desk is at the correct height.

Printer
Position your printer near the system unit. Make sure there is sufficient space around it for loading the paper trays.

⚠️ **Watch out**
Repetitive Strain Injury (RSI) is muscle strain due to repeated actions. Home PC users are unlikely to experience problems but a good posture and typing technique is still essential. When working at your PC, stand up, stretch and move around regularly.

Hardware and software

Understanding how these operate is key to success

Hardware and software work together to allow you to perform the wide variety of functions possible on your PC.

Hardware is the actual "body" of the system, comprising the system unit and all the elements that you can plug into it, like the keyboard. Your computer's hardware determines which type of operating system you can use. Note that it is not always possible to use one type of system on another computer.

Software is the thinking part, or brain, of your computer, putting all the hardware to work. The most important piece of software on your computer is the operating system. By translating your instructions into a language the hardware can understand, the operating system lets you communicate with various computer parts and control how the com-

puter and its accessories work. Microsoft® Windows® is the most popular operating system for PCs. An operating system is so important to the workings of a computer that, without one, you cannot open any files, use a printer or see anything on the screen.

However, in order to perform specific functions, such as editing a report, playing a computer game or keeping a check on your household spending, your computer also needs to use special software, called applications or programs. There are thousands of programs available, each designed to perform different, sometimes specialized, tasks. Programs enable you to do almost anything, from writing formal letters and compiling spreadsheets, to editing your digital imagery and even making your own movies.

The other big player

The Apple Mac works similarly to the PC in that you access documents via a desktop. These days, many programs are available for both platforms, often with very little difference between the two versions, though the Windows version of a given application must be run under Windows, while Mac versions run only on the Mac.

Modern Macs can run Windows alongside their native Mac OS, but this book assumes that you are running Vista on a PC.

Introducing your software

Understanding what software does will help you to get the most out of your PC. This introduction describes the operating system and the different types of programs available.

The operating system

The operating system allows you to interact with the computer's hardware. It manages the saving of files on the hard disk, translates commands given through the keyboard and mouse, and sends data to the screen or printer.

It also interacts with other programs you may be running, allowing them to communicate with the hardware.

Any software packages you use rely on the operating system to provide this basic level of communication with the hardware. Most new PCs are supplied with Windows Vista as their operating system. Earlier versions include Windows XP and Windows Me.

Which program?

SPREADSHEET PROGRAM

For making complex budget calculations and carrying out financial analysis you can use a spreadsheet program. These programs can also show figures as a chart or graph, making it easier to understand.

WORD-PROCESSING PROGRAM

To write letters, reports and any other documents that are mainly text-based, use a word-processing program or the word-processing tool in software suites. Most include a range of fonts and style features and allow you to insert pictures in the text.

GRAPHICS PROGRAM

To work with pictures, use a graphics program. This will help you to create greeting cards, invitations, posters and personal stationery. You can use the graphics libraries available on your PC or from CD-ROM galleries. You can even use your own photographs.

DATABASE PROGRAM

To make address lists, or lists of contact details, use a database program. Software suites often feature a database tool, or you can use a separate database program for more complex work.

GAMES

Playing games is an entertaining way of becoming more adept on the computer. You usually have to buy each game separately, although some systems come with some simple games included.

OTHER PROGRAMS

Whether you want to access the Web and send e-mail, install specialized financial software or edit your digital photos, there are many programs available to suit your needs.

Mozilla® Firefox® is a registered trademark and Thunderbird™ is a trademark of the Mozilla Foundation.

Keywords

Software suite *A software suite like Micro-soft Office incorporates several programs into one package, often with a high degree of inter-operability and a much better price than the individually-boxed programs offer. Low-cost suites, such as Microsoft Works, offer even better value for money and let you do many of the same things as the more pro-level versions*

Storing software on your hard disk

All software, whether it be the operating system or programs, uses storage space on your hard disk. This space is measured in terms of "bits" and "bytes."

A bit is the smallest unit of computer storage. A combination of eight bits makes up a byte.

A kilobyte (KB) is 1,024 bytes; a megabyte (MB) is 1,024 KB; and a gigabyte (GB) is 1,024 MB.

A typical home computer will have about 60GB of hard disk space. This space is soon used up – the Microsoft Office suite alone can use several hundred megabytes of disk space, and the Microsoft Works suite uses around 40MB.

Making the most of hardware

Get the most out of your PC **by** understanding **the purpose of** each part

Once you have unpacked your PC and set up the different hardware elements, it's worth taking the time to get to know exactly what each part does.

All personal computers have the same basic elements. Knowing how they fit together and operate as a unit – and understanding where you fit into the picture – will help you and your family to get the most out of home computing. Your computer is simply a tool that, given the correct instructions and data, will make your day-to-day life easier and more enjoyable. You enter instructions and information into the computer via the mouse and keyboard. The results can be seen on your monitor's screen and printed out on your printer. The most important part of the system – the system unit – links all these elements together.

Whatever make of computer you have, it will have these same key components that allow you to use it. Although most computers look similar, there are variations between models, so always check instructions in the computer manual to make sure you're using your equipment correctly.

The mouse

A mouse is used to select items on screen and move the text cursor (a flashing line that identifies where new text appears). You move the mouse around with your hand and a mouse pointer moves around on the screen, allowing you to select menus and click on commands.

The monitor

Your monitor's screen shows you what your computer is doing. Monitors come in different sizes and, in the interests of preventing eye strain, the bigger the better. LCD (liquid crystal display) flat screens take up less space and can give much sharper pictures than older CRT (cathode ray tube) designs.

The keyboard

A keyboard is used for typing in data and commands, and has the familiar typewriter keys plus a number of extra ones. On the right is a separate numeric keypad, plus navigation keys (with arrows) that help you to move around the screen. There is also a series of function keys along the top that allow you to give special commands.

⚠ Watch out
Always use the Shut Down command from the Start menu before turning the power switch off. Never turn the power switch off when Windows is running. Most newer PCs automatically switch off power when shutting down.

💡 Bright idea
If environmental issues are a concern for you, look out for "green" hardware. Some manufacturers use plastics and packaging in their computer systems that can be recycled.

The system unit

This is where all the cables plug in. Your system unit will contain disk drives such as a CD-ROM drive. In new PCs, a CD-RW drive or perhaps a DVD-RW drive may be included.

Optical drive
Your PC has a CD-ROM and/or a DVD-ROM drive. Use it to install new software, and play music CDs or DVD movies. You may also have a CD-RW and/or DVD-RW for saving files.

Floppy disk drive
Found on older PCs, this allows you to store or transfer files to your computer on a floppy disk.

USB ports
Ports on the front of a PC makes it easier to connect devices.

Integrated sound ports
You can connect a microphone, headphones and speakers to these ports.

Power switch
This is used to turn your PC on. Some much older PCs also use this button to switch off.

Power socket
This is where the power cable plugs in.

Serial ports
Older PCs may have serial ports to connect the mouse, keyboard and an external modem to the PC.

Integrated sound ports
If you have speakers, a microphone or headphones with colour-coded plugs, they can be connected to these colour-coded ports. There may be other ports elsewhere on your PC for these peripherals.

USB ports
Use these ports to connect items such as music players, scanners, cameras and joysticks. They are also used to connect a mouse, keyboard and an external modem, if you have one. There may also be convenient extra ports on the front of your PC.

Printer (or parallel) port
On older PCs this provides the connection to the printer, although most now use USB ports.

PC expansion card slots
This is where you plug in the monitor. You'll also find a sound card here, and possibly an internal modem or networking card.

All-in-one devices

If you are buying a printer, you might consider an all-in-one device (AIO). This combines the job of several different hardware devices – a printer, a photocopier, a scanner and a fax machine. Some can also print directly from digital cameras. Not only do AIOs save on space and avoid the messy and confusing jumble of connecting cables, they produce good quality printouts at relatively fast printing speeds and are easy to set up and use.

Laptop computers

All the components of a laptop computer are in a single unit. The screen is smaller than that on a desktop computer. The keyboard is smaller and does not have the extra keys. The mouse is built-in, either as a tiny joystick or touchpad.

Laptops can be plugged in or powered by a rechargeable battery, but don't expect more than 6 hours use from a single charge.

17

Starting up your computer

You've set it all up – now switch on and begin using your PC

Once your computer's been set up properly, you're ready to get going – so remember to make sure it's plugged in!

Turn on the computer via the power switch on the system unit. You also need to turn on the monitor. The Windows Vista logo then appears above a set of scrolling green lights, showing that the computer is checking itself over. After a few moments you will see the Logon screen. Click on your username (you will need to enter a password if you use one). After a few moments you'll see a colour screen that Windows calls the Desktop. Small pictures (called "icons") will appear on the Desktop, and you may also see a message asking if you would like to find out about new features in Vista.

The Desktop icons

Through the Desktop icons you can access important utilities and all your work. To open an icon place your mouse pointer over the top of it and double-click with the left mouse button.

 In Windows Vista, click on the Start button to see the **Start Menu**. This contains links to all of your programs, files, photographs and music, and to system utilities and help text. The programs and files you use most often have their own links. Despite its name, the Start menu is also the place to go if you want to lock your computer, shut it down, or switch to another user. When you first start Vista, you'll see at least one icon on your Desktop, the Recycle Bin. Your PC manufacturer may have added others.

 Recycle Bin is where files or folders are moved for deletion. The bin can be emptied for permanent deletion, or items can be retrieved if you made a mistake.

 Computer shows you all your computer's disks (hard drive and CD/DVD drive).

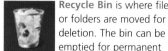 **Documents** leads to a folder that you can use to store any files you create.

Network allows you to access and view other computers connected to your own.

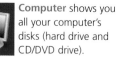

The Windows **Taskbar** is the area that, by default, is located at the bottom of your screen and contains taskbar buttons. It is divided loosely into three areas. On the left is always the Start button followed by the Quick Launch toolbar containing shortcuts to your favourite programs, such as Microsoft Internet Explorer. On the right is the notification area containing a clock and icons giving access to programs and important status information. As you open new windows, they will appear as buttons in the middle of the Taskbar, so you can always see what's open, even when other windows cover them.

Basic window features

Active programs and files are displayed inside windows, and your computer can display several windows at once. This key will help you find your way around.

Address bar
This shows you where you are, and also allows you access to other files and folders.

Minimize button
This reduces the window to an icon on the Taskbar.

Maximize button
This enlarges the window to fill the screen. Click on it again to return it to its original size.

Title bar
This displays the name of the window. To move the window, click on the Title bar and, with the left mouse button pressed down, move the mouse pointer across the screen. This is called "dragging."

Close button
This closes the window.

Scroll bars
To view any hidden contents of a window, click on the arrows at the ends of the scroll bar or click on and drag the slide bar up.

Menu bar
This contains drop-down menus through which you issue commands.

Window borders
To resize windows, place the mouse pointer over the window's border. When the pointer changes to a double-headed arrow, hold down the left mouse button and drag the window into the size you require.

Toolbar
Toolbar buttons provide shortcuts to common commands.

Status bar
This gives information about the contents of the window.

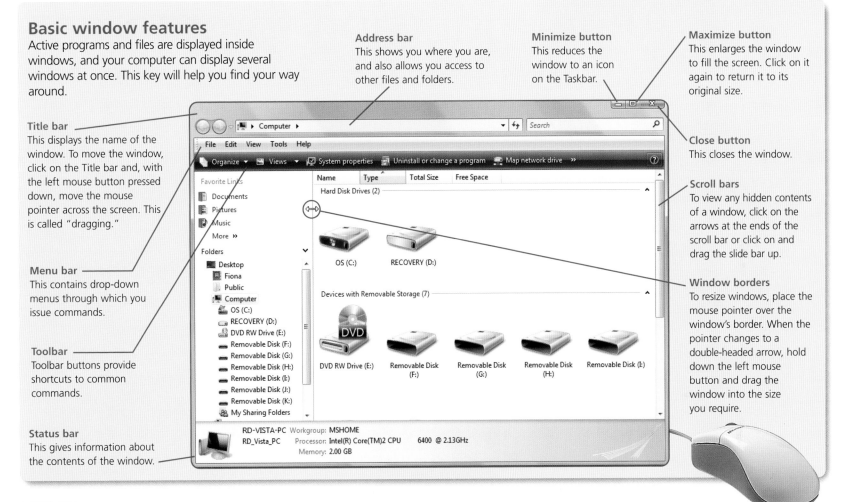

Windows Sidebar

A new feature in Vista is Windows Sidebar. This is a panel on the right-hand side of your Desktop, where you can place special "Gadgets." The Sidebar is normally open and displays a clock, slide show and news feed headlines. If it isn't open, right-click on its icon (found towards the right of the Taskbar) and select **Open**. To add a new gadget to your Sidebar, move your mouse to the top of the bar and click on the "**+**." To add the Weather gadget, for example, right-click on it and then on **Add** in the pop-up menu. To customize it (i.e. to change the location on the weather report), right-click on the gadget and select **Options**. Type in the location you want and click **OK**.

Using the mouse

Once your computer's switched on, you can really see how the mouse works. Moving the mouse on your desk moves the mouse pointer on screen.

Place your mouse pointer over an icon and a box will appear telling you what the icon does. When you want to look "inside" an icon, press the left mouse button twice quickly. This is known as "double-clicking." The double-click principle applies to the opening of programs or files.

An introduction to programs

Improve your skills **more** quickly **by getting to** know your PC's programs

Windows, the operating system, helps connect each element of your PC together but it can't perform practical tasks such as letter writing and calculating your bills. For these jobs you need to use additional software – called applications, or programs – which is designed to carry out specific tasks.

Personal computers are often purchased with a varied package of programs already installed – these are known as bundled software or software suites. Two of the most popular packages are Microsoft® Works and Microsoft® Office.

Your package explained

Works, a package of "mini-programs" grouped together, offers you tools to perform most of the tasks you might want to carry out on a home computer, and it also includes many pre-set documents, known as wizards, that you can customize for your own purposes (you are given step-by-step guidance on how to do this).

Works Suite is an expanded version of Works. It uses Word as its word processor, and contains some extra programs, such as an encyclopedia.

Office comprises several individual programs (Word, Outlook®, PowerPoint® and Excel). The more sophisticated capabilities of each of these programs, compared with their equivalent in Works, means that they can be used to produce a wider range of documents. Because they are more advanced, together they use up more of your hard disk space than Works. You will find templates available for both Office and Works.

Understanding your software suite

Knowing what each program in your software package can do will help you decide which will be the most appropriate for the tasks you want to perform.

Microsoft Office

Word is an extremely powerful word processor which is able to produce text documents of all kinds, including letters, memos, newsletters and posters. You have the option to create documents from scratch or, for many types of documents, to use one of the program's templates. Templates have a pre-set layout into which you enter your own text. This is a much quicker and easier way to create new documents.

Excel is a spreadsheet program, used for organizing and calculating numerical data. It is ideal for keeping track of all types of budgets and accounts. Like all spreadsheets, it takes the form of a grid containing "cells" into which you input figures and formulas to make calculations. Excel allows you to have several spreadsheets, or "worksheets," within the same document, and enter calculations using figures from each of the worksheets. This is particularly useful when organizing, say, a major event that comprises mini-projects. Once data is entered, you can then select, or "filter," specific information to analyze.

Excel can also produce a range of charts and graphs that can be used to illustrate your spreadsheet figures.

These are particularly useful as they simplify complicated numerical information, presenting it in a clear, easily understandable manner.

Outlook is an information management program. It contains an address book into which you can enter contact details for friends, family and business associates. It also has an agenda and calendar that will help you to keep track of your current schedule and forthcoming appointments. Outlook can also be used to send and receive e-mails through the Internet or through an internal company network (intranet).

PowerPoint is most often used in business. It enables you to create presentations for conferences, company meetings and marketing projects. It gives you the means to structure information efficiently and incorporate graphics within your text. It even offers animation effects to maximize the impact of your presentation. You can create notes for your own use in addition to handouts for your audience.

As well as being a useful business tool, PowerPoint can also be used at home to make a computerized slide show for your friends and family.

Microsoft Works

Word Processor. This program allows you to create a range of word-based documents, and has many templates to help you design pages. It is similar to Microsoft Word, but slightly less sophisticated – Word allows you to add colours and borders to text boxes needed to create business cards.

Calendar. This feature lets you keep track of appointments, important dates, birthdays and anniversaries. It integrates with the Works **Address Book**, so that you can be reminded automatically about a friend's birthday, for example.

Spreadsheet. This program allows you to monitor and analyze numerical data. It also offers a number of templates for common documents such as household bills, invoices and accounts, which you can customize and use.

Database. This program is ideal for recording details about related items. For example, you can record details of your household contents. Using its ReportCreator function you can sort and group selected information (say, to update your household insurance), perform calculations and add some explanatory notes.

Accessory programs

Accessories are small programs within Windows that perform specific tasks. Your computer will almost certainly contain a calculator, a drawing program (Paint), simple games and a basic word-processing program (WordPad).

To open an accessory program, go to the **Start** menu and click on **All Programs** then **Accessories**. Click on the program you want to use.

Getting around a document

Learn how to open a program and navigate around the screen

Opening a program and creating a new document will be among the first things you do on your computer. The process is similar in most programs. The steps are the same whether you are using a spreadsheet, database or word-processing program.

All programs can be accessed by clicking on the **Start** button on the Taskbar that runs along the bottom of the screen, then clicking on **All Programs** in the menu that pops up. Another menu appears listing all the programs on your system. Click on the program you wish to open. The program opens and a blank document appears. You can now start typing.

Before you do this, it's useful to understand the different parts of the window. The window shown below is from the Microsoft Word word-processing program.

Inputting commands

Whichever program you are using, you input commands using your mouse and keyboard. These commands might relate to the look of the document or to the material it contains.

The mouse

The mouse is the best way to access the command options available through the Ribbon in Office programs or through menus and toolbars in Works documents or in Windows Explorer. To activate items onscreen (a button on the Ribbon, for example), use the mouse to move the cursor over them and press your left mouse button down then release it (this process is known as "clicking").

If you are asked to "click," press and release the left mouse button once; to "double-click," press and release the left mouse button twice in quick succession.

If you are asked to "drag" (you will do this to move items on the screen or to select text), press the left mouse button and, holding it down, move your mouse. As you do so, a section of text will become highlighted, or the onscreen item you clicked on will also move. When the desired text is selected, or the item has moved to the correct position, release the mouse button.

"Right-clicking" – that is, clicking with the right mouse button – anywhere on screen will activate a pop-up menu offering formatting functions and other options. Click on an option to activate or open it.

The keyboard

The most obvious use of the keyboard is for typing in text and data, but it is also possible to issue commands by using special combinations of keys (these keyboard commands are discussed on page 74).

It is also possible to use the arrow keys at the bottom of your keyboard to move your cursor around within a document. Most people find this more laborious than using the mouse.

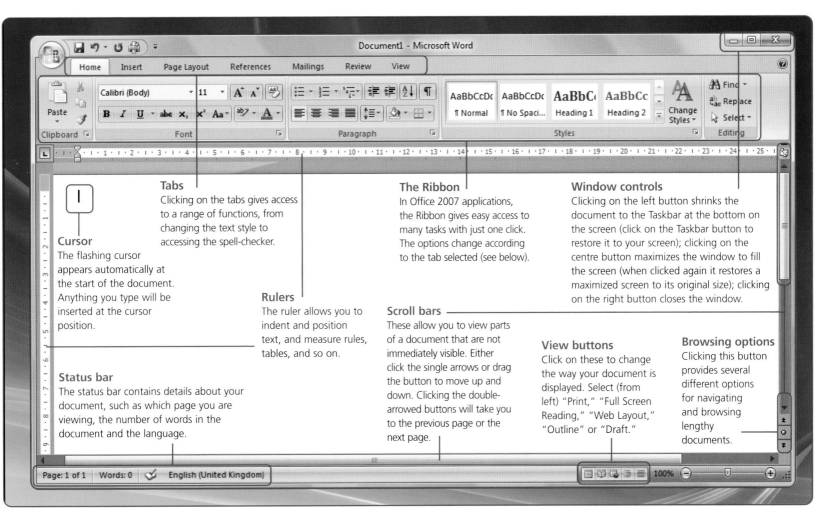

Tabs
Clicking on the tabs gives access to a range of functions, from changing the text style to accessing the spell-checker.

The Ribbon
In Office 2007 applications, the Ribbon gives easy access to many tasks with just one click. The options change according to the tab selected (see below).

Window controls
Clicking on the left button shrinks the document to the Taskbar at the bottom on the screen (click on the Taskbar button to restore it to your screen); clicking on the centre button maximizes the window to fill the screen (when clicked again it restores a maximized screen to its original size); clicking on the right button closes the window.

Cursor
The flashing cursor appears automatically at the start of the document. Anything you type will be inserted at the cursor position.

Rulers
The ruler allows you to indent and position text, and measure rules, tables, and so on.

Scroll bars
These allow you to view parts of a document that are not immediately visible. Either click the single arrows or drag the button to move up and down. Clicking the double-arrowed buttons will take you to the previous page or the next page.

View buttons
Click on these to change the way your document is displayed. Select (from left) "Print," "Full Screen Reading," "Web Layout," "Outline" or "Draft."

Browsing options
Clicking this button provides several different options for navigating and browsing lengthy documents.

Status bar
The status bar contains details about your document, such as which page you are viewing, the number of words in the document and the language.

Using the Ribbon

Office 2007 no longer uses toolbars and menus to access commands although these features are still present in Works. The new versions of Office's popular programs, including Word, Excel and Powerpoint, instead feature the Ribbon.

The Ribbon only presents options that relate to the currently selected object. The displayed functions change depending upon the tab chosen – "Insert" or "View," for example – and will also change as different items, such as a table or paragraph, are selected.

The buttons on the Ribbon are grouped by similar functions. Click on the buttons to access commands or click on the small arrow at the bottom of a group – called a dialogue box launcher – to see extra options. When you start using Office 2007, the Ribbon's one-click functions will quickly become second nature.

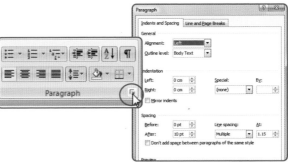

The basics of word processing

Learn the essentials of working with text in documents

Once you have opened a new document in Word, Office 2007's word-processing program, you can start typing in text. The great advantage that computers have over typewriters is that they allow you to revise and refine your text as much as you wish. You can also adjust the appearance of your text, its size, shape, colour and position on the page, and the spacing between individual letters, words and lines. You can even add special effects such as shadows. This is known as "formatting."

Becoming familiar with the terms used in word processing, and the basics of working with text, will enable you to create and modify documents with ease.

Setting up your document

Before you start typing you should set up the page as you need it. To do this, click on the **Page Layout** tab, then click on **Orientation** and select **Portrait** or **Landscape**. You can then click on **Size** and choose the paper size from the drop-down menu. Finally, click on **Margins** and adjust the settings if you need to, then click on **OK**.

Typing in text

> I would like to raise several points:
> • Seventy people have confirmed that they are
> • Twenty people have confirmed that they are
> • Four people have yet to respond

To enter text, just type on the keyboard. As you type, the words will appear at the cursor position on your screen. When you reach the end of a line, the text will automatically flow on to the next line. To start typing on a new line before reaching the end of the current one, press the **Return** key on your keyboard and continue to type.

Highlighting text

To format a section of text you first need to select, or "highlight," it. To do this, place your cursor just before the relevant section and

> Maureen Brooks
> 58 Somerfield Close
> Aldershot
> Hampshire

press and release your left mouse button once (this is called "clicking"). Press the mouse button again and, keeping it pressed down, move the mouse to the right (this is called "dragging"). As you do this the text appears in a blue bar. Release the mouse button when the relevant text is highlighted.

To highlight all the text in a document, press the **Ctrl** key and, keeping it pressed down, press the "**A**" key.

Formatting the text

Once text is highlighted it is ready to format, or style. Go to the **Home** tab and click on the **Font** dialogue box launcher (see "Using the Ribbon" below). Many of Word's formatting options can also be quickly accessed on the new Office 2007 Ribbon.

Fonts

Your word-processing program offers a range of fonts (particular styles of type).

Brush Script
Impact
Perpetua

To view the list of fonts, click on the arrows (this is called "scrolling"). Click on your choice of font (it becomes highlighted).

Colour

To alter the colour of text, click on the arrow next to the "Font color" box, scroll through the colours and click on your choice.

You can choose a whole range of different colours

Remember that too many colours on one page can be overpowering.

Effects

You will be presented with a number of special effects that you can apply to text.

Shadow
Outline
Engrave

To choose one, click in the relevant box (a tick will appear). Click the box again to remove the effect.

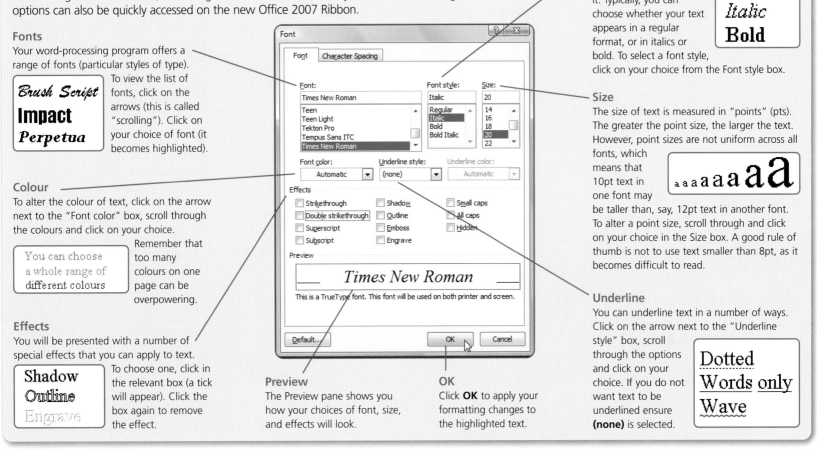

Font style

Once you have chosen a font, select a font style for it. Typically, you can choose whether your text appears in a regular format, or in italics or bold. To select a font style, click on your choice from the Font style box.

Regular
Italic
Bold

Size

The size of text is measured in "points" (pts). The greater the point size, the larger the text. However, point sizes are not uniform across all fonts, which means that 10pt text in one font may be taller than, say, 12pt text in another font. To alter a point size, scroll through and click on your choice in the Size box. A good rule of thumb is not to use text smaller than 8pt, as it becomes difficult to read.

Underline

You can underline text in a number of ways. Click on the arrow next to the "Underline style" box, scroll through the options and click on your choice. If you do not want text to be underlined ensure **(none)** is selected.

Dotted
Words only
Wave

Preview

The Preview pane shows you how your choices of font, size, and effects will look.

OK

Click **OK** to apply your formatting changes to the highlighted text.

Using the Ribbon

Most of the styling options shown above also appear in the "Font" group that sits under the Home tab. The tools within the "Font" group can be easily accessed with just one click – often launching a pop-up menu to choose from. If you would like to make a number of changes, it might be quicker to launch the Font dialogue box – click on the small arrow at the bottom right of the "Font" group.

To style your text, first highlight it and then click on the appropriate button on the Ribbon. (To see what a button does, place your mouse pointer over the button – a small box describing its function will pop up.) Buttons for changing text size, alignment and colour can all be found on the Ribbon. You can also change the font – select your text and click on the arrow by the font name. Hover over a font name and your text will change on the page.

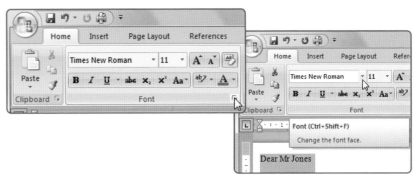

Laying out your document

Word allows you to adjust the structure of your documents, making them easier to read and drawing attention to important information.

Adding borders

To add a border around a section of text to give it definition, highlight the relevant text (here, the company address) then go to the "Paragraph" group under the **Home** tab and click on the arrow beside the **Border** button. Click on your choice of style.

Paragraph indents

A simple way to distinguish where each new paragraph begins is to indent its first line. Click in the paragraph, then launch the Paragraph dialogue box by clicking on the arrow at the bottom right of the "Paragraph" group. Click on the arrow beside the "Special" box and select **First line**. In the "By" box set the space required then click on **OK**. You can indent entire paragraphs by highlighting them and clicking on the **Increaseindent** button within the "Paragraph group.

Aligning paragraphs

To position, or align, text in your document, highlight the relevant section then go to the "Paragraph" group and click on the button:

Centre text

Align to left margin

Align to right margin

Justify text

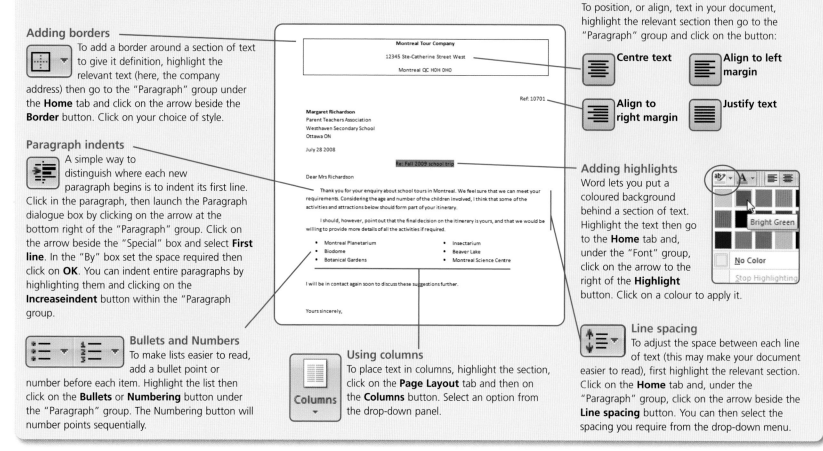

Adding highlights

Word lets you put a coloured background behind a section of text. Highlight the text then go to the **Home** tab and, under the "Font" group, click on the arrow to the right of the **Highlight** button. Click on a colour to apply it.

Bullets and Numbers

To make lists easier to read, add a bullet point or number before each item. Highlight the list then click on the **Bullets** or **Numbering** button under the "Paragraph" group. The Numbering button will number points sequentially.

Using columns

To place text in columns, highlight the section, click on the **Page Layout** tab and then on the **Columns** button. Select an option from the drop-down panel.

Line spacing

To adjust the space between each line of text (this may make your document easier to read), first highlight the relevant section. Click on the **Home** tab and, under the "Paragraph" group, click on the arrow beside the **Line spacing** button. You can then select the spacing you require from the drop-down menu.

What if I make a mistake?

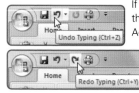

If you make a mistake, click on the **Undo** button on the Quick Access toolbar. You can continue to click on it to undo previous commands. If you undo an action you then want to redo, click on the **Redo** button. (In Works, you can undo the 100 previous commands. Go to the **Edit** menu and click on **Undo** or **Redo**.)

Moving or copying text

To move a section of text, go to the **Home** tab and use the buttons in the "Clipboard" group. Highlight your text and click on the **Cut** button

(left). The text will disappear. Position the cursor where you want the text to reappear, click once, then click on the **Paste** button (right) – the text will reappear in your document.

To copy a section of text so that it appears more than once in a document (you can also copy text from one document to another), highlight it then click on the **Copy** button (middle). Position the cursor and click where you want the text to appear, then click on the **Paste** button.

Finishing touches

Once you have finished formatting and laying out your document, it's a good idea to check it for spelling and grammatical errors. Also, you can now add extra features, such as headers and footers.

Spelling and grammar check

When you type in text, some words may appear with a wavy red or green line underneath. A red line indicates a possible spelling error; a green line indicates a possible grammatical error. When you have finished typing your document, go to the **Review** tab

and click on **Spelling and Grammar**, or press the **F7** key.

Your PC scans your document, selecting the underlined words for you to check and suggesting how to correct the "error." If you don't agree with any of the suggested changes click on **Ignore Once** or **Ignore All**; if you agree, click on the relevant suggestion then on **Change**.

Thesaurus

The Thesaurus function will help you find alternatives to repeated words, and suggestions for more suitable words. To do this, highlight the word you would like to find an alternative for, go to the **Review** tab and click on **Thesaurus** (in Works, click directly on **Thesaurus**). Or, press the **Shift** key and, keeping it pressed down, the **F7** key.

In the column on the right you will see a list of alternatives. Click on the word you want to use, then click on the arrow to the right of it and select **Insert**. In Works, you will see a dialogue box when you click on Thesaurus. Select a replacement word and then click on **Replace**.

Counting your words

If you are writing a long article or essay, it can be useful to know how many words you have written. Go to the **Review** tab and in the "Proofing" group click on **Word Count**. Word will also count the pages, paragraphs and even characters used. (In Works, you are given a total word count for your document, including footnotes, headers and footers.)

Headers and footers

Word-processing documents can include a section at the top and bottom of each page – known as headers and footers, respectively. Text entered into these sections automatically appears on each new page of your document. This is useful if you want to include a title at the top of each page or a date or page number at the bottom. To add a header or footer in Word, click on the **Insert** tab and go to the "Header and Footer" group. Click on **Header** and/or **Footer** and choose from the pre-formatted templates in the list.

In Works, click on **Header and Footer** from the **View** menu. Type your text into the "Header" box and add any repeating text in the "Footer" box. Then click **Close**.

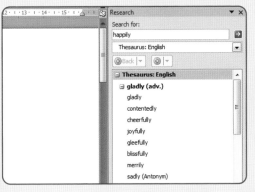

Templates

Microsoft Office 2007 has built-in and online templates to help you quickly construct a professional-looking document. Go to the **Office** button and click on **New**. In the "New Document" dialogue box select a category from the first column – its options will be shown in the second column and a preview in the third. Click on **Download** to use the template.

In Works, click on **Templates** and select a category from the left pane to see options in the right (if a subcategory appears, make a further selection). Then click on **Use this style** to finish. You are now ready to create your document from the template.

Figuring out spreadsheets

Learn how to use spreadsheets for financial planning and budgeting

O f all the computer functions, spreadsheets are the hardest to come to grips with. But a small investment of time and effort will soon pay dividends, because once you have the hang of them, spreadsheets can perform very complex financial calculations. You can, for example, set up a spreadsheet to work out the true cost of running your car, including such invisible expenses as depreciation and wear and tear. All you have to do is "explain" the task to the program once: it will do all the math for you, month after month, year after year.

Opening a new spreadsheet

This book deals with the two most widely used spreadsheet programs: Microsoft Excel and the spreadsheet tool in Microsoft Works. To open a document in either program, go to the **Start** menu and select **All Programs** then **Microsoft Office Excel 2007** or **Microsoft Works**.

If you open Excel, a new blank document will automatically appear onscreen. If you open Works, the Works Task Launcher will open. Click on the **Programs** tab, then on **Works Spreadsheet** button, then on **Start a blank Spreadsheet**.

Using templates

Microsoft Excel provides a number of templates that you can use to create your own spreadsheet. When you open a new document, click on the **Templates** button to see those available. Some will have been supplied within your Office 2007 software, but the majority need to be downloaded for free from the Microsoft Online Web site.

Saving your document

After opening a new document in Excel, go to the **Office** button and select **Save As**, then **Excel Workbook**. In the Save As dialogue box, name your document and click on **Save**. In Works, go to the **File** menu and click on **Save As**. The Save As dialogue box appears. Click on the arrow at the side of the "Save in" box and scroll down to select a folder in which to save your document. Enter a file name, then click on **Save**.

Finding your way around

Identifying the various elements of your spreadsheet document will help you to navigate around it more easily, and so use it more effectively. Most elements are the same for all spreadsheet programs.

Understanding spreadsheets

A spreadsheet is a grid of "cells." The columns are like the columns in a ledger – you can use them to make lists of figures and perform calculations. Each column is identified by a letter of the alphabet, and each row by a number. So every cell has its own unique address, comprising the letter of the column and the number of the row it is in (A1, A2, and so on). You can type numbers, text or formulas into these cells. The formulas make it possible to get the program to do all the complicated and laborious math for you.

Using the Formula bar to input data

When you first open a spreadsheet, cell A1 is automatically selected as the "active cell" – indicated by a thick black line around the cell – and you can type directly into it. To make entries into other cells, click on them first. As you make entries, they will appear in the Formula bar located below the toolbars. You can view and edit the contents of a cell in the Formula bar.

To the left of the Formula bar are two buttons (marked "**X**" and "**✔**") that only appear after you type something in. If you make a mistake, click on the **X** button to cancel it; otherwise, click on the **✔** button to enter it (or press the **Return** or **Tab** keys).

What you can see

Spreadsheets look quite complicated. However, once you understand how they work and how to find your way around them, they are easy to use. The documents displayed here are from Microsoft Excel. The main difference between these and Works documents is that there are fewer toolbar options in Works.

When using spreadsheets, the mouse pointer becomes a thick white cross, rather than the normal arrowhead you will see elsewhere.

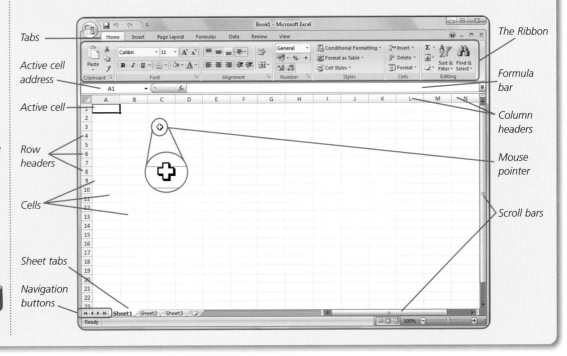

Tabs

Active cell address

Active cell

Row headers

Cells

Sheet tabs

Navigation buttons

The Ribbon

Formula bar

Column headers

Mouse pointer

Scroll bars

Moving around a spreadsheet

You can move from one cell to the next in several ways. You can either click on the next cell using your mouse, navigate to the cell you want using the four arrow keys on your keyboard, or press the **Tab** key. To move to a previous cell, press the **Shift** key and, keeping it pressed down, the **Tab** key.

In Excel, unless you want to move to a new row, do not press the **Return** key, as this will activate the cell below the one you are currently in.

Selecting cells

You can select cells for styling, cutting and copying in several ways. To select a column or row of cells, click on the blue column or row header. To select cells that are adjacent to each other, click on the first cell and, keeping the left mouse button pressed down, drag the cursor across or down the screen until the entire range of cells is selected, then release the mouse button.

If the cells you want to select are not adjacent, but are dotted throughout the spreadsheet, press the **Ctrl** key on your keyboard and, keeping it pressed down, click on each of the cells in turn.

Tips for using spreadsheets effectively

When you are dealing with numbers, it pays to give some thought to how to lay out the spreadsheet. When you type in information, be as careful as possible.

Adding titles and headings

To make it easier to identify your spreadsheet and navigate around it, it is helpful to enter a title at the top of the sheet, and to give separate headings to columns and rows. To do this, click on a cell and type in your text.

Adjusting column widths

If an entry is too long for its cell, adjust the width of the column. Place your mouse pointer over the right-hand edge of the blue column header. When it becomes a double-headed arrow, press the left mouse button and, keeping it pressed down, drag it to the desired width. Release the mouse button. You can make the column automatically adjust to include the widest entry in any of its cells by placing the mouse pointer in the same position and double-clicking.

Locking row and column headings

Often, column and row headings can disappear off screen when you scroll through large spreadsheets, making it difficult to keep track of which figures relate to what. To keep the headings viewable at all times, drag the small button at the top of the scroll bar down. This splits the worksheet into two independent panes, one to house the headings, one for the rest of the spreadsheet.

Enter identical data in multiple cells

To enter the same data into adjacent cells in a row or column – or common data that has a set sequence, such as the months of the year or days of the week – use the Fill function. Type an entry into the first cell. Place the mouse pointer in the lower right-hand corner of the cell. When it becomes a small black cross, press the left mouse button, keep it pressed and drag it over the cells you'd like filled. Release the mouse. To enter the same number into several columns and rows at once, select the cells and type in the number. Now press the **Ctrl** key and, with it, the **Return** key.

Moving and copying data

To move data, use the Cut, Copy and Paste commands found under the **Home** tab. Highlight the cells you want to place elsewhere (the source range). To remove the source range, click on the **Cut** button (left). The cells become selected. To leave the source range in its position and copy it, click on the **Copy** button (middle) instead. Now click on the top left-hand cell of the position where you want the moved information to appear (the target range). Click on the **Paste** button (right).

Insert and delete columns and rows

Your spreadsheet design can be edited according to your needs. For example, you can insert a new column or row. To do this in Excel, click on the blue column or row header (these contain either a letter or number) where you'd like your new one to be placed. Go to the **Home** tab and in the "Cells" group click on **Insert**. You can then select **Insert Sheet Rows** or **Insert Sheet Columns** from the drop-down menu. A new row/column appears before the one where your cursor is positioned. To delete a row or column, click on its header, then on the **Delete** button.

In Works, all four commands – Insert Row, Delete Row, Insert Column and Delete Column – are found in the Insert menu.

Sorting by rows

Spreadsheet entries can easily be sorted, or prioritized. You can, for example, have items appear in order of expense. To do this, select the column(s) to be sorted. In Excel, go to the **Home** tab and in the "Editing" group click on **Sort & Filter** then on **Sort**. In Works, go to the **Tools** menu and click on **Sort**. Both Excel and Works allow you to choose which column or columns you want to sort. You can choose whether you want to list the results in ascending (A-Z) or descending (Z-A) order. Make your choices then click on **OK**.

Formatting cells

To change the style of the text or figures in your spreadsheet, first select the cell or cells to be formatted. Next, go to the **Home** tab and in the "Cells" group click on the **Format** button. Select **Format Cells** at the bottom of the menu.
In the Format Cells dialogue box, click on the **Font** tab. Select a font, style, size and colour as desired, then click on **OK**. Alternatively, select the cells then click on the relevant buttons in the "Font" group.

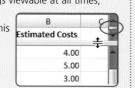

Performing calculations

It is the ability of spreadsheets to perform complex calculations which makes them such a powerful tool. It is worth the effort to learn how to use formulas correctly.

Adding figures

In Excel you can add together the contents of columns, rows or any combination of selected cells. Select the cells and their total is displayed on the Status bar at the bottom of the screen.

| 10 |
| 10 |
| 10 |
| 10 |
| Sum: 50 | 10 |

Using the AutoSum function

Both Excel and Works have an AutoSum toolbar button to calculate figures.

In Excel, to add figures in adjacent cells in a column or a row, select the relevant cells then go to the **Formulas** tab and click on the **AutoSum** button. The total will be displayed in the next cell of the column or row.

In Works, you must click on a blank cell in the column or row you want calculated, then click on the **AutoSum** button. The cell references, or addresses, for the cells will appear in a formula. If they are correct, press **Return**; if not, type in the correct cell references. The total will appear in your selected cell.

`=SUM(C2,D2,D3,` In Excel, to add up figures in cells that are not adjacent to each other, click on an empty cell, then on the **AutoSum** button. The selected cell will display the legend "=SUM()". Enter the cell references of the cells to be calculated. You can do this manually or by clicking on them, inserting a comma between each one. Each co-ordinate will be added to the formula automatically. Press the **Return** key.

To add up figures in cells that are not adjacent to each other in Works, click on an empty cell then press the "=" key on your keyboard. Works now knows you want to enter a formula. Enter the cell references of the cells to be calculated, either manually or by clicking on them, inserting a "+" sign between each one. Press **Return**.

To delete a formula in a cell press the **Delete** key.

Further functions in Excel

There are a number of preset functions in Excel that can take the effort out of spreadsheet calculations. Click on an empty cell to make it active and type in "=". Click on the arrow button between the Active cell address box and the Cancel button near the top of the window. A drop-down menu will appear. Click on an option and a dialogue box will appear, giving a brief description of the function it performs, such as the average value of selected cells, or depreciation of an asset (for example, a car) over a specified time period.

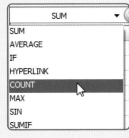

SUM
SUM
AVERAGE
IF
HYPERLINK
COUNT
MAX
SIN
SUMIF

Further functions in Works

For other calculation functions in Works, click on the **Easy Calc** button on the toolbar. A dialogue box appears, listing common calculations and more specialized ones. Click on the **Other** button at the bottom of the box for a scrollable menu of the program's 76 pre-set functions with more detailed descriptions.

Easy Calc
Click the function you want to use in your formula.

Common functions
Add — Adds together two or m
Subtract — using a formula.
Multiply
Divide
Average

Other functions
Other — Displays a complete list of functions

Cancel | < Back

More complex equations in Excel and Works

You are not restricted to simple sums – you can create formulas for any type of calculation. Click on an empty cell and press the "=" key. Then type in the cell references of the cells to be calculated in your formula, separating them by the relevant "operators" – the symbols for addition (+), subtraction (-), multiplication (*) and division (/). Press the **Return** key.

Item	Units ordered	Price per unit	Total	Disc
Gloss Paint	6	9.99	59.94	
Brushes	4	5.99	=B3*C3	
Sandpaper	3	6.99		

Spreadsheet programs automatically process some operators before others (for example, multiplication and division before addition or subtraction) so, to ensure that one part of the equation is calculated before the rest, enclose it in brackets.

| Final Total | =(D2-E2)*(D3-E3) |

Setting number formats

To help prevent incorrect calculations in Excel, it is wise to format cells for currency, dates, percentages, times, and so on. Select your cell(s) then go to the **Home** tab and in the "Cells" group click on the **Format** button. Select **Format Cells** from the drop-down menu and in the dialogue box click on the **Number** tab. Choose "Number" from the menu of options, select the number of decimal places and, if a negative number, a style, then click on **OK**. Works offers fewer options: go to the **Format** menu and choose **Number**.

| Number | Alignment | Font | Border | Fill | Protection |

Category:
General
Number
Currency
Accounting
Date
Time
Percentage
Fraction
Scientific
Text
Special
Custom

Sample
1,436.16

Decimal places: 2

☑ Use 1000 Separator (,)

Negative numbers:
-1,234.10
1,234.10
-1,234.10
-1,234.10

An introduction to databases

Learn **how to use** database programs **to keep records that** you can sort

Databases are used for storing and organizing large amounts of data about related topics. For example, you can create a database to catalogue your recipe collection and then search it to find all the lamb dishes or all the dishes using coriander.

A database's ability to organize and prioritize data in different ways also makes it suitable for storing names, addresses and contact details. If you forget someone's last name, you can search the database by first name only, by phone number or by address.

But databases are far more than just deposit boxes for information. They can also make useful calculations – for instance, enter the value of each item of your household contents, then add up the total value to provide a guide to how much you should insure your possessions for.

Working with fields

The building blocks of a database are fields. Each field represents a category of information. In an address database, they might be last name, first name, address, telephone number, and so on. To build a database, you must first create fields for it.

Membership No.	First Name	Surname	Street Address	To

Creating records

Once the fields have been created you can begin to make your entries – each entry is known as a record. For each record, you fill in the fields.

First Name: Gillian
Surname: Foster
Street Address: 1234 1st Str
Town or City: Vancouver

The database allows you to organize the records in a number of ways – for example, you can list them in alphabetical order or by date. You can also browse through the records, search for a particular entry and print out selected aspects.

Opening a new database

In the **Start** menu select **All Programs** then **Microsoft Works Task Launcher**. From the Quick Launch menu on the right-hand side click on **Works Database**. When the Microsoft Works Database dialogue box appears, select **Blank Database** and then click on **OK**.

Building a database

When you open a new database, the Create Database dialogue box appears, in which you specify fields. Don't worry if you leave one out, or enter them in the wrong order, as you can edit your database later.

Setting up fields

As you enter field names you are given a chance to format and choose a style for them.

Field name

Type your field name into this box. Field names should not be more than 15 characters long (this includes spaces between words). The more fields you create, the greater the flexibility of your database. It is sensible, for example, to create separate fields for first and last names so you can search by either category.

Try to enter field names in the order that you wish them to appear in your database. It's good practice to be as organized as possible at this stage.

Format

You have a choice of formats for your field names. These relate to the type of information you are entering. The date field, for example, is automatically set up for the day, month and year. Select an option by clicking it. A small black dot indicates that the Format is active. Choose the following formats for the appropriate information:

General This is the default setting for all field names. Text entries are aligned to the left, and numbers to the right.

Number This lets you specify the way that numbers are displayed. For example, you can select the number of decimal places, or whether negative numbers appear in red.

Date Select this to specify how dates are displayed – by month only, with or without the year, or with the month as text rather than a number.

Time Select either "AM" or "PM," and whether to include seconds as well as hours and minutes.

Text Use this if you want to display numbers as text rather than figures, or if you wish to include dashes or spaces (these are particularly useful when entering telephone numbers).

Fraction If you want to store fractions – 2¾, for example – choose this format. When entering data, type a space between the whole number (2) and the fraction (3/4) to let Works tell them apart. The decimal equivalent appears in the Entry bar when the cell containing a fraction is selected.

Serialized Choose this format to get Works to automatically add a serial number to each record. This unique number is useful if you need to sort records into the order in which they were entered.

Appearance

You will be given style choices for how you want your number, date, time, fraction and serialized formats to appear. For example, you may want to include decimal values in your numbers, and to have months written out in full in dates. Scroll through the lists and click on your choice.

Add/Exit

After you have created a field and selected a format and appearance for it, click on the **Add** button to confirm your selection and move to another field. When you have created all your database fields click on **Exit**. Your database will appear in List View, with your field names as headings at the top of columns.

✓		Membership No.	First Name	Surname	Stre
☐	1				
☐	2				

Database programs

Microsoft Works includes a database tool. It also contains a selection of database templates – you can open these and use them as they are, or customize for your own needs.

Microsoft Office The Standard edition of Microsoft Office does not include a specific database program, but its spreadsheet program, Microsoft Excel, can perform many of the same tasks (see page 35).

Saving your database

When your database appears for the first time in List View, it is called "Unsaved Database." You should save it immediately with an appropriate name.

Click on the **Save** toolbar button or go to the **File** menu and click on **Save As**. A dialogue box appears. In the "File name" box type in a name for your database. Click on the arrow beside the "Save in" box to see the destinations to which you can save your file. Select a folder then click on **Save**. For more detailed information on saving documents, see page 36.

Save As

Save in: Business Records

Name	Date modif...	Type

File name: Club Database

Save as type: Works (*.wdb)

Getting around your database

Your new database appears in List View, which looks similar to a spreadsheet. There are three other ways to view your database, too. Become familiar with them before entering any records.

Different points of view

You can view your database in four different ways, each of which lends itself best to a particular use. All the views can be accessed via the **View** menu, or by clicking on the appropriate buttons on the toolbar.

List View

Immediately after you create your fields, your database is displayed in List View. This view allows you to see a number of records at the same time. It is useful when you simply want to browse your records, move data (copy and paste) from one record to another, or when entering a series of numbers or dates.

You can enter information into your database in List View by first clicking on a cell then typing your entry (it also appears in the Entry bar at the top of the window). List View is also used to display the results of any searches that you run.

Form View

Each record can be viewed separately using Form View. Most people prefer to enter information using this view – it means you can see the entries for all the other fields as you enter new data into the database.

Membership No:	00001
First Name:	Gillian
Surname:	Foster
Street Address:	1234 1st Street
Town or City:	Vancouver

Form Design

In Form Design you structure the look of the Form View. You can rearrange fields and their adjoining field boxes to suit your own needs.

You can also style the field labels by using a contrasting font or adding a colour and other elements. Here, for example, we have used colour and a border to give focus to the club name.

To move field names around the page, click on them and drag them into place.

To adjust the size of a field box, first click on the right or bottom edge, or the bottom right-hand corner of the field box, and then, with the left mouse button pressed down, drag it until all the information you want to include fits in the box.

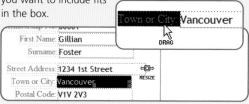

Report View

A good database allows you to extract data. Through Report View you can design and print out a report that organizes your information by related subjects. It also lets you perform calculations on fields, such as the total of subscription fees club members have paid to date.

Club Database.wdb - Money Owed

Membership No	Surname	Total Due
00001	Foster	$700.00
00002	Ianni	$500.00
00003	Kingsley	$0.00
00004	Beaulieu	$0.00
00005	Davidowicz	$700.00
00006	O'Riordan	$500.00
TOTAL Total Due:		$2,400.00

Inputting your records

You can enter data into your database in either List View or Form View.

In List View, click on the relevant cell and type into it. To move to the next cell, either click in it using your mouse, or press the **Tab** key on your keyboard. (To return to a previous field, or cell, press **Shift** and **Tab**.) Unlike spreadsheet programs, pressing the Return key will not move your cursor to the next cell or row in a database.

In Form View, click the field box adjoining the field name and type your data. Press the **Tab** key to move to the next field (or the next record when you come to the end of the current one), and the **Shift** and **Tab** keys to return to a previous field, or record.

Navigating through forms

In Form View and Form Design you can view other records by clicking on the appropriate arrows displayed on each side of the current record number at the bottom of the window.

The arrows immediately to the left and right of the current record name take you to the previous and next records respectively. The arrows to the outside of these take you straight to the first and last records.

Finding information and sorting your records

Databases allow you to prioritize and organize your information as you please, and to search for specific entries quickly and easily.

Finding information

A single database in Microsoft Works can store up to 32,000 records. To locate a record quickly, you can initiate a search. In List View go to the **Edit** menu and click on **Find**. The Find dialogue box appears on screen. In the "Find what" box type in a keyword or words (be as specific as possible), select the **All records** option then click on **OK**. The records containing your keyword will appear in a list. To return to your full list of records, go to the **Record** menu, select **Show** then **All records**.

You can search in Form View in the same way but the records are displayed one at a time. To move between them, click on the arrows at the foot of the screen.

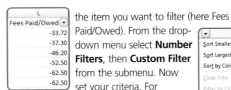

Sorting records in your database

You can use the Sort function in Works to reorder your database. Go to the **Record** menu and click on **Sort Records**. In the Sort Records dialogue box you can choose to have your records prioritized by up to three fields. For example, by first sorting by "Date of birth" in ascending order, the oldest person in your database will appear at the top of the list, and the youngest person last. If you then sort by "Surname" in ascending order, those who share the same date of birth will then be listed alphabetically. Sort a third time by town in ascending order. Now those who share the same birthday and name will be listed alphabetically by town.

Click on the arrows beside each Sort box, scroll through the lists and select your choice of field. You have the option of sorting records in Ascending or Descending order (Ascending lists entries A to Z, or 1, 2, 3...; Descending lists entries Z to A, or 10, 9, 8...).

Editing your database

After you have created a database, you can add and delete information, and perform calculations.

Inserting new records

To insert a new record between existing records, click on the row number where you want to insert it in List View. Go to the **Record** menu and select **Insert Record**. To delete a row, click on the row number, go to the **Record** menu and select **Delete Record**.

Adding and moving fields

To add a new field, click the field heading where you'd like it to appear in List View. Go to the **Record** menu and select **Insert Field**. Choose to insert it before or after the selected one. A dialogue box appears – give the new field a name and click on **OK**. To delete a field, click its heading then go to the **Record** menu and select **Delete Field**.

To move a field, click on the field heading in List View. Move the mouse pointer to the edge of a highlighted cell. When it changes to a "drag" pointer, drag the field to its new location. To move a record, click on the row heading and do the same. In each case you must be able to see the intended destination in the window.

Calculating data

You can perform calculations on values in two or more fields and display the results in another. If you have fields for "Price" and "Deposit," create a third called "Total Due." Click its heading and type "=Price-Deposit" in the Entry bar to show the balance.

Microsoft Excel as a database

Microsoft Excel can be used to perform database functions. Instead of entering field names, headings are typed into the spreadsheet, in cells along the same row. Records are entered into the rows below. (Records must be numbered manually, so create a heading for "Record No.")

To look at a subset of your data, use AutoFilter. First, highlight the data to be filtered. Go to the **Data** tab and click on the **Filter** button in the "Sort & Filter" group. Each column appears with a menu arrow on the right. Click on the arrow on the item you want to filter (here Fees Paid/Owed). From the drop-down menu select **Number Filters**, then **Custom Filter** from the submenu. Now set your criteria. For example, in a "Fees Paid/ Owed" column, you can select records to see only those people who owe money. In the Custom AutoFilter dialogue box, specify records for which the fees paid/owed are less than "0", then click on **OK**. To remove the filter, click on the down arrow beside the column heading and then on **Clear Filter From "Fees Paid/Owed"**. To return to the full database, click on the **Filter** button.

Saving and printing

Transform **your work into** printed documents

Your computer stores work in much the same way as a conventional filing system. The documents that you create on your PC are kept in folders. Within the folders are subfolders that help you organize the different areas of your work. For example, if you create a folder for office work, you could then create subfolders for business correspondence and accounts. As with any filing system, it's vital to organize it well right from the start.

Windows Vista helps by automatically creating folders for different types of files. You can easily set up each family member as a new user of the computer, each with his own set of files and folders. A well-ordered system makes it easy to save and retrieve your work – far easier, in fact, than with a traditional paper-filled filing cabinet.

Printing is easy

Printing your files (these are the documents you create, rather than the folders in which you store them) is one of the most useful skills you can master on your computer. Depending on the type of printer you have, you can print on a variety of paper sizes and weights (thicknesses). You can print out sticky address labels and even print directly onto envelopes.

By using the many font styles, colours and graphics available on your PC, it's possible to produce printed work that looks professional.

As soon as you create a new document, save it. Continue to save it as you work. This way, should your PC crash, your work will not be lost.

SAVING YOUR WORK

1 To save a file, click on the **Save** button on the Quick Access toolbar or click on the **Office** button and choose **Save As**. A dialogue box appears. In the "File name" box, type in the file's name. At the top of the box you can see the place in which your file would currently be saved.

Page settings

To adjust how your document prints out, click on the **Page Layout** tab and then on the dialogue box launcher in the "Page Setup" group. Click on the **Margins** tab to choose the space around your page and either "Portrait" or "Landscape" orientation. Click on the **Paper** tab to select your paper size. Click **OK**.

*In Works, if a subfolder is selected but you wish to return to the main folder (moving up one level), click on **Up One Level** button. To return*  *to a main drive, click on the arrow beside the "Save in" box, scroll through the list that appears and click on the drive.*

Bright idea
*You can set some programs, including Word, to save files automatically – reducing the risk of losing work. Launch Word and then go to the **Office** button and click on **Word options** at the foot of the menu. Click on **Save**. Now click next to "Save AutoRecover info every:" and set a time interval. Finally, click on **OK**.*

2 To change where your file is saved, use the arrows to the right of the destinations at the top to navigate to the location you'd like to save your new file in. If you would like to create a new folder, click on the **New Folder** button. A new folder will appear, ready for you to type in a name.

3 Your new folder automatically becomes the new destination for your file. Click on **Save** to save your document into it. The document name now appears on the document's Title bar, and an icon and the filename for the Word file, appear in the new subfolder.

4 When you are ready to print your document, go to the **Office** button, click on **Print** and then select **Print** from the options that appear. In the Print dialogue box you are offered several options, such as printing multiple copies and printing a range of pages. Make your selections and click on **OK**.

Saving and printing in Works

To save a file, click on the **Save** toolbar button or on **Save As** in the **File** menu. The Save As dialogue box appears. In the "File name" box, type in the file's name. Click on the arrow to the right of the "Save in" box to choose where to save

your file. Click on **Save**. To create a subfolder within, say your "Household" folder, click on the **Create New Folder** button. Type in a name for the "New Folder" that appears and click on **Open**, then on **Save**. To print your file click on **Print** in the **File** menu, select the options for copies and page range, click on **OK**.

Print preview

To check how your document looks before printing, click on the **Office** button and choose **Print**, then **Print Preview**. To return to your original document layout, click **Close Print Preview**.

How your computer works

Discover what happens inside your PC when you switch it on

When you switch on your PC it has to complete several automatic operations before it is able to process the commands you will subsequently input via your keyboard and mouse.

To ensure that the operating conditions are as they should be, all your hardware components (like your memory and keyboard) are checked to make sure that they are undamaged and are able to communicate with each other and with your software.

This process is called "booting up." It takes only a minute, but it's the most important minute of your PC's working day: It makes sure that the hardware and software are communicating properly. Otherwise, nothing on your PC will work.

Your computer's memory

The basic functions of your computer are governed by different types of memory.

RAM

Random Access Memory (RAM) is the memory used by your computer to temporarily store the files and programs you are working on. It can process your commands extremely quickly. This type of memory only works when the computer is switched on; when it is turned off, anything left in RAM is lost.

ROM

Read Only Memory (ROM) holds basic details about the computer and a small, self-test program that runs every time you switch the computer on. ROM is part of your computer's "identity," and is retained when your PC is turned off. You can't change or remove what's stored in the ROM, which is why it's called "read only."

CMOS

Complementary Metal Oxide Semiconductor (CMOS) memory stores your computer's settings, such as which type of hard disk it uses. The CMOS also remembers the date and time. It is powered by a small battery that recharges itself when the computer is switched on (switch it on at least once a month for an hour or two).

BIOS

The Basic Input/Output System (BIOS) memory controls your computer hardware. The BIOS tells the operating system which hardware to expect to come into operation and how it is arranged. It is as if your computer were a chef, and the BIOS his assistant, checking he has all the necessary ingredients. The BIOS is stored within the ROM.

Watch out
If your PC was not shut down properly the last time you used it, a message will flash up the next time you switch it on. If this happens, allow your PC to boot up, then restart it immediately. This ensures that the shutdown mistake has no lingering after-effects.

Close-up
As well as switching on your computer, you may also have to turn on your monitor, and other peripheral units, such as a scanner or printer. You can make this easier by using a power bar.

When you switch on…
The first two minutes after you switch on are vital to the performance of your computer. Here's what happens after you press the power button.

Start up your computer
The first sound you will hear is the whirr of the fans. These regulate the temperature inside the system unit, and run for as long as the computer is switched on. Be careful not to cover any of the air vents on your PC as this will cause overheating. A modern computer can have as many as three fans blowing air over critical components, such as the graphics card.

Roll call
The first task your computer performs is the POST (Power On Self Test). This checks that the most important components such as the hard disk are present and working correctly. While your PC is going through this test you should see lights flickering on and off as the computer tests the CD drive, hard drive and keyboard. During these initial tests, the computer also checks the CD or DVD drive for a startup disk – this allows you to make repairs in case of a major problem.

Once the POST is complete, Windows Vista starts to load. You'll see a black screen with the Windows Vista logo and a series of green lights scrolling from left to right. These show that Windows is loading all the information it needs to coordinate the various components of your system. The tasks it performs at this stage include loading drivers – special programs that enable components like video cards and printers to work – into memory; looking for new devices that may have been added to the computer since it was last switched on; and detecting any networks that your computer may be attached to.

When this process is complete you will see the initial Windows Vista screen. Click on your user name (if you use a password, type it in and then press **Return** or click on the green arrow). Windows will play a sound and load your personal configuration – your choice of Desktop pattern and icons on it.

A quicker start
If you have used PCs with older versions of Windows, you will notice that Vista starts up more quickly than its predecessors and doesn't show pages of numbers and letters before it starts to load. One of the reasons for the quicker start is that Vista can stop the computer from doing certain time-consuming tests before starting to load Windows. Also, the operating system loads in a more efficient way, so that it can take as little as 30 seconds before you are ready to get to work on your PC.

The Welcome screen
Once you have logged on as a user, you will see the Welcome screen. From here you can access many useful tools to get you started with your Vista experience. The screen gives you immediate access to information about your PC and some online resources that can help to protect your PC or give you information about Vista features.

Click on an item in the "Get started with Windows" panel, then on **Show more details**, at the top right of the screen, to see in-depth information on that topic.

The hard disk
This is a series of magnetized metal disk platters. They are read by a small arm that passes over them – a little like an old-style record player. However, the arm never touches the disks – it skims thousandths of a millimetre above the platters, which you can hear spinning.

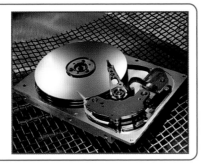

Clutter-free Desktop
What you will see on your Desktop will depend on the PC manufacturer. You may have an almost empty Desktop, showing just the Recycle bin. In this case, to access your Documents, Pictures and Music folders, click on the **Start** button and select the folders from the right-hand pane. You can make these folders appear on your Desktop if you prefer – see page 83 for instructions on how to do this.

Storing all your data

How to make space for everything you need

Your computer's hard disk is where all your programs and documents are stored. The more programs and documents you have, the less disk space there is in which to store them. As the hard disk fills up, your computer will slow down. Disposing of unwanted documents in the Recycle Bin and uninstalling software you no longer use will help to conserve hard disk space (for more details, see pages 54-55). However, you may eventually need to use extra storage devices.

Your first choices

Your computer will probably have a CD-RW drive built in. This is like an ordinary CD-ROM drive in that it can read music and data CDs. However, it can also "write" information onto special blank CDs. As much as 750MB of data can be stored on each disk, and Windows Vista makes it simple to store data this way. If you don't have a CD-RW drive, it's easy and cheap to add one.

Many new computers now have a combined CD-RW and DVD-RW drive. This enables you to watch DVDs – films or music videos, for example, on your PC – and record to DVD. Each DVD can hold as much as 4.5GB of data, and can be a great way to hold a large number of digital photos. The downside is that the disks are still quite expensive.

If you are looking to move files from one PC to another, then a flash drive is a good option. These small devices connect to your PC through a USB port. They are quite cheap, and have a number of memory options.

On older computers you may find a floppy disk drive. Floppy disks can store up to 1.44MB of data each, which many users now find rather limited.

You should be aware that sharing data on any portable storage device is a common way of spreading viruses, so ensure you have up-to-date antivirus software on your PC.

Connecting a drive

The storage devices described here are separate items that need to be connected to your system unit. Almost all devices of this type will connect to your PC using a USB port. Most drives use USB 2.0 interfaces, which allow for extremely fast transfers – as long as your PC is similarly equipped.

Close-up
The units for memory and storage on a PC are:
1,024 Bytes = 1 Kilobyte (KB)
1,024 Kilobytes = 1 Megabyte (MB)
1,024 Megabytes = 1 Gigabyte (GB)
1,024 Gigabytes = 1 Terabyte (TB)
Generally, however, the 1,024 is rounded to 1,000.

Which storage device?

These devices are all suitable for storing large quantities of information. If you need to transfer data to other PCs, make sure each PC has the same type of drive.

Flash drive

Flash drives are small devices that are powered through your PC via one of the USB ports. They are economical to buy and highly portable. There is a range of memory options to choose from – the cheapest carry 64MB of data and the highest capacity flash drives hold 32GB.

DVD-RW

Many PCs now have DVD-RW drives, which can read and write to DVD disks as well as ordinary CD-ROMs. These drives offer huge amounts of storage – as much as 4.5GB per disk – but can be expensive, as are the special disks used for recording.

CD-Rewritable Disks

One of the most cost-effective forms of storage for your PC is a CD-RW (Rewritable) drive. This will write to CD-R disks, which cannot be erased, or to CD-RW disks that can be overwritten as many times as you like. CD-RW disks can hold up to 750MB of data.

External hard drives

If you have a lot of space-hungry programs on your computer or want an easy way to back up your files, you should consider buying an external hard drive to supplement your existing hard drive. External hard drives from manufacturers such as Seagate, Lacie and Western Digital can offer a capacity up to 2TB (Terabytes) – which is more than enough for most people's needs.

Formatting CDs or DVDs

Before you can copy files to a CD or DVD, the disc must be formatted. Insert a disc into your PC's CD or DVD drive. When the Autoplay dialogue box appears, click on **Burn files to disc**. Click on **Show formatting options** and select either **Live File System** to copy files to disc immediately as you would to a USB flash drive or **Mastered** to select an entire collection and burn them all at once. Click on **Next** to prepare the disc.

Supplementary hardware

Extend **your computer's** capabilities **with** added devices

Once your computer knowledge and confidence grows, you will be eager to expand your PC's capabilities. A wide range of devices is available that will make working with your computer even more interesting and enjoyable.

If you like to use images in your work, a scanner is a surprisingly cheap way to get high-resolution images into your computer. Not all images need to be scanned. Digital cameras allow you to take photos and

With added hardware, you can really make the most of your computer, turning it into a complete home office and entertainment centre.

transfer them to your PC without a scanner. It's also possible to buy a small video camera called a webcam to connect to your computer. As well as being fun, you can hold video conferences with colleagues who also have webcams. Making home movies is possible when you attach a digital camcorder to your PC.

You can also buy hardware to make the most of today's onscreen entertainment. The new generation of joysticks, for instance, really take game playing to a new dimension.

These extras can be built up over time. You don't have to buy everything on the same shopping trip.

Modems

Almost all home computers now have an internal modem that allows you to connect to the Internet using a phone line. If your computer doesn't have an internal modem, you can add an external model, which can also act as a fax and answering machine. To take advantage of an always-on, broadband Internet connection, you'll need a cable modem or an ADSL model – either wired or a wireless "router" (see right).

 Bright idea
Most computers come with a built-in standard modem these days. However, they can go wrong and often aren't worth the cost of repair. Instead buy a new external modem, which attaches to your computer by a USB cable.

Watch out

While wireless routers are popular, there is an increased security risk. Make sure you always password-protect your router and install a firewall on your PC.

Scanners

A scanner will transform your paper images and photo prints into graphic files that you can then edit and use on your PC. The most versatile kind of scanners are "flatbed" scanners.

Picture quality is described in terms of resolution, measured in dots per inch (dpi). The more dots that make up an image, the higher the resolution and the better the quality of the image. Buy a scanner with a resolution capability of at least 600 dpi.

Wireless router

Home users are increasingly opting for a wireless router for access to their broadband service. These "hubs" require a power outlet and a phone line or cable connection and then, after the installation of their linked software, will allow more than one computer to have access to the same service, without a jumble of wires.

Digital cameras

These cameras take photographs without using any film. You transfer pictures directly to your computer through a cable or digital memory card reader. The price of digital cameras has decreased rapidly in recent years, so good-quality images can now be taken with quite low-cost cameras.

When you consider that you won't need to buy film and get it developed, they are very good value.

Joysticks

If you're a fan of computer games, a joystick is essential. These devices plug into a port in your system unit. The best joysticks are those that also provide feedback – recoiling as you fire guns, or shaking as you drive over rocks – but these "force feedback" devices only work with games that support them.

It's also possible to buy steering wheels and pedals for driving games.

Webcams

These are small video cameras that connect to your PC. They can be used for video conferencing, but are now popular with home PC users for "live chats" with friends and family that live far away. For the best sound and picture quality, you will need a powerful PC and a high-speed connection.

Microphones

Most microphones are fine for common uses – recording a narration for example.

They come as external devices or are built in. You can also buy microphones with speech-recognition software, so you don't have to type: just speak your thoughts, and the words appear in your document. This software may take a long time before it recognizes your voice and gives the best results.

Installing drivers

Additional hardware often needs software called a driver to allow Windows to control the hardware. Many devices now resolve this problem because they are "plug and play" – this means that the software is automatically installed on your computer when the device is added. In other cases Windows Vista does the work for you. It recognizes the hardware as soon as it is added to your PC and connects to the Web to find a suitable driver. You may need to run the set-up program provided on a CD with the hardware. When buying a peripheral device, always check that it will work with Windows Vista and that suitable drivers are available.

Driver Software Installation

Your devices are ready to use

The software for this device has been successfully installed.

| USB Mass Storage Device | Ready to use |
| ST66022C F USB Device | Ready to use |

Close

More software for your PC

Extend the uses of your computer with extra programs

When you bought your PC, a selection of software may have been included. Packages often focus on Microsoft products, including Microsoft® Works Suite and Microsoft® Office. These packages contain a number of programs that allow you to perform a wide range of functions, such as word processing and spreadsheet work. The software packages that come with your computer are known as "bundled software."

Although this bundled software allows you to perform many different tasks on your PC, you're bound eventually to want to use more specialized software. If you have a digital camera, for example, you may want a photo editing program, such as Photoshop Elements. Or, if you have children, you may want a selection of games to play. You should also use antivirus software to be sure your computer is kept free from viruses. All such software is readily available, and easy to load onto your PC, but there are a few points you should check.

Checking the requirements

Before you buy a new piece of software, check the information on the packaging to ensure it runs on your version of Windows. You should also find out how much memory (RAM) and hard-disk storage space it requires.

To see how much disk space you have available, go to the **Start** menu, click on **Computer**, then on **System properties** to see detailed information about your PC.

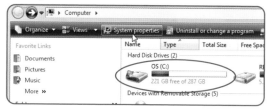

Close-up
When buying goods by mail order or online, make sure that the retailer has an actual address, rather than just a PO box. Also, bear in mind that most credit cards, as well as online payment services like PayPal, usually have consumer protection systems in place. You can also turn to Canada's Office of Consumer Affairs if something goes wrong.

Watch out
Copying programs from friends is not obtaining software for free – it's stealing. Unless you have purchased a licence, you are breaking copyright laws and could be prosecuted.

'Free' software

You don't always have to buy new software for your PC. Some of it can be obtained free, if only for a limited period.

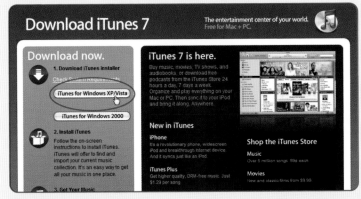

Freeware, shareware and evaluation software

Freeware describes software that's available completely free. Most of the programs have been written by PC enthusiasts and are of good quality.

Shareware and evaluation software are offered free for a limited period (usually 30 days), after which you will not be able to operate the program.

If you want to continue to use a shareware program you must pay a fee (usually much lower than the price of similar, commercial packages). To continue using evaluation software, you must purchase a full copy.

Sources of software

Specialized computer or electronics stores are good places to start, but the other sources outlined below may save you money.

Downloading programs

It's possible to download shareware, freeware and evaluation software (including "beta," or pre-release versions) from the Internet. Locate a dedicated website (see below), then follow the onscreen instructions.

Your PC will tell you how long the download will take – a big program can take hours on a dialup connection. Once it has downloaded, you will need to install the program before running it.

PC magazines

Look out for free, cover-mounted CD-ROMS on PC magazines. Some CDs will hold "full product" or complete programs, while others will offer beta, demonstration or shareware versions.

Buying mail order

Mail order or "direct" software vendors can offer better pricing than brick-and-mortar retailers. Look at the ads in PC magazines to compare prices. Software can be downloaded from the Internet or mailed to you.

Where for wares?

JUMBO (www.jumbo.com) is a website that lists many of the shareware and freeware programs that are available to download. We've downloaded a version of the popular "Sudoku" puzzle. Always make sure that your download is compatible with Windows Vista.

Filing your work

Learn how to name and save your files,
and to organize your work efficiently

It can be far easier to locate your work in a well-organized filing system on your computer than it is in a normal paper filing system

Your computer is an electronic filing cabinet. Each piece of work is stored in folders (as are all the programs you use). Folders can be stored in other folders which are like the drawers in the cabinet. It is tempting to keep all your files on your computer Desktop where you can see them but, as with a real desk, it makes life easier if you tidy things up before the clutter gets out of hand.

Filing made easy

Don't worry that you will forget where you put files, because Windows makes it easy to find them. It is like having an efficient personal assistant – or it is as if your filing cabinet could tell you exactly what is in all its drawers.

You can access your computer's filing system through a handy facility called Windows Explorer. Through it, you can move folders and files around, make new folders and even copy, or duplicate, folders and documents.

There are several ways to create folders. The method you use will depend on how you save your work.

CREATING FOLDERS

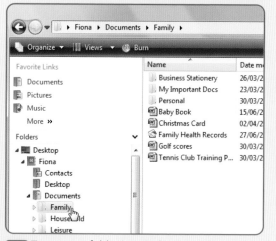

1 To create a folder in Windows Explorer, go to the **Start** menu, select **All Programs** then **Accessories** and click on **Windows Explorer**. Alternatively, hold down the **Windows** key and press **E**. In the left pane, click on the drive or folder in which you want to create the new folder.

Naming your files

Always name your files logically so that, should you misplace one and not remember its full name, you can still activate a search for it. If several members of the family are using the computer, Vista creates separate folders in which each person can store work. In shared folders, use your name or initials when naming documents so that you don't get confused as to whose files are whose.

Bright idea
To rename a file or folder, right-click on it and select **Rename**. *Type in the new name over the highlighted old name.*

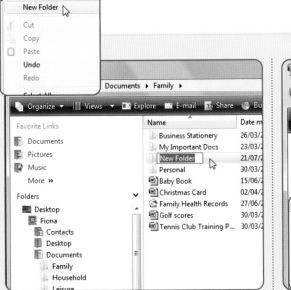

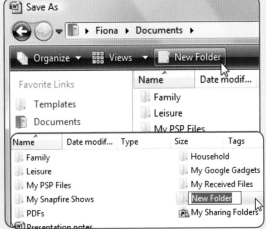

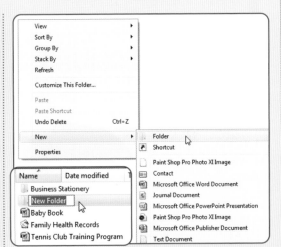

2 Click on the **Organize** button and select **New Folder**. In the right pane a new folder appears, with its name highlighted. The default name, "New Folder," will be replaced as soon as you begin typing in the new name.

You can also create new folders in which to store work as you save your documents. In the Save As dialogue box click on the **New Folder** button. A new folder will appear, ready for you to name.

It is possible to create new folders by using your right mouse button. When you need to create a new folder, click on the right mouse button, select **New** and then **Folder**. The default name on the folder that appears will be replaced as you type in the new name.

Finding lost files

To find work you have misplaced, go to the **Start** menu and select **Search**. Type the keywords you can remember into the search bar – any matching files will be listed on the right pane, below the search bar. Click on one to see information about it appear at the foot of the box. For more search options, click on **Advanced Search** – here you can search on the date the file was created or last modified, or by the type of file or person who created it.

Maximizing disk space

How to make the most of the space on your computer

Ensuring that your computer works efficiently means organizing your folders and files effectively and using the available storage space properly.

As you create files and folders you will use more and more hard-disk space. This won't be a problem initially but, as the hard disk fills up, your computer may slow down as it searches for the correct file or folder, or performs a task. You will also find it more difficult to install new programs.

Deleting out-of-date folders and files, and uninstalling old software, will free up disk space, allowing your PC to run smoothly.

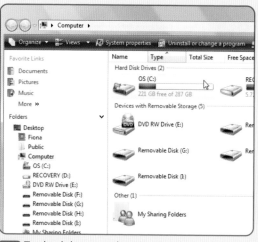

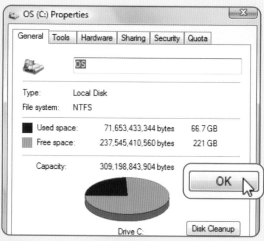

1 To check how much space you have on your hard disk, click on the **Start** button and select **Computer** on the right. In the pane on the right, you will see a list of "local disks." Your hard disk is the drive icon marked "(C:)" – here it is "OS (C:)".

2 Right-click on **OS (C:)** and in the Properties dialogue box click on the **General** tab. Here you can see the amount of Used and Free space, as well as the full hard-disk capacity. A pie chart gives an instant overview. Click on **OK** to close the window.

How much space do I need?

To keep your computer working efficiently, it's important that you keep a minimum of 700MB of hard-disk space free. If you want to install new software, check how much disk space the software requires.

To do this, insert the software CD, set up the installation and look for the screen that lets you know how much space is required. If you don't have enough space available, quit the installation by following the onscreen instructions.

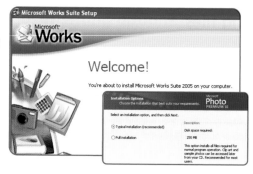

*To delete files or folders, go to the **Start** menu, select **All Programs**, then **Accessories** and click on **Windows Explorer**.*

DELETING FILES

If you send a file to the Recycle Bin by mistake, Windows allows you to restore it to its original location.

RESTORING FILES

1 Click on the file or folder you wish to delete. Click on the **Organize** button and select **Delete**, or press the **Delete** key. A prompt will ask you to confirm your command. Click on **Yes** to send the files or folders to the Recycle Bin on your Desktop.

2 Files in the Recycle Bin continue to take up space until the bin is emptied. To completely remove an item from your computer, double-click on the **Recycle Bin**, click on the file, click on the **Organize** button and select **Delete**. You will be asked to confirm your choice.

The Recycle Bin has a useful safety net if you make a mistake in deleting an item. To rescue a file from the bin, double-click on the **Recycle Bin** Desktop icon, click on the file you want to rescue and then, keeping the mouse button pressed, drag it across to the Desktop.

Empty your bin

If you want to empty the Recycle Bin completely, double-click on its Desktop icon. A window will open showing the contents.

Now click on the **Empty the Recycle Bin** button. Confirm the command at the prompt.

Watch out

To remove program files, use the special Uninstalling function described on page 54. Do not drag them into the Recycle Bin.

Tidying your hard disk

Learn **how to** uninstall **software to** create space **on your PC**

Over time, your PC's hard disk may become clogged up with programs you no longer use. Removing them is often the best way to create space and ensure that your computer continues to run smoothly.

It is essential that programs are removed completely. Simply dropping them into the Recycle Bin is like pulling up a weed and leaving the roots behind.

Get it right

To ensure effective removal, programs may have their own uninstall facilities, found in each program's folder. For the many that do not, use the "Uninstall a Program" function in Windows.

The steps here are a guide only, as each uninstalling process is unique.

1 Windows Vista has a built-in utility that helps you to remove unwanted programs properly. In the **Start** menu, click on **Control Panel**. In the panel that appears, click on **Uninstall a program** under "Programs."

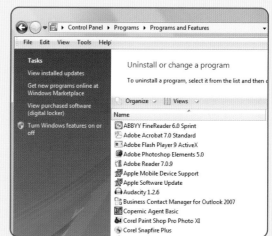

2 The Uninstall or change a program window appears, with a list of all the programs that can be removed using this process. Scroll through and click on the one you want to remove.

⚠️ **Watch out**
Before uninstalling any programs, check that nobody else in the family wants to keep them. Then close down all active programs before starting the uninstall process.

Uninstalling software

Some programs do not come with an uninstall option which means Windows will not put them into its "Uninstall or change a program" list. Other programs may be listed but then throw up problems while you are trying to uninstall them. To deal with these programs, consider buying some of the specialized uninstaller software that is available. Most of this software is inexpensive and can sometimes be obtained as shareware (software distributed free with magazines for a trial period).

Bright idea
Before you uninstall software, back up any related data that you wish to keep and ensure that you still have the original installation CDs in case you want to reinstall the program later.

If you have placed a shortcut on your Desktop to the program you have deleted you will need to remove the shortcut separately yourself.

REMOVING SHORTCUTS

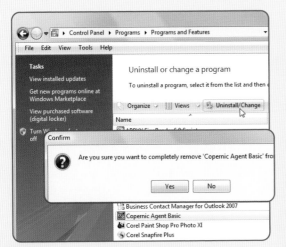

3 Click on the **Uninstall/Change** button (some programs may have a "Remove" button instead). Your PC will open an uninstaller program designed for the software you have chosen. It will ask you to confirm your decision to uninstall. Check that you have selected the right program, then click on the **Yes** button.

4 Your PC will now uninstall all relevant files. A dialogue box will show you the operation in progress. (If some program files are shared with other programs, you will be asked whether you want to remove them. To be safe, choose **No**.)

5 To remove a shortcut on the Desktop to a program that you have deleted, first minimize all your windows to view your Desktop. You can do this by holding down the **Windows** key and pressing **M** at the same time. Right-click on the shortcut icon that you want to remove and choose **Delete** from the pop-up menu.

Deleting other shortcuts

If you are using Windows Vista "Classic view," when you uninstall a program the removed program might still appear in the list of your most often used programs in the Start menu. To clear the list, click on **Start**, right-click in an empty part of the Desktop and choose **Properties**. From the Start Menu tab, click on **Classic Start menu**, then **Customize**. Then click on **Clear**.

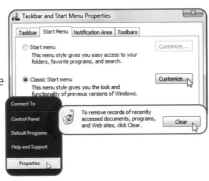

Understanding computer viruses

Take **the right** precautions **to keep your** computer healthy

Vigilance pays when it comes to viruses. Make sure you install an antivirus program on your computer and run it regularly.

Viruses are computer programs that are designed to cause harm rather than good. Once inside your PC they can cause all sorts of problems, from making unwanted messages appear on your screen, to causing programs to crash, or your printer to stop working. In very rare cases, they can even delete all the data on your hard disk.

There are several ways a virus can infiltrate your computer. When they first appeared, viruses were most often passed on via floppy disks. Nowadays, however, the biggest danger is from the Internet. Viruses are most often "caught" by downloading infected files attached to seemingly innocent e-mail messages.

Antivirus software

No matter how your computer catches a virus, you probably won't be aware of it until something goes wrong and damage has been done. However, you can take precautions and limit the risk of catching a virus.

The first step is to buy an antivirus program, such as McAfee's VirusScan. You should also subscribe to an update service, so that your PC will be protected against new viruses. Last, install a firewall, especially if you use an "always-on" broadband service.

Then it's a matter of using your common sense. Treat all e-mail attachments with caution. Set up a weekly routine where you install any new updates to your antivirus software and run a full check on your hard disk.

How viruses infect your PC

Identifying the different sorts of virus, and knowing how they spread from one computer to another, will help you keep your PC infection-free.

TYPES OF VIRUSES
File virus

A file virus infects program files. Once the affected program is running, it can infect other programs on your hard drive.

Macro virus

A macro virus infects individual documents. It affects files created in programs that use macro programming language, such as Microsoft Office's Word and Excel programs. One way to protect against this family of viruses is to set a high level of Macro Security. Go to the **Office** button and click on **Excel Options** at the bottom of the window. Then click on **Trust Center** and select **Trust Center Settings**. Click on **Macro Settings** in the left pane and choose the level of security you want from the options in the right pane. Click on **OK**.

Boot and partition sector viruses

Boot and partition sector viruses infect the system software; that is, the special parts of the hard disk that enable your computer to start, or "boot" up. These viruses may prevent you getting your computer working at all. They work by removing your PC's startup instructions and replacing them with their own set of instructions. You may need the help of a specialist if your computer catches this type of virus.

THE WAYS VIRUSES ARE SPREAD
Portable storage devices

Always be wary of portable storage devices, such as Flash drives, as they are made to move files or programs between computers. The more machines that a portable drive or disk is used on, the greater the chances of it picking up a virus and passing it on.

E-mail

You should be very cautious about opening a file attached to an e-mail as the file itself may carry a virus. As a general rule, do not open up files attached to unsolicited e-mail. However, some e-mail programs can catch viruses simply by opening an infected e-mail message.

CD-ROM

You are safe with a CD-ROM (except in the extremely unlikely event that it was made with a virus). "ROM" stands for Read Only Memory, which means it will not accept viruses – or, indeed, any other kind of information. However, with recordable or rewritable CDs you need to be as careful as with other portable storage devices.

Wksstecd4 (D:)

Internet

Don't download software of dubious origin from the Internet. Use a reputable company providing software that you know about, such as Corel, Norton, Microsoft or McAfee.

Internet Explorer

 Watch out

Be careful when buying software on a disk. Ensure it comes from a reputable source and that the packaging has not been tampered with. If the disk has been used there is a chance that it carries a virus. Remember, pirated software is illegal and greatly increases the chances of catching viruses.

 Keywords

Computer bug *A computer bug is different from a virus in that bugs are accidents or mistakes in programming, rather than programs specifically designed to cause harm.*

Keeping up to date

Update Windows **so it stays** stable and secure

Microsoft Windows Vista is an extremely secure operating system and many home users will never experience any problems. However, even a system as stable as Windows Vista occasionally needs minor revisions. These are made available via Windows Update and the easiest way to get them is over the Internet (see page 88 for how to get online).

The Microsoft website can check out your system and prompt it to download any recommended updates. You can even set up your machine to do the checking automatically, so that it alerts you when a new update has been released.

Windows Update can fix minor Windows problems – nine times out of ten you won't even have noticed that there was a problem – but these updates are often made to improve the security of your computer. Security updates are almost inevitable, as no manufacturer can think of every way that a malicious mind might try to break down their product, and obscure security lapses are only discovered after a product has been released to the general public.

Whenever an update to Windows is released, Microsoft publishes information on its website about what is being updated and the problem that it is correcting. Using this information, you can decide whether or not you need to update your system – often the problems addressed on the website aren't relevant to home users.

Microsoft also occasionally releases "Service Packs" – collected packages of updates and improvements that can be downloaded from Microsoft's website or ordered on CD-ROM.

You need an Internet connection to use Windows Update (see page 88). Make sure your modem is plugged into a phone line or cable connection.

(see page 88)

BEFORE YOU START

Bright Idea
Office Update works in a similar way to Windows Update to keep Microsoft Office fully up to date.

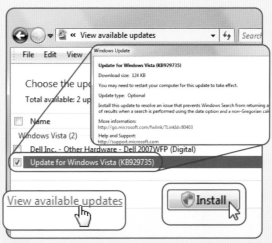

1 Go to the **Start** button, click on **All Programs**, then on **Windows Update**. If you aren't already, you will be asked to connect to the Internet. An Internet Explorer Window will open with the Windows Update and a check of your system will automatically run. This process may take some time.

2 After the scan is complete, a results window opens stating the number of critical and/or optional updates available. There may be none. Click on **View available updates** for more detail. Double-click on an entry to read a review of the update and click on a Web link for even more information. When ready, click on **Install**.

3 A progress bar will appear during the installation and, when complete, a results window will show a summary of the update. Read and accept any licence agreements and wait while the installation finishes. When this is completed you will be asked to restart your PC.

Auto updating

Your PC can automatically check for updates when you are online. The process can be slow, so a fast connection is preferable. To set automatic updates, go to the **Start** menu and click on **Control Panel** in the right-hand pane. Next, click on **System and Maintenance** and under "Windows Update" click on **Turn automatic updating on or off**. Click on the **Install updates automatically (recommended)** option and then set your frequency and time options. Finally, click on **OK** to save this setting.

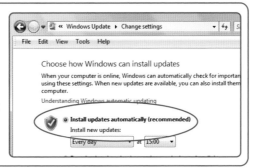

59

Defragment and clean up the hard disk

How to help your computer to perform at its best

Taking care of your computer means ensuring that the hard disk is working at its optimum level. Defragmenting and cleaning the hard disk on a regular basis will help it do this. Defragmenting makes sure large files can be stored in such a way that access to them is as easy and quick as possible. Removing unwanted files from your hard disk will free up space and make your computer work much more efficiently.

Windows Vista has two useful tools – Disk Defragmenter and Disk Cleanup – that carry out these tasks. You should use these tools on a regular basis to maintain the smooth running of your PC.

Larger disks can take an hour or more to defragment. Don't set the process in motion if you haven't got the time to spare.

DISK DEFRAGMENTING

Disk Defragmenter

Disk Defragmenter consolidates fragmented files on your co performance. How does Disk Defragmenter help?

☑ Run on a schedule (recommended)

Run at 01:00 every Wednesday, st

Last run: 18/07/2007 17:28

Next scheduled run: 25/07/2007 0

Control Panel
Disk Cleanup
Disk Defragmenter
Internet Explorer (No Ad
System Information
System Restore
Task Scheduler
Windows Easy Transfer

◀ **Back**

Start Search

✓ **Scheduled defragmentatic**
Your disks will be defragme

1 Go to the **Start** menu, select **All Programs**, then **Accessories**, then **System Tools**, then click on **Disk Defragmenter**.

Close-up
When you save a large file, your computer will often split it up into fragments and store it in different locations on the hard disk. Your computer can still find the file but it takes longer to do so. Disk Defragmenter rearranges the fragments of a large file so that they are stored next to each other. This makes it easier and quicker for your computer to access files.

Bright idea
If you use your computer to edit your home videos, you will be placing many Gigabytes of data onto your hard disk. Even a large disk can fill up quickly and become badly fragmented, so it's a good idea to regularly defragment the disk drive.

Find files you don't need on your hard disk and delete them to free up memory.

DISK CLEANUP

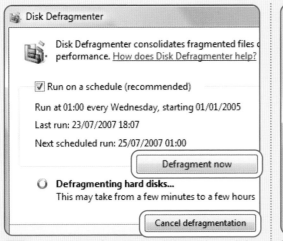

2 In the Disk Defragmenter dialogue box, click on the **Defragment now** button to start the process. The Vista "circle" starts spinning, showing that the process is working. If you need to stop the process, click on **Cancel defragmentation** and continue at some other time.

1 Go to the **Start** menu, select **All Programs**, **Accessories**, then **System Tools**, then click on **Disk Cleanup**. Click on either **My files only** or **Files from all users on this computer**. In the Disk Cleanup: Drive Selection dialogue box select the drive to clean from the drop-down menu. Then click on **OK**.

2 In the dialogue box that opens, click in the check boxes next to the file or files you wish to delete. Click on **OK** then in the Disk Cleanup dialogue box click on **Delete Files** to confirm the operation.

Set the schedule

You can set the schedule so that your PC runs the defragmentation program overnight once a week. In the Disk Defragmentation dialogue box, click on the **Modify schedule** button (to the far right of the box), then select how often and at what time you'd like it to run. Then click **OK**. Just remember to leave your PC switched on that night.

Modify schedule...

Disk Defragmenter: Modify Schedule

Run disk defragmenter on this schedule:

How often:	Weekly
What day:	Wednesday
What time:	01:00

Caring for your equipment

Cleaning hardware **regularly will** prevent problems **in the future**

Your computer needs simple but regular maintenance to stay in good condition. Problems like your mouse seizing up, or the keys on your keyboard becoming stuck, can be easily avoided if you clean your equipment regularly. And keeping your workspace clean and tidy will create a more pleasant environment for everyone to work in.

Simple measures include making a rule that you don't drink or eat near your PC, and that you protect it with a suitable dust cover when not in use. When cleaning, spare a few minutes to check that those "spaghetti" wires are out of harm's way, too.

Stock up

Establish a cleaning routine that you carry out once a month. As with any type of cleaning, ensure that you have the right materials for the job. Computer stores offer a variety of cleaning products, but a multi-purpose cleaning kit is probably the best choice for the home user. A typical kit comprises PC wipes, swabs, cleaning cloths, cleaning fluid and a cleaning card. You should also consider buying a dust spray.

Before you start cleaning, make sure your equipment is turned off and unplugged – it is never safe to use liquids with electricity.

Dust and stains on your screen can make it difficult to read.

Watch out
Never use ordinary household spray polish or liquid spray cleaners on your keyboard. If liquid gets between or under the keys, it can damage the mechanism.

Bright idea
Before cleaning your keyboard, turn it upside down over a garbage can and shake it gently. Much of the debris that has slipped between and under the keys will fall out.

Cleaning your hardware

A few minutes of light maintenance every month is all you need to keep your machine running at peak performance and in showroom condition.

The keyboard

Because your keyboard is an exposed component of your computer, dirt will inevitably accumulate between and under its keys. To remove it, wipe the keys with special cleaning swabs or use dust spray to blow away dust. If you have them, work cleaning cards dipped in cleaning solution between the keys.

The printer

Check your printer's paper path to ensure that it's clean and free from ink or toner. Use wipes to remove any spillage, but be careful not to get toner on your hands or clothes as it is difficult to remove. Don't touch the printing mechanism itself unless the print manual gives cleaning advice on this. Perform a print test (consult your print manual for instructions) to check on the ink or toner level. Replace print cartridges or toner as required.

CD and DVD drives

Keeping your CD and DVD drive clean ensures that programs and files can be accessed smoothly and are less prone to data loss.

Special CD/DVD cleaning disks are available from computer stores. Simply insert the appropriate cleaning disk and follow the onscreen instructions.

The monitor

It is important that you keep your monitor in pristine condition. Using a dirty, stained screen leads to unnecessary eye strain. Use a PC cleaning wipe to keep the screen clean, clear and safe – the non-smear varieties are best for the job.

The mouse - Follow this routine to keep your mouse running smoothly.

1 Turn a mouse upside down and wipe the base firmly with a special PC wipe.

2 Twist the mouse-ball cover so that it opens and the ball falls out into your hand.

3 Clean the mouse ball with a lint-free cloth. Dab it with sticky tape to pick up any dust or dirt that has accumulated on it.

4 Using a PC swab, remove dust from inside the socket, focusing on the rollers that make contact with the ball. Finally, put the ball back and replace the cover.

Cleaning an infrared mouse
1 Turn the mouse upside down and then wipe the base.

2 Using tweezers or a PC swab, gently work out any dirt or dust that has built up around the infrared sensor eyehole.

Welcome to the world of Windows

Fast and flexible – **your PC's** operating system **lets you use your PC with** confidence

To drive your car you don't need to know the intimate workings of an engine. It helps should you break down, but it's not essential. So it is with Windows. You don't need to know the layers of code that make it run, you just need to know the best way to drive it, while getting the most out of it.

Windows gets its name from the fact that every program – word processor, database, spreadsheet – operates inside its own window on your PC's Desktop.

Keeping your house in order

Windows is an "operating system" (or OS) – the set of instructions that make sure your computer runs smoothly. It keeps your files in order, and allows your PC to perform basic jobs, such as printing.

You can personalize Windows to suit your needs by, for example, giving your computer its own background (a picture or pattern that covers your Desktop).

Windows Vista has a choice of dramatic images to decorate your Desktop.

Keywords

Start menu *This is where you can quickly access key functions, such as customizing Windows controls. Click on the* **Start** *button and a menu pops up. Select an item by clicking on it.*

Advances in Windows

Since Windows first appeared, it has been updated to keep pace with new technology. Windows Vista is the latest version but Windows XP is still widely used.

Vista contains many familiar features – a Desktop with a Recycle bin, a Start button and Taskbar. Like earlier versions, Vista can only run software which is compliant with Windows.

Vista retains the Windows Start menu, with dedicated folders for music, pictures and other types of file. It also integrates with the Internet very closely and is much more stable than earlier versions.

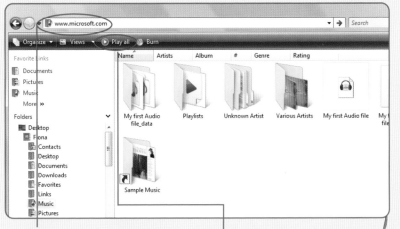

Windows Vista lets you connect to Internet sites by typing a Web address into the Address box. You have to be connected to do this.

Vista puts buttons on the toolbar which are linked to tasks relevant to the folder being looked at. In "Music," for example, there is the option to Play all.

Changing face of PCs

In the days of DOS (the PC operating system before Windows) the way to print a file, say, was by typing in commands (below). The birth of Windows 3.1, then

```
Command Prompt
Microsoft Windows [Version 6.0.6000
Copyright (c) 2006 Microsoft Corpor
```

Windows 95 and 98, literally changed the face of PCs. The visual nature of Windows lets you see exactly what you are doing on your PC's Desktop.

The mouse became the new steering wheel. It allows you to move and organize files by picking them up and dropping them into the folders that you have created and named.

The Start button and Taskbar introduced in Windows 95 meant that you could find files, open programs and use Windows' many tools in just a few moves of the mouse. Windows Vista has stream-lined many features and added some extras – such as "see-through" windows (see page 82) and a way of arranging windows in a three-dimensional stack.

Bright idea

Help is always at hand. Click on the **Start** *button and select* **Help and Support** *from the right-hand menu. Alternatively, simply press the* **F1** *key on your keyboard to get assistance relevant to the program you are using.*

Coming to grips with windows

Organize your Desktop for maximum efficiency and ease of use

Your computer's Desktop is much like a conventional desk in that it holds files, folders, documents and tools. These are all represented on your PC by icons.

By double-clicking on any icon you will open its associated file or program, which will appear as a separate window on your Desktop, and its size, shape and position can all be set by you.

Having several windows open on your Desktop at once can be just as confusing as having a pile of papers scattered all over your desk. But there are ways to keep your work area tidy and boost your efficiency.

Controlling the size of windows
The buttons in the top right-hand corner of a window control its appearance.

The Minimize button
Click on the **Minimize** button to shrink the window to a button on the Taskbar. Clicking on the Taskbar button will restore the window to the Desktop.

The Maximize button
Click on the **Maximize** button to expand the window to fill the whole screen. When a window is maximized, the button changes to a Restore button. Click on this to restore the window to its original size.

The Close button
Click on the **Close** button to close a window or program.

Scroll bars
Often, you won't be able to see all the contents of a window. When this happens, scroll bars appear to the right of, and/or bottom of, the window.

To view the window's contents, click on the arrows at each end of the scroll bar, or click on the slider itself and, keeping your finger pressed down on the mouse button, drag it along.

Resizing windows
To adjust the height or width of a window, click on any of the window's edges (the mouse pointer will change to a double-headed arrow when you are in position). Keeping your finger pressed down on the mouse button, drag the window in or out.

To resize the width and height at the same time, click on the window's corner and drag it diagonally.

Shortcut
You may find it easier and quicker to maximize windows by double-clicking on the Title bar that runs across the top of them.

Close-up
*To see what's behind a maximized window, press the **Alt** key and then the **Tab** key (with Alt still pressed). Open windows appear as icons in a blue panel. Press the **Tab** key to move along the icons and when the one you want is selected, press the **Return** key to open it up onscreen.*

Bright idea
*If several windows are open and you need to see your Desktop, right-click on the **Taskbar** and click on **Show the Desktop** in the pop-up menu. To restore the windows to your screen, click on **Show Open Windows**.*

Arranging windows on your Desktop

Windows is extremely flexible when it comes to organizing open folders and documents.

Working with windows
Ideally, it is best to have just one or two windows open on your screen at any one time. This not only keeps your Desktop tidy, but also makes it less likely that you will file documents in the wrong place.

Stacking your windows
You can arrange your windows so that you can see the contents of each one at the same time. Individual windows can be "stacked" in a neat arrangement across your screen so that every open window is visible on the Desktop.

Right-click on the **Taskbar** and select **Show Windows Stacked**. This arranges all your folders and open programs into a tile-like layout. To revert back to your former screen, right-click on the **Taskbar** and select **Undo Show Stacked**.

Cascading windows
Another handy option is Cascade Windows, which arranges windows so that each one overlaps the one before, diagonally, from the top left-hand corner of your screen. This is useful if you have several windows open, as you will still be able to see the name of each one filed behind the other. Clicking on a cascaded window will bring it to the front of your stack.

To operate this function, right-click on the **Taskbar** then click on **Cascade Windows** from the pop-up menu. To revert back to your former screen, right-click on the **Taskbar** and select **Undo Cascade**.

Exploring Windows

Windows Vista offers new ways of managing open windows. Here are three new features which are all part of the new "Aero" technology in Vista. Flip 3D (shown left) can be opened by pressing the **Windows** key and the **Tab** key at the same time. This will show you all open windows in a 3D display. Hold the **Windows** key down and press the **Tab** key to move through them. Windows Flip (top right) displays all your open windows on a blue bar in the centre of your screen. Press **Alt + Tab** to open it, and tab through them. Aero will also give you a "thumbnail" image of an open document (bottom right) if you hover the mouse over an item on the Taskbar.

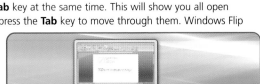

Personalizing your Desktop

Decorate your PC to make it feel like part of the furniture

We all like to add individual touches to our houses. The colour that we paint our front door and the layout of our front yard make us feel that our home truly belongs to us. It is just as easy to put a personal stamp on Windows.

If, for instance, you don't particularly like the background colour or pattern of your Desktop you can change it by selecting a different background from Windows' library. Options include land-scape scenes, flowers, shapes and animals. You can easily change your Desktop back-ground again if you get bored with it.

Background design

To change the background on your Desktop, right-click anywhere on the Desktop and select **Personalize** from the pop-up menu. In the box that appears, click on the **Desktop Background** option. You can then choose from a list of different background styles – Windows Wallpapers are shown, but you can click on the arrow to the right to choose other options. For example, select **Pictures** and then click on **Browse** to find one of your own images.

Click on an image to view it in the preview window (you also need to click on Open, if it is not a Wallpaper image). You can choose to centre, stretch or tile the image. Centre places the image in the middle of the screen, Stretch fills the screen with the image and Tile repeats the image to fill the screen. When you have selected your new background, click on **OK**.

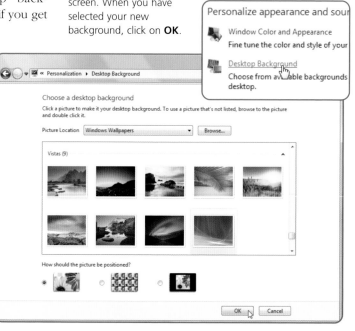

Keyword

Properties Nearly everything you see in Windows has its own "Properties," which gives valuable information about your PC's resources and allows you to alter its settings. To see an item's properties, right-click on the object and select **Properties** from the pop-up menu.

Bright idea

To remind yourself of an important or amusing message or slogan, select the **3D Text** screen saver. Type in your text and select a font, colour and style for it, along with the speed at which you wish it to travel across your screen.

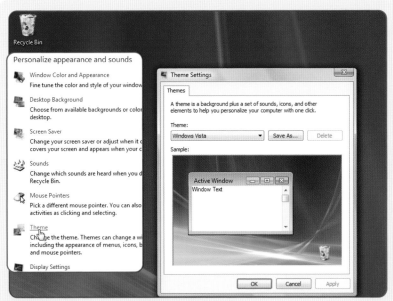

While you were away...

Screensavers appear when your PC is on but not in use. They can be fun and also protect work from prying eyes. To select a screensaver, right-click anywhere on the Desktop and select **Personalize** from the pop-up menu. Click on the **Screen Saver** option. Scroll through and select an option in the "Screen saver" box. It then appears in the preview window. (You can choose **Photos** to display the images in your Pictures folder as your screensaver.) Set the length of time your PC waits before activating the screen saver in the "Wait" box, then click on **OK**.

On some PCs the Screen Saver tab has an energy-saving option that reduces the amount of power to your monitor and/or hard disk after a set period of inactivity. Click on **Change power settings** (left) and select an appropriate wait period from the list.

More than just a Desktop

Themes allow you to change your background, sounds and colour schemes, and are standard with Windows Vista. To apply a theme, right-click on the Desktop and then on **Personalize**. In the Personalize appearance and sounds screen, click on **Theme**. Select a theme from the list. Click on **Apply** then on **OK** to save the theme.

Setting passwords for users

If your PC has more than one user, each can have his or her own personalized version of Windows Vista. They can access the PC without interfering with other users' settings. Each has their own background, folders and Start menus.

Users with administrator rights can set up accounts. Go to the **Start** menu, click on **Control Panel** then click on **Add or remove accounts** under "User Accounts and Family Safety." Beneath the main pane in the box that appears, click on **Create a new account**. Enter a user name and account type, then click on **Create Account**. The account appears in the User Accounts window. Click on it and select **Create a password**.

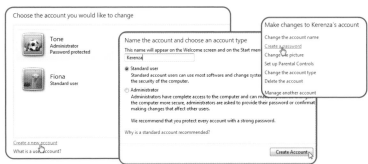

Customizing Windows controls

Tailor **your** computer's settings **to make it work the way** you want

When you are using your PC it's helpful to know that you can tailor Windows controls to suit your needs. For example, you can change the speed at which your mouse double-clicks, alter the size and shape of the mouse pointer, and change the appearance of your screen. Left-handed users can even swap the role of the mouse buttons.

If you are visually impaired, changing the shape and size of your mouse pointer may help you see it more clearly onscreen.

Mouse settings

To customize your mouse settings, go to the **Start** menu, select **Control Panel**, then click on **Mouse** under the "Hardware and Sound" category. There are five tabs at the top of the Mouse Properties dialogue box – Buttons, Pointers, Pointer Options, Wheel and Hardware.

Buttons allows left-handed users to swap the role of the mouse buttons; Pointers lets you choose a "scheme," or style, for your onscreen pointer; in Pointer Options you can alter the speed at which your mouse pointer moves; and in Wheel you can adjust how far your mouse wheel scrolls down the page.

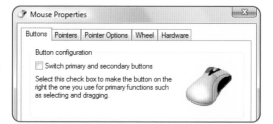

Bright idea
*Windows is aware of Daylight Savings Time and can change the clock in spring and fall. In the Date and Time dialogue box, you can request a reminder. Tick the box by **Remind me one week before this change occurs** and then click on **OK**.*

Date and time
The current time is displayed on the right-hand side of the Taskbar. To see the current date, place your mouse pointer over the time display. The date will pop up in a second.

To set the date or time, click on the Taskbar Clock. A calendar pops up. Click on **Change date and time settings...** beneath the calendar. Under the Date and Time tab, click on **Change date and time...** You can then click on the arrows to change the time, or click on the calendar to change the date. Click on **OK**.

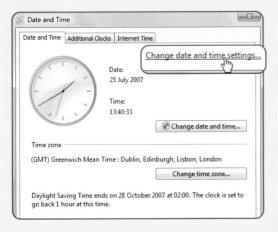

Setting sounds
If your PC has a sound card you can configure Windows to play a number of built-in sounds. Go to the **Start** menu, select **Control Panel**, then **Hardware and Sound**, then click on **Change system sounds** under the "Sound" category.

In the Sounds tab, scroll down and click on an event in the "Program" box. Now click on the arrow under the "Sounds" box, scroll through and click on your preferred sound (or None for no sound). Click on **OK**. To preview sounds, select a sound from the list and click on **Test** to hear it.

Disability options in Windows
Windows offers help to users with disabilities. Go to the **Start** menu, select **Control Panel**, then **Ease of Access**. These are some of the options available within the Ease of Access Center:

● If you are hard of hearing, set your PC to send out visual warnings. Click on the **Replace sounds with visual cues** option. Check the box and then choose a sound. Click on **Save** to store the settings.

● If you have trouble moving your mouse, click on **Change how your mouse works**. Switch on Mouse Keys to use the numeric keypad on the right-hand side of your keyboard to move your mouse pointer.

*To prevent pressing the Caps Lock key accidentally and typing in capital letters, use Toggle Keys, which will alert you with a warning sound. In the Ease of Access Center, click on **Make the keyboard easier to use**. Then click in the box next to **Turn on Toggle Keys** and click on **Save**.*

● If you are visually impaired, click on **Optimize visual display** and select the high-contrast viewing mode. You can also have text and descriptions read aloud by clicking in the box next to **Turn on Narrator**. Click on **Save** to keep your settings.

● Users with slight visual impairments can also use the Magnifier. At the foot of the "Optimize visual display" box, click in the box next to **Turn on Magnifier**. This will create a separate window at the top of the screen that displays a magnified portion of the screen.

Close-up
*Windows Vista lets you decide how you open folders on your Desktop (with one click or two), and whether folders open within the same window or separate windows. Go to the **Start** menu, click on **Control Panel** and then on **Appearance and Personalization**. Under "Folder Options," click on **Specify single or double-click to open**. In the General tab of the dialogue box, click beside the setting you want and then click on **OK**.*

Create your own shortcuts

Fine-tune **the way you work on** your PC, **and** save **yourself** time and energy

Once you are familiar with the basic workings of Windows and you have a reasonable understanding of which programs and commands you use most often, you can begin using shortcuts to help you launch or activate them quickly.

You can create simple shortcuts to folders, documents and to almost anything else, including a printer, program and a drive. These can then be activated directly from the Desktop or Start button. You can also arrange for programs to launch when you start up Windows.

The Start menu

The Start menu in Windows Vista watches how you use your computer and changes its contents accordingly. For example, the lower part of the left-hand column will gradually fill up with a list of programs that you use most often – there's no need to tell Windows to do this.

Like almost everything in Vista, the Start menu is fully customizable. You can choose how many programs it displays and whether it shows a list of the ten documents that you most recently worked on. If you choose, you can also customize the Start menu to show links to the documents you have opened most frequently.

You don't have to rely on Windows Vista to put programs in the Start menu for you. You can also choose to "pin" a program to the menu so that it's always quickly available for you to start up.

Click on **Start** to open the Start menu, click on **All Programs** and choose the program you wish to add. Right-click on it, and choose **Pin to Start Menu**. The program's icon will now appear in the upper left-hand part of your Start menu.

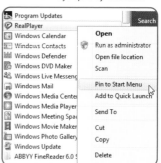

Bright idea
Windows Vista allows each user of a computer to set up the Start menu, Taskbar and Desktop to suit his or her preferences. When you log in to the computer, your Desktop and menus will appear just the way you like them.

Customize the Start menu to suit the way you work

You can change the Start menu to suit how you use your computer. Choose whether you want to view items in new windows or as further menus – you're the boss.

Viewing folders as menus

It can sometimes be quicker to view commonly used items, such as the Control Panel, as a menu attached to the side of the Start menu, rather than cluttering up the screen with a new window.

To view the Control Panel as a submenu, right-click anywhere on the Taskbar at the bottom of the screen. In the pop-up menu select **Properties** then click on the **Start Menu** tab. Click on **Customize**. Under the "Control Panel" section, click on the **Display as a menu** option. Click on **OK**, then on **Apply**, and on **OK** again to close the Taskbar and Start Menu Properties dialogue box.

Now when you open the Start menu and move your mouse pointer over Control Panel on the right pane, a list of all your Control Panel items will open to the right. You can use the same procedure for other Start menu items – you might add the Computer, Pictures and Music folders, for example.

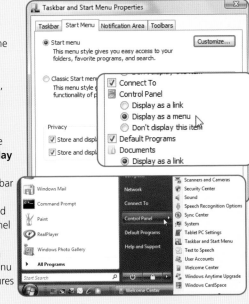

Show on Desktop

It often helps to be able to reach your most commonly used items from the Desktop.

To place an icon for Documents on the Desktop, click on **Start** to open the Start menu. Right-click on **Documents**, and choose **Send To** from the drop-down menu, then **Desktop (create shortcut)** from the submenu of options that appears. Every time you start up your PC now, a shortcut for Documents will appear. Double-click on the icon to access all the files within the folder.

Vista will allow you to place as many shortcuts and/or files and folders on the Desktop as you like. Try to avoid too much clutter though.

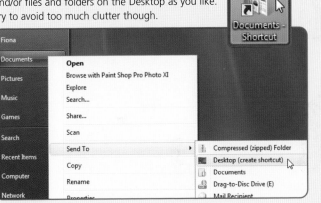

The ultimate time-saver ...

You can arrange for a frequently used program to launch whenever Windows starts. Go to the **Start** menu, click on **All Programs** and navigate through the pop-up menus to find the program you want. Right-click on it and choose **Copy**. Click on **Start** and then **All Programs** again and double-click on **Startup**. The Startup items folder will open. Right-click in it and choose **Paste Shortcut**. A Shortcut icon for the program you have chosen will now appear in the Startup items folder. When you next restart your computer and log in, your chosen program will start automatically.

Quick keyboard commands

Save yourself time by using hot keys instead of your mouse

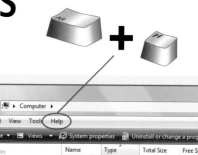

Nearly all the actions or commands you perform with your mouse can also be done by pressing "hot keys" – these are single keys or a combination of keys on your keyboard. For example, in Microsoft Word you can access the spelling and grammar facility by pressing one of the "F" (or function) keys at the top of your keyboard, or print by pressing the Ctrl and "P" keys at the same time.

Using the hot keys is quicker than using your mouse, especially if you do a lot of work from the keyboard, such as word processing.

Taking control with shortcuts

There are a number of keyboard options that can help you to quickly perform everyday tasks on your PC. Once you have a program running, you can hold down the **Ctrl** key and press **N** to open a new file or window from that program. To close a file – in any program – hold down **Ctrl** and then press **W**. Cut, copy and paste functions can also be easily accessed with keyboard combinations. Hold down the **Ctrl** key and press **X** to cut, **Ctrl + C** to copy and **Ctrl + V** to paste.

Some options in menus allow you to use the keyboard to choose them. For an example, launch Word, go to the Office button and look at the "Exit Word" button. The "x" is underlined, indicating that you can press **X** to select it. Look out for similar, underlined shortcuts.

Shortcut
*Most PC keyboards have a Windows key – found between the Ctrl and Alt keys. Press it to open the Start menu and use the cursor keys to move around the menu items. Press the **Return** key to open a highlighted option or program.*

Watch out

*When you use a key combination that involves the Ctrl or Alt keys with a letter or function key, press the **Ctrl** or **Alt** key first. Otherwise, you may issue the wrong command.*

Keywords

***Keyboard shortcut** This describes a key combination that replaces a mouse command. It can take the form of pressing just one key, such as a function key, or several keys, such as **Ctrl + F4**.*

Accessing the Quick Access bar

The Quick Access toolbar present in the Microsoft Office 2007 programs – including Word, Excel and PowerPoint – allows you to use many of the most common functions with just one click. Initially, it will include only the Save, Undo and Redo commands, but you can choose to add others.

To customize the Quick Access bar, click on the down arrow to the right of the bar. A menu appears, showing all the functions that can be added. Click on one to select it – a tick appears on its left, and an icon will be added to the toolbar.

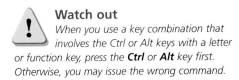

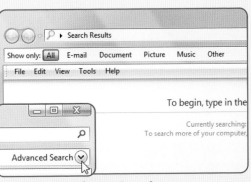

Using the function keys

The function keys along the top of your keyboard perform pre-assigned duties, or functions.

Press **F1** to access a program's Help facility. This helps you to solve software problems.

From the Window's Desktop, press **F3** to access the Find: All Files dialogue box (above). This allows you to search your hard disk to find a file.

You can use function keys in combination with other keys. To close a window or program, for example, press the **Alt** key and the **F4** key at the same time.

Moving around the Desktop

You can use keyboard shortcuts to move around your Desktop. For example, click on the **Computer** icon then press the arrow keys to move around your various Desktop items. They become highlighted when selected. (Against the default Windows Vista Desktop this is very subtle in appearance.) Press **Return** to open a selected icon. Try this on your Documents folder.

The same principle applies inside the folders. In Documents, use the arrow keys to move around the folder's contents. Press **Return** to open a file or folder.

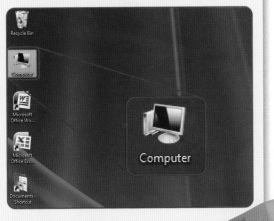

Important command keys

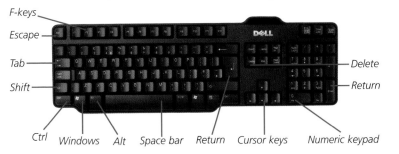

F-keys

Escape

Tab

Shift

Ctrl   Windows   Alt   Space bar   Return   Cursor keys   Numeric keypad

Delete

Return

Becoming an old hand

If you have more than one window open, you can bring each one to the front of your Desktop using the **Alt + Tab** keys. Press (and hold) **Alt** then **Tab** and a bar will appear with icons showing all the windows you have open. The uppermost window's icon will have an outline around it. To move to the next and subsequent icons, press the **Tab** key while still holding down **Alt**. Release on the window you want to view.

Windows' included programs

Learn about these mini-applications and they'll soon become indispensable

Windows comes with a number of programs, known as Accessories. These are really useful and – even better – they don't cost a cent extra.

If you need to open a text document created in a program you don't have, you can use the Notepad text editor. You can play music on your computer and create compilation CDs using Windows Media Player. Once you familiarize yourself with Windows' accessory programs, you will be surprised how often you use them.

Where to find accessory programs

To find Windows' accessory programs, go to the **Start** menu, select **All Programs** then **Accessories**. A menu with the accessory programs will drop down.

These include a calculator, Paint for image editing and Notepad for very basic word processing.

The Accessories menu contains other useful system tools to keep your computer up to date. For example, Disk Cleanup will remove unwanted files and Character Map will help you find those accented characters that are always hard to locate.

Start menu showing:
- Internet — Mozilla Firefox
- E-mail — Microsoft Office Outlook
- Microsoft Office Word 200
- Microsoft Office Excel 200
- Windows Explorer
- Microsoft Works Task Launc
- Internet Explorer
- Windows Media Player
- Windows Mail
- Command Prompt
- Paint
- RealPlayer
- Picasa2
- All Programs
- Start Search

All Programs submenu:
- Accessories
- Adobe
- Corel Pa
- Dell
- Dell PC
- Dell Prin
- Dell Sup
- Extras a
- Family

Accessories submenu:
- Calculator
- Command Prompt
- Connect to a Network Projecto
- Notepad
- Paint
- Remote Desktop Connection
- Run
- Snipping Tool
- Sound Recorder
- Sync Center
- Welcome Center
- Windows Explorer
- Windows Sidebar
- WordPad
- Ease of Access
- Entertainment
- System Tools

Bright idea
Windows Media Player can "rip," or extract, music data from your CDs and store it on your hard drive. To save hard disk space, the music is stored in a special read-only format called WMA, which stands for Windows Media Audio.

Close-up
*Notepad will only let you work in one font and font size per document. Go to the **Edit** menu and click on **Set Font**. Select a font and size. These will then be applied to the whole document.*

Everything you need from a word processor

WordPad is an effective word processor that has many features in common with Word. It includes a toolbar that lets you do tasks quickly, has a good selection of fonts and font sizes and even lets you format text. The only important function it lacks is a spellchecker.

Notepad is far more basic. Referred to as a text editor, rather than word processor, it creates only plain text files – that is, files that lack formatting, such as bullet points or multiple fonts. Notepad is the program to use if you need your document to be readable on any type of computer.

For your entertainment

Windows Media Player allows you to play many different kinds of audio and video files, as well as extract audio from CDs to store and play back from your hard drive (see below left). Using Media Player, you can create your own playlists and burn personalized CDs. You can also have psychedelic images swirling on screen while your songs play, and choose from a number of offbeat "skins" that change the complete look of the program – from ultra-modern to plain surreal!

Special characters

Character Map lets you view the characters that are available in a selected font, but do not have a dedicated key on the keyboard – accented letters, for example. To use them, copy individual characters or a group of characters to the Clipboard. From there, you can then paste them into your document.

Working with images

Paint is a simple drawing package with which you can undertake some basic photo editing. You can also, with practice, create your own artwork. It can be a very useful tool but if you plan to take a lot of digital photography, it might be worth purchasing a full photo-editing program.

Making your sums add up

Calculator carries out basic addition, subtraction, multiplication and division.

To use it, click on **Calculator** in the Accessories menu. Then, either click the onscreen calculator keys using your mouse, or use the numeric keypad on the right-hand side of your keyboard.

The Copy and Paste options in the Edit menu let you transfer numbers to other programs. If you want advanced functions, go to the **View** menu and click on **Scientific**. Choose **Standard** to return to the basic form.

Make the right connection

Speed **costs** – how **fast** do you want **to go?**

SATELLITE
ADSL
CABLE
GPRS
56K
3G

Today's computers are designed to communicate with each other, and the wider world, using the Internet. It's rare to find a new PC that doesn't come complete with a modem designed to use ordinary phone lines. Your PC will probably have a built-in 56K modem, able to download data from the Internet at a rate of 56,000 bits each second. Windows Vista's Internet connection wizard makes it a simple job to get online using that modem and an Internet Service Provider.

Many users will be happy with this kind of Internet connection, known as a "dialup" connection. However, if you use the Internet for more than a few hours each day, or need to send and receive large files, you may want to consider other ways to connect.

Broadband connection

You can now surf with cheap, high-speed Internet access, known as "broadband," using either ADSL or Cable technologies. Broadband is available in most towns and cities, and can give you access to the Internet at many times the speed of a normal dialup connection. The connection is "always on," so you don't have to wait for a modem to dial in and log on before you get your mail and files. Most broadband providers are ISPs, and their connections have high enough maximum transfers (called "caps") that normal everyday use won't incur any extra fees.

online radio

Broadband doesn't just give you faster downloads, it vastly improves the quality of many Internet technologies, fundamentally changing what your PC can do. For instance, you might find yourself using your computer where once you would have used a radio. With thousands of radio stations around the world sending CD quality sound to your Desktop, traditional radio is hard-pressed to compete.

Keyword
ADSL (Asymmetric Digital Subscriber Line)
Internet technology that uses ordinary phone lines but is much faster than a dialup connection, and lets you make phone calls while you're online.

⚠ Watch out
Some rural areas cannot receive conventional broadband. Use a phone number search (see below) or call your supplier to check availability. If ADSL and Cable are ruled out, consider a satellite connection.

Picking a broadband connection

Broadband costs have plummeted, but it's worth considering your requirements before you sign up.

ADSL

Using an ADSL (or simply DSL) modem to connect your computer to your local telephone company's exchange, a huge amount of data can be squeezed through an ordinary telephone line. The technology has quickly become popular, proving stable and easy to use.

To use ADSL on your PC you will need software to drive your new modem, and you will also need to configure some system settings – in most cases the software CD supplied by your ADSL provider will take care of that for you.

In Canada, ADSL offers download speeds of up to 11 Mbps and upload speeds of 512Kbps or 1 Mbps – business users can pay for even faster connections, but the standard package should suit most home users.

However, ADSL is not available everywhere – your local exchange needs to have been converted. Also the rate at which data can be transmitted decreases dramatically with distance. So if you live more than a few kilometres from your nearest phone exchange, ADSL may not be available to you. Check with your local phone company.

Cable

If you live in an area where cable TV is available, you may find that the company can also offer you high-speed Internet access over the same connection. However, this will only be the case if the cable network in your area is digital – many areas still have the older analogue version. But for those with suitable networks in their area, cable offers a fast and cheap alternative to ADSL.

Like ADSL you will need a special modem, and again you will need to install the software supplied. Some cable operators offer a low-price 128Kps service

that may fulfill your needs. While it doesn't offer the pace of ADSL or full-speed cable, it is an "always on" service that provides surprisingly rapid downloads. However, if you aim to use your broadband connection mostly for large video or audio downloads then this slower kind of service is probably not the best option.

Satellite

As fast as cable and ADSL connections are, they're just not always a practical choice for rural Canadians, or those who live beyond a certain distance from a phone exchange or the territory covered by "terrestrial" service providers (in other words, there aren't any wires stretching that far).

For these people, satellite-based broadband is a good choice. The thin-air nature of the data transfer for a satellite-based system makes it susceptible to signal degradation during heavy rainfall (called "Rain Fade") and the data transfer rates don't match the blazing speed of wired services like cable or ADSL (partly due to the incredible distances that the data must travel each way), but in some areas it's the only practical choice, and it's still a *lot* faster than dialup access.

A satellite connection is also more expensive than cable or ADSL, though some regional governments may offer grants to small businesses or organizations to help offset the costs.

The mobile Internet

Laptop users can now choose from an array of wireless cards for genuinely mobile Internet access.

The latest technologies are Wi-Fi, which connects users when they are in small "hotspots" such as specially equipped coffee shops, airport lounges and hotels, and 3G, the next generation mobile phone technology offering very high connection speeds. Wi-Fi ties users to an area in the vicinity of a particular base station whereas 3G, like other mobile phone systems, allows users to wander from place to place. However, 3G networks are only in place in a few areas around the globe, and the

costs of using the system may remain high for some years.

GPRS, an older phone system, offers much lower data rates of around 30–40Kps, but works almost anywhere that there is an ordinary mobile phone network, and is ideal for checking e-mail while on the move.

Making the most of broadband

Connect your whole family with a home network

Many households these days have more than one computer, each in a different room. It can make sense to join these computers up in a home network, so that they can all share a single printer or scanner. And, with the rapid adoption of broadband Internet connections, it also makes sense to allow all the computers in a household to share fast Internet access.

There are many different ways to join PCs together in a network, both wireless and wired. However, if there are more than two computers in the house, or if you are likely to be moving computers around (most likely if you have a laptop computer), a wireless network is probably the best solution. This sort of network uses a hub, a device that communicates via radio waves with adapters fitted to all the PCs around the home. The adapters can be cards fitted inside computers or devices attached to the PC by a USB connector. Such a setup can cost surprisingly little, and does not involve any messy wiring or the installation of jacks.

Wireless networks most often use a standard called 802.11, often known as the much friendlier "Wi-Fi." With a Wi-Fi network you'll be able to surf the Web in bed or the backyard, and add new computers to your setup quickly and easily. Although the standard range from network hub to PC is around 25 to 32 metres, some enthusiasts have extended this to many kilometres, using antennas made from old tin cans!

Your Wi-Fi network connects to a broadband Internet connection using a separate device called a router. As well as directing Internet traffic to the different computers on the network, most routers also work as firewalls, protecting your network from unwanted intrusions via the Internet.

⚠ Watch out

The Wi-Fi standard should guarantee that products from different manufacturers will function together perfectly, but this is not always the case. For best results, ensure all your Wi-Fi components come from the same supplier. Many retailers offer hardware bundles for just this purpose.

Building a wireless network
Connect computers and share fast Internet access without any messy drilling.

The hardware setup
The heart of your network is a combined router, firewall and wireless hub. These unobtrusive boxes are best mounted on a wall for maximum range, and will need to be located as near to the centre of your home as possible, to ensure that the signal is strong throughout your property.

Detailed instructions for the setup and configuration of your router will depend on the particular model and manufacturer you choose. However, networks like this are becoming increasingly popular, so suppliers produce extremely user-friendly devices. They are generally configured using setup "wizards" just like those used to set up other hardware in Windows.

Security issues
A wireless network lets you surf the net from your back porch. However, it will also let anyone else in the vicinity to do the same unless you choose the best security options your setup wizard suggests. At the very least, ensure that all users log in with a password; better still, use additional security built-in to the Wi-Fi standard, such as WEP (below left). This will prevent any passing hackers or mischievous neighbours from using your network and Internet connection or reading your files.

The physical side of things is simple – there are just two wires to plug into the box; a power cable, and the connection to your ADSL or cable modem.

The final touches
Once the router is connected and working, you will need to attach adapters to each of your desktop computers, together with the appropriate drivers for each device (older laptops may also need cards to be added). All the software you need will come with the hardware, and this is a simple task that you will carry out only once. Next, configure your network on one of your computers. In the **Start** menu, click on **Control Panel**, then **Network and Internet**, and then click on **Set up a new wireless router or access point**. You should then click on **Next**.

The "Set up a home or small business network" wizard will then take you through the steps necessary to set up your network. At each stage, make your selections and then click on **Next**.

Wireless and safe
All Wi-Fi standard equipment should be able to broadcast and receive using something called Wired Equivalent Privacy (or WEP). This is a method of encrypting the data that passes between PCs and the hub so that it cannot be intercepted by a hacker. There are stronger forms of protection available if your data is particularly sensitive, but the standard version is quite safe enough for most home users.

Discover new features

Getting the most out of Windows Vista and Microsoft Office 2007

The latest version of any software package will give the PC user some new features to try out. In this case, both Microsoft Windows and Microsoft Office have been greatly revised. The new "look and feel," as well as the new features, may initially be disconcerting for PC users accustomed to the previous versions, but it doesn't take long to adapt and discover that the changes are designed to make the software more user-friendly.

Here we give you a quick run-through of some of the most useful features in Windows Vista and Office 2007. It should be helpful both to new PC users, and to those who have upgraded from previous versions.

Windows Vista

When you first start up your PC in Windows Vista, you are presented with the Welcome Center screen. This displays a set of links to various features to help you get started. Double-click on **What's new in Windows Vista**. This will explain some of the important features of Windows Vista.

Searching

Every Windows folder contains a Search box in the top right corner. When you type in the Search box, Windows immediately searches the current folder and subfolders

"Contextual" tabs appear only when necessary, to aid you with the current task. If, for example, you are inserting a picture into an Office document, you will see "Picture Tools" displayed in the bar above the additional contextual tab "Format," giving you an extra ribbon of commands related to that task.

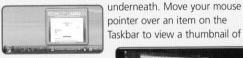

for filenames and any other details that match your search text. Windows then creates a Search Results folder at the bottom of the Folders list in the left pane. If no items are found, click on **Advanced Search** and enter further search criteria, such as Date, Size and Authors.

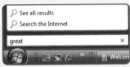

Alternatively, you can use the Search box on the Start menu. Click on the **Start** button and type a word, or part of a word, into the box. As you type, items that match your text will be displayed on the Start menu above.

Windows Media Center

You can enjoy live or recorded TV, movies, music and pictures with the Windows Media Center. Click on the **Start** button and select **All Programs**, then **Windows Media Center**. The first time you do this, you will be presented with a Welcome screen inviting you to choose a "Setup" option – Express or Custom. Make your selection and click on **OK**.

Windows Aero

This special feature gives a translucent glass frame design to your windows, letting you view whatever is underneath. Move your mouse pointer over an item on the Taskbar to view a thumbnail of

the contents of the window. This feature incorporates Windows Flip 3D. Hold down the **Windows** key and press **Tab** to preview your open windows in a three-dimensional stack. With the Windows key held down, continue to press **Tab** until the window you want appears at the front, then release.

Power off

Click on the **Start** button. At the bottom left is a circular icon – the "Sleep" button. Click on it to put your PC into a low power mode. The padlock icon locks your PC – you will need to enter a password to unlock it. Click on the arrow for options to Switch User, Log Off, Restart and Shut Down.

Microsoft Office 2007

The Ribbon

This toolbar gives easy access to many tasks with just one click. The tools change according to the tab selected. (See page 23 for more information on the Ribbon.)

Dialogue box launcher
Click on the small diagonal arrow next to a group name on the Ribbon to access the related dialogue box.

Customize the Quick Access Toolbar
To add a command to the toolbar, click on the **Customize Quick Access Toolbar** button. Choose a command from the drop-down list, or select **More Commands** to view more categories. Select one, click on **Add**, then on **OK**.

Viewing and zooming
Click on the viewing percentage at the bottom right of your window to access the Zoom dialogue box, which will allow you to zoom in or out of your document. Alternatively, drag the slider bar.

Control Panel

Windows Vista, by default, displays the items of the Control Panel in "Category" view – showing items grouped together under a common heading. If you have used earlier versions of Windows, you might find using the Control Panel in "Classic" view easier – this shows items as icons in alphabetical order. To change the view, click on the **Start** button and select **Control Panel**. In the left pane, click on **Classic View**. To switch back again, click on **Control Panel Home**.

CONNECTING TO

The **Internet** and the **World Wide Web** (the collection of websites created by businesses, organizations and individuals) are expanding at a staggering rate. Users can now find **information** on almost any subject. The Internet also allows users to send messages across the globe in the form of **e-mail** (electronic mail). Find out how to **connect** to the Net, then go and **explore** this vast storehouse of information.

THE INTERNET

Welcome to the Internet

A meeting place, shopping centre, travel agency and library in one

The Internet is made up of a network of millions of computers throughout the world that allow people to access a wide range of information and services. It comprises the World Wide Web, through which people access this information, and facilities such as electronic mail (e-mail), chat rooms, forums and newsgroups.

E-mail is a major feature of the Internet. Messages are typed into a computer then sent via an Internet connection to other e-mail users thousands of kilometres away – without incurring huge long-distance charges. If you have a particular interest, forums and newsgroups provide an opportunity to exchange opinions and ideas. Many Internet Service Providers (or "ISPs," the companies that provide connection to the Internet) set up discussion areas in which you can comment on issues that interest you.

A spider's web of information

The World Wide Web (or just "the Web") is the public face of the Internet. It is a vast conglomeration of websites, made up of Web pages. The text and images you see on the Internet are part of a Web page.

Web pages are written in a computer language called HTML, or HyperText Markup Language, that allows pages to be linked together. A collection of linked pages forms a website, which in turn can be linked to other sites around the world, forming a global spider web of connected sites.

All websites have unique addresses, called URLs (for "Uniform Resource Locator"). These act like phone numbers, connecting your computer to the computer that holds the Web page you want to view.

To find your way around the huge tangle of websites (or "surf the Net") you need a Web browser. This is a program that allows you to view pages and move around the Web. The most popular Web browser is Microsoft Internet Explorer, which is usually installed with Windows Vista and is free of charge. Other Web browsers include Mozilla Firefox, Safari and Google's Chrome.

Once you are online, the Web is your oyster. You can use it to buy goods – including books, CDs, food and clothes – to book holidays, research any subject, and even play computer games. For key areas you can explore on the Web, see opposite.

All you need to connect to the Internet is a modem and an account with an ISP.

The world at your fingertips

Once connected to the Net, you are ready to explore the potential of the World Wide Web.
This is made up of a collection of websites that promote a multitude of subjects and interests.

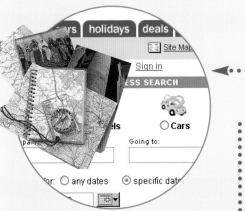

Travel

Use the Web to access travel guides, check the latest weather reports, book flights and accommodations, view exchange rates, and find out what other visitors thought of a place.

Research

Whether you are studying for a qualification or pursuing a personal interest, there are websites to help you. You will even find online encyclopedias. (See pages 120, 124 and 130 for research projects on the Internet.)

Health and medicine

The Web is an invaluable resource when it comes to health matters (but it is not a substitute for going to the doctor). You can find out about medical conditions, research treatment options and even get online advice – but not a diagnosis – from doctors and other health experts.

The media

The Web allows you to access the latest news from newspapers, magazines and broadcasting companies. Many of these services are free. With the correct software you can watch live television broadcasts from the other side of the world. You can even get news of events before they reach the TV news bulletins or the papers.

Shopping

You can buy virtually anything on the Internet – from new shirts to a new home. There are even sites that can help find you the best price on the item you're looking for. (To find out how to shop on the Internet, see page 106.)

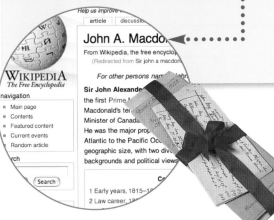

Health Canada homepage, Health Canada, August 2008. Reproduced with the permission of the Minister of Public Works and Government Services Canada, 2008

What you need to get online

To surf the Net you must have a PC, a modem and an Internet Service Provider

Getting connected to the Internet is very easy and usually inexpensive. To begin with, you need a modem or other connecting device (see opposite). This provides your link to the Net. Then you need to arrange an account with an Internet Service Provider (ISP). The ISP you choose is your gateway to the Internet. It allows you to browse the World Wide Web and to send and receive e-mail. Your ISP is also the place where any Web pages you have created are stored. It makes them available to other users of the Internet.

An ISP could be a large organization, such as Rogers Communications Inc, Bell Canada and America Online (AOL), or a small, independent operation that might only serve the area in which you live. Finding an ISP to suit your needs is the most important aspect of getting online.

Types of Internet Service Provider

The term ISP is a catch-all term that describes all the various companies that provide you with your online access. However, just what they offer can vary pretty widely. Generally, the types of ISP break down into two camps:

● Internet Access Providers (IAPs) offer basic services like an Internet connection and e-mail account. Often, you will receive a CD or DVD with a Web browser and e-mail application, but Vista already includes these. An example of an IAP is Rogers Communications, Inc. (below).

● Online Service Providers (OSPs) provide not only a gateway to the Internet and e-mail access, but also a degree of content, like news and information, entertainment and chat or shopping services. An OSP will have a home page designed to make it easier for a beginner to get to the information he or she needs. One of the best-known OSPs is America Online (below).

Keyword

Web browser *This is a software application that acts as your window to the Web (Internet Explorer, for instance). Your ISP will provide you with this in its start-up kit, though most operating systems come with one already included.*

Questions to ask about ISPs

There are many different ways to go online nowadays. The type of connection you choose will likely depend on how much you will be using the Internet, though for some, location can be a factor as well.

If you already have a phone line, the simplest way to connect to the Internet is via a dialup account and a standard modem. However, the multimedia nature of today's Web, the growing number of online services (shopping, bill-paying, and so on) and the increasing time that people tend to spend on the Internet mean that your best bet is likely to be an always-on broadband connection, such as cable or ADSL – or satellite, if you live in a rural area.

What's are the rates, speeds and limits?

Dialup accounts are usually metered. That is, your monthly charge covers Internet use up to a certain number of hours, time used beyond this resulting in extra charges. Broadband accounts are technically metered as well, but the limits are so high that most people's normal use won't incur extra charges.

Data transfer rates listed by service providers are often "best-case" rates based on optimal running conditions (in other words, a couple of users on an uncrowded phone or cable line). With some systems, as the number of users in a given area increases, the speed of each connection goes down as the lines become saturated. Find out how increased traffic will affect the speed of connections in your area. Also, some service providers put speed caps on their lines in order to accomodate more customers.

Do you get any added extras?

Find out how many e-mail addresses you can have on one account. Having more than one means that each family member can have their own address and send and receive e-mail from the same computer. Or, if you work from home, you could have one e-mail address for personal mail and another for business use.

Your account usually will likely include some Web space in which to put a Web page or site. how much space do you get for your monthly fee? Is it enough for a site you might want to put up?

Ask whether calls to the support helpline are free or charged to your account or credit card. Some ISPs that offer "free" services charge premium rates for support calls, while other ISPs offer 24-hour-a-day support. You should also check on the ISP's reliability: will you get through to your dialup account on your first try? Does your local cable provider suffer a lot of service interruptions? Will your satellite connection go down in moderate rainfall? Speak to your friends and relatives to see who is happiest with their service.

Get a real feel with a free trial

Some ISPs offer a free trial of their services, usually for 30 days. If you take up a trial offer make sure that all sections of the service are user-friendly.

Are you impressed with the standard of content? Also, how easy is it to send and receive e-mail through the ISP? (See page 90 for more details on sending and receiving e-mail.)

Cable, ADSL or dialup?

Most users of the Internet prefer an always-on, broadband connection, via either **cable** or **ADSL**. ADSL stands for Asynchronous Digital Subscriber Line, and is a technology that allows very fast connections to be made using ordinary phone lines. The availability of the service depends on your telephone provider and your distance from the local phone exchange. Another access option for users in some areas is **satellite**, though this option can be pricey.

Cable TV companies offer fast Internet services in many areas, through the same cable as the TV signal. Both ADSL and cable connections require special modems, normally provided as part of the package by the ISP.

A modem and dialup connection is another way of accessing the Internet from home. A modem sends information to, and receives information from, the Internet. But dialup modems work slowly – connecting at a maximum of 56 Kbps (kilobits per second).

Send and receive e-mail

Using your PC to revolutionize the way you keep in touch

In addition to the World Wide Web and all its resources, the Internet also provides electronic mail, or e-mail. Many people find that e-mail is the single most useful feature of the Internet.

E-mail functions at a staggering speed. A message can reach a computer on the other side of the world in minutes. And because it's operated from your Desktop, it's extremely convenient, too.

Every e-mail program has its own look, but all operate in a similar way. Here, we take Microsoft Windows Mail as an example.

1 Click on **Start** then on the **Windows Mail** icon. A dialogue box will appear inviting you to connect to the Internet. Using dialup? Click on **Cancel** – composing your message offline reduces the amount of time your line will be busy.

Choosing your email program

Windows Vista reserves a space in the Start menu for your choice of e-mail program, so it's always easy to find. To set Windows Mail as your chosen e-mail program, click on **Start**, then right-click in a clear space. Click on **Properties**, then **Customize**. The section at the bottom of the dialogue box lets you choose which programs you want to appear in the Start menu as your e-mail program and Web browser.

Close-up
E-mail addresses take the form of name@somewhere.com. "Name" refers to the sender's name, and "somewhere.com" refers to the host system where mail is stored until it is collected by the recipient. In Canada, many addresses end in ".ca".

Keyword
Online/offline *online refers to when your computer is connected to the Internet; offline refers to when it isn't.*

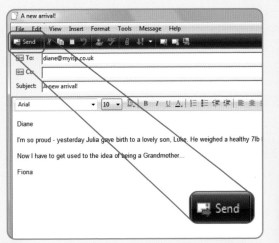

2 To write an e-mail message, click on the **Create Mail** button. A blank message appears. Type your recipient's e-mail address in the "To" box, a title for your message in the "Subject" box and the message itself in the main panel.

3 When you have completed your message, click on the button marked **Send** (or similar). If you're using a dialup connection, you will be asked whether you want to connect to the Internet. Click on **Connect** to activate your modem, connect to the Internet and send your message.

4 To collect e-mail from your ISP, click on the **Send/Receive** button. Your PC will dial up to the Internet and look for messages. If there are any, it delivers them to your Inbox. To read a message, click on it. To reply, click on the **Reply** button, then follow steps 2 and 3.

Sending attachments

You can send pictures and other documents with e-mails. To add an attachment to a message in Windows Mail, go to the **Insert** menu and click on **File Attachment**. A dialogue box will open. Navigate to the folder containing the file you wish to send, click once on the file, then on the **Open** button. The file will be added to the message.

Address books

Windows Mail stores your contacts' details in its Address Book. To send a message to someone in your address book, go to the **Tools** menu and choose **Windows Contacts**, or click on the **Contacts** button in the main Mail window. Click on your recipient's name, then on the **E-Mail** button. Complete your message as in step 2 above and finally click on **Send**.

Starting out online

Set up your Web browser and you are ready to surf the Net

Many people are daunted by the idea of venturing onto the Internet. But, in fact, going online for the first time is a simple matter. It is no more difficult than installing a new piece of software. To connect to the Internet you will need an Internet Service Provider (ISP) and a modem or ADSL – see pages 88 and 89 respectively. You also need a Web browser. This is a piece of software that opens the door through which you enter the world of the Web. Once your browser is set up, you can explore the fascinating world beyond.

Understanding Web browsers

A Web browser is a piece of software that allows you to access websites and navigate between them. All Web browsers are the same in principle. They contain an address box, in which you type a Web address, and an area in which Web pages are displayed.

The most popular browser is Microsoft Internet Explorer which will almost certainly have come pre-installed on your system, and will also be added if you install Microsoft Works, Works Suite or Office. It's a good idea to keep your Web browser up to date so that you are able to view new types of content on the Internet.

Whether or not your PC came with its own browser, your ISP may also provide you with one in its startup kit. This could be Microsoft Internet Explorer or Mozilla® Firefox®, but some ISPs, such as AOL, provide you with their own specially designed Web browser. You can have more than one Web browser, just as you can have more than one word processor or spreadsheet program.

Mozilla® Firefox® is a registered trademark of the Mozilla Foundation.

Many ISPs offer CD-ROMs that make it simple to set up an Internet connection. You can also set one up using the New Connection Wizard in Windows Vista.

GETTING ONLINE

Get to know your way around your Web browser

Your browser gives the Internet a face and allows you to view all its resources.
Learning to use it effectively will make surfing the Net more enjoyable and rewarding.

Use the Back and Forward buttons to navigate backwards or forwards through downloaded pages. Some browsers clearly label them Back and Forward.

Most browsers have a main menu bar containing drop-down menus. Using these menus you can print Web pages, configure your ISP settings and access help facilities.

The Address box is where you type Web addresses. Press the **Return** key to download the Web page.

Many sites list their content in a "navigation panel." Underlined text in blue indicates a link – click on it to see the relevant page.

When you have a number of Web pages open, each one is displayed on a separate tab. Just click on the tabs to switch between Web pages.

Most browsers include some form of search facility to help you find information. Type a key word or words into the search box then click on the magnifying glass icon (or press the **Return** key).

This is the main viewing area, into which Web pages are downloaded and displayed.

Use the scroll buttons to see all the information on a long Web page. A mouse with a scroll wheel makes this easy.

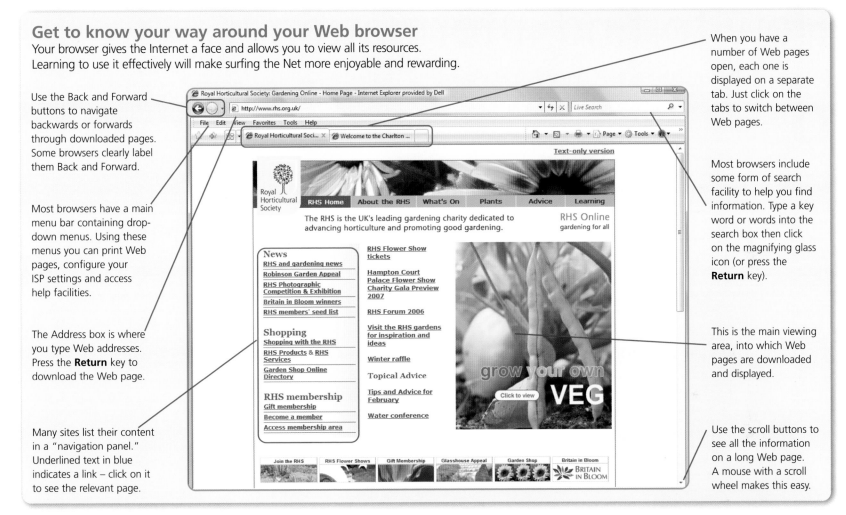

Web addresses explained

Every Web address (or URL) is unique, in just the same way as your telephone number. In fact, it can be helpful to think of a URL as a telephone number, whereby you "dial" the site's address to view it.

The "www" prefix tells you that the site belongs to the Web. After the "www" you are told the domain name (this "points" to the server that holds the website) and where that computer is located (".ca" for Canada; ".au" for Australia; and so on). Addresses do not always end in the country of origin. If you see ".com" at the end, for example, this indicates that the site is commercial. If you see ".org," the website is an organization.

For many pages, extra text appears after the domain name. This shows the location of the page within the website.

http://www.cbc.ca/

How to find information

Exploring **the** Internet **is easy** once **you know where to** start

O nce your Internet connection is up and running you are ready to explore the World Wide Web. The quickest way to find information is to type the Web address of a site you want to visit into your browser's address box and press the Return key on your keyboard. The site's first page (known as the home page) will appear onscreen. You can move around the site by clicking on links.

If you do not know the address of a Web site, you can find information using a search engine. This will search for keywords or categories that you select, then present you with a list of sites to visit. Click on the links to view the sites. The key to effective use of the Internet is narrowing your searches by using more specific keywords so that the number of sites yielded is manageable.

> Be as specific as you can in your search and tell the search engine exactly what you are looking for. You can get tips on better searching from the engines themselves.

USING A SEARCH ENGINE

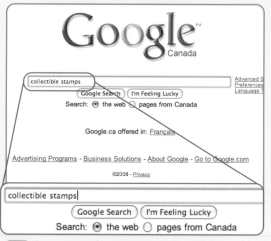

Google™ Canada

collectible stamps

Google Search   I'm Feeling Lucky

Search: ⦿ the web ◯ pages from Canada

Google.ca offered in: Français

Advertising Programs - Business Solutions - About Google - Go to Google.com

©2008 - Privacy

collectible stamps|

Google Search   I'm Feeling Lucky

Search: ⦿ the web ◯ pages from Canada

1 Connect to the Internet. In your Web browser's address box type the address of a search engine (here, www.google.ca). Click on **Go**. The site's home page will appear in a few seconds. Type your keywords into the search box and press the **Return** key on your keyboard.

Which search engine?

The Web site at www.searchenginewatch.com explains how the main search engines work and how efficient they are. Here are the addresses of some popular search engines:

● www.google.ca
● www.altavista.ca
● www.alltheweb.com
● www.excite.com
● www.lycos.ca
● www.yahoo.ca

Your Internet Service Provider might also have its own search facility (see pages 88–89).

Most text that is a certain colour within a site is a link to another part of the same site or to a new site. Click on the coloured (or sometimes underlined) text to activate the link.

Watch out
Do not type a Web address into a word search box. You will not be taken to the website. Type only keywords for your search.

CyberStamps.com is your online store for all your **stamp** collecting desires. Our catalogue and supplies store is designed to serve the large community ...
www.cyberstamps.com/ - 25k - Cached - Similar pages

Collectible Stamp - Find **Collectible Stamp** items for sale on eBa
eBay - Find **Collectible Stamp** on eBay. ... So what are some **collectible stam**
"off the beaten path?" Souvenir **stamps**, which can sometimes be found ...
popular.ebay.com/ns/Stamps/Collectible-Stamp.html - 44k - Cached - Similar

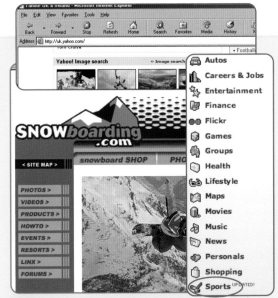

2 A list of related websites will appear. (Some engines tell you how many sites have been found.) Use the scroll bar to the right of the page to view the list. To view a site, click on its underlined title. Use your browser's Back button to return to previous pages.

3 Most search engines, including Yahoo (www.yahoo.ca), allow you to search by category. Click on a category (sometimes they will be underlined) and you will be presented with subdivisions to narrow your search. Continue to click on subdivisions until a list of sites appears.

Reproduced with permission of Yahoo! Inc. ® 2008 by Yahoo! Inc.
YAHOO! and the YAHOO! logo are trademarks of Yahoo! Inc.

4 To find information on snowboarding, for example, click on **Sports** in the "Web Directory" section on the Yahoo home page. Then click on **Snowboarding**. This reveals a list of sites, resources and chat areas. Click on a site to open it.

Search by batch

Most search engines present their list of sites in batches per page (usually of ten). When you reach the bottom of the first page in Google, click on **2** for the next page, and so on.

Information collected for you

Some websites have databases of information that make searching easy. For example, www.bigfoot.com has a variety of directories that offer everything from a simple name lookup to reverse phone number lookup, e-mail address searching and a friend finder. Google Groups indexes all messages sent to its newsgroups.

Goole Groups has its own search engine that will find information for you. Type, say, "apple pie recipe" into the search box and press enter. The search results will list messages from the various discussion groups about your search topic.

Your PC can use more than one search engine at a time. Copernic is a program that collects results from many search engines. Download it free of charge from the Internet.

SERIOUS SEARCHING

Watch out
Make sure your Internet connection is running before you double-click on the Copernic icon. Otherwise, you will not be able to use it.

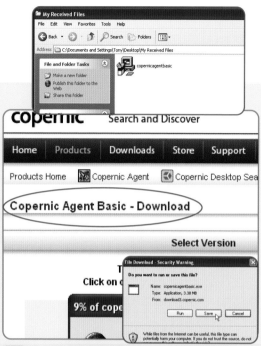

5 Type www.copernic.com into your browser's address box and press the **Return** key on your keyboard. Then, from the Top Downloads panel, click on **Copernic Agent 6.12** (or whatever is the latest version). In the Select Version panel, click on **Download Copernic Agent Basic – English**.

6 The File Download dialogue box appears. Click on **Save** to save the program to your hard disk. Then specify which folder to save it to. Once the file has downloaded, double-click on it to install. Follow the onscreen instructions until the installation is finished.

7 To use Copernic, connect to the Internet, then double-click on its Desktop icon (you may need to register). To find Web data, click on **The Web** in the Category panel on the left. In the New Search dialogue box type a word into the "Search for" box and click on the **Search** button.

Bookmarking Web pages

Browsers allow you to record the addresses of favourite Web sites you have visited. This saves you having to remember the addresses and means you don't have to spend time online searching for the sites again. As long as you are connected to the Internet, a click on a bookmarked address will open up the site.

The process of bookmarking websites is similar in all browsers (look for "Bookmarks," "Favorites" or "Favorite Places" on your browser's toolbar). To bookmark a site when you are on the Internet, first open the site, then go to the **Favorites** menu and click on **Add to Favorites**. The Add Favorite dialogue box appears with the address of the site you are visiting. Click on **OK**.

To access this site again, click on the **Favorites** icon on the toolbar. A list of your bookmarked addresses will appear in a column on the left. Click on the relevant address to load the site.

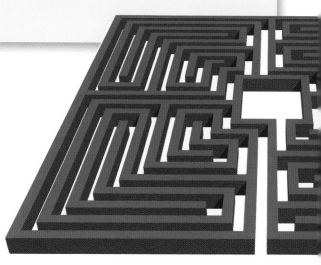

8 Copernic now searches through a variety of search engines. It collates the findings and downloads them into your Web browser, ready for you to view. Click on a link to open the Web page. (Your search keywords are highlighted in yellow.)

9 Copernic can search newsgroup and e-mail address databases in the same way. Select a category – such as Newsgroups – in the New Search dialogue box, type your keywords in the "Search for" box and click on **Search**. Copernic will then search the websites that monitor messages posted to newsgroups.

10 The results of the search are listed in your browser, with keywords highlighted in yellow. Click on a link to investigate it. Once you have opened the link, it appears blue in the list so that you know you have viewed it.

Close-up
Don't forget to use links to track down information. Links are a key part of the World Wide Web. They appear as underlined text on a Web page and let you jump directly from one page or site to another. Most websites have links to other similar sites, so you may find the information you want browsing from one to the next.

Security on the Internet

How to ensure users **of your PC** are protected **when** online

Internet newcomers are naturally concerned about security. They worry about whether it's safe to send credit-card details over the Internet, or whether children will come across undesirable material. Many people also have concerns over the privacy of e-mail and the unauthorized issue of their e-mail addresses, as well as the threat of computer viruses.

All these concerns are valid, but there are measures you can take to guarantee the integrity of the sites your family visits, and that your personal details are kept confidential.

Keeping it safe and sound

Whether shopping, browsing or e-mailing, there are ways to guarantee your security on the Internet.

Shopping and security

If a shopping website states that it uses "encryption" technology to transfer credit-card details (a complex, almost unbreakable, scrambling system), there should be no security problem. However, a good website will also offer alternative methods of payment, such as issuing an invoice, offering to call you and take details over the phone, or faxing or posting an order form.

amazon.ca

| WELCOME | YOUR STORE | BOOKS | MUSIC | DVD | VIDEO | SOFTWARE |

Search Amazon.ca

Help > Privacy and Security > Safe and Secure Online Transactions

Help Topics

Vous voulez voir cette page en français ? Cliquez ici.

Privacy and Security
> Your Amazon.ca Charter of Rights
> Credit Card Safety
> Amazon.ca Privacy Notice
> Safe and Secure Online Transactions
> Safe Shopping Guarantee

Customer Security: Buying and Selling

Amazon.ca is concerned about the safety and sec we have put a number of technological protection transaction process is extremely safe and that ou

Additionally, Amazon.ca takes a number of steps seller platforms are safe and that our sellers are keep in mind that customer protection is a two-w any online venue, caution must always be practic

Ordering
> New Customers
> Amazon Marketplace
> 1-Click Ordering
> Search Tips
> Pricing Policy

The overwhelming majority of online transactions While the possibility of being defrauded by a thir some risks. Amazon.ca has developed the followi to help ensure that your online shopping experier

NETNANNY
www.netnanny.net

Home   FAQ   Support   Buy   Review   Contact

Children and the Internet

The best way to protect children from coming across undesirable material on the Internet is to use special software. Programs such as Cyber Patrol and Net Nanny block access to sites known to have offensive content.

You can also get software that creates a log of all the sites that have been visited from your PC, and so keep a check on what your children have seen. You can also use the History button on your Web browser to do a similar job (see below right).

In Windows Vista you can set up a "Content Advisor" ratings system to control how much of the Internet a person can view according to levels of language, nudity, sex and violence. To do this, click on the **Start** button, then **Control Panel**. Click on **Network and Internet**, then on **Internet Options**. Click on the **Content** tab

and then on the **Enable** button. In the Content Advisor dialogue box, select the Ratings tab and click on each category then adjust the slider to set a rating level. Setting all categories at "Level 1" effectively bars all access to the Web, apart from the most child-friendly sites. Click on **OK** when you have finished and you will be prompted to set a supervisor password. You must type it in every time you change the Content Advisor settings, so don't lose it.

Watch out

It is possible, but very unlikely, that your e-mail could be intercepted as it is sent across the Internet. However, anyone who uses your PC could read your incoming e-mail once it has been received, which is a good reason for being discreet in what you write.

Viruses and the Internet

Computer viruses can seriously damage your PC. The best way to avoid getting a virus from the Internet, or from any other source, is to use an antivirus utility.

There is also a risk of infection from "macro viruses" that enter your PC via e-mail attachments. You can set a high level of Macro Virus protection in any Microsoft Office program (Word, Excel, PowerPoint or Outlook). Go to the **Tools** menu and click on **Options**. Click on the **Security** tab and then on **Macro Security**. Choose a level of Macro security in the dialogue box, then click on **OK**.

A computer on an "always-on" broadband connection to the Internet can be open to malicious attack. To protect against this, Windows Vista includes a "firewall" – software that prevents unauthorized access to your machine. Go to the **Start** menu, then **Control Panel** and click on **Security** then **Security Center** to set and adjust your Windows firewall and virus protection settings.

Safeguard your e-mail address

Sometimes, your e-mail address can be obtained by companies or individuals who send you junk e-mail, known as "spam." Try to avoid this by omitting your e-mail address from forms that you fill in by hand or on the Internet.

Only give your e-mail address to individuals of your choice. Good Internet trading companies should give you the option of withholding your address, even to reputable, third-party vendors. Never reply to an unsolicited e-mail; this confirms yours is an active address.

History button

A simple way to keep an eye on the websites that have been visited from your PC is to use the History button that comes with Internet Explorer. When you press it, a log of all sites that have been accessed will appear to the left of the Explorer window.

You can set the number of days that the History button monitors in Internet Explorer. Go to the **Tools** menu and click on **Internet Options**. With the General tab selected, go to the "Days to keep pages in history" box and input the number of days that suits you. You can also choose to clear the History folder.

Explore the world of multimedia

Watch video and animations, play games and listen to the radio on your PC

The term "multimedia" describes the capability of modern computers to deliver many different kinds of information at once: the elements of multimedia are generally pictures, text, animations, sounds and video. For example, you might find a short clip to accompany a film review, or a live radio feed at a news site. The quality of what you experience depends on the speed of your Internet connection: if you have a fast, broadband Internet connection, you will be able to download and view long videos and animations, take part in interactive games and listen to high-quality music files.

Sights and sounds on the Internet

In order to enjoy the extra dimension of multimedia, you may need to add extra features to your browser.

Bring your Web browser up to speed

Microsoft Internet Explorer and almost all other Web browsers can handle basic forms of multimedia. However, to view video clips and animation on some sites you need mini-programs called "plug-ins." These vary in sophistication but the best, such as Shockwave, can play animations, video and interactive games.

The most popular plug-ins are Flash^{TM} and Shockwave$^®$, both from Macromedia, Inc., and RealPlayer$^®$ from RealNetworks$^®$. Flash uses ingenious programming to pack complicated animations, games and interfaces into small files that download quickly. Shockwave allows more complicated games and interactivity to be displayed within your browser, even including video images.

RealPlayer is one of the most popular plug-ins for "streaming" audio or video content to your PC. Streaming means that you can start listening to or watching a file before it is completely downloaded – the file plays while the download continues in the background, saving you a long wait. The quality of the streamed sound and pictures depends on the speed of your connection: the faster the better.

Keyword

Plug-in *This is a piece of software that adds new features to your Web browser. After a plug-in has been installed, your browser will use it automatically whenever necessary.*

Watch out

If you have a pay-as-you-go dialup connection, listening to Internet radio stations can become expensive. But if you have a broadband contract, you can listen for as long as you like.

Downloading a plug-in

This section tells you how to download the RealPlayer plug-in from RealNetworks. The procedure for downloading other plug-ins is similar.

Connect to the Internet and launch your browser. In the address bar, type www.real.com and press the **Return** key. Then, click on the **Start Download** button for

http://www.real.com/

the player (or similar: The site changes often). An installation dialogue box will appear, asking if you want to run the installer. Click on **Run** to start the download. Click on **Run** again to launch the RealPlayer Setup application. A dialogue box will ask your connection speed. Click on

the button corresponding to your speed and click on **Next**. You will be asked to read and accept the licence agreement, to select an installation location and whether you want a Desktop shortcut. Click on **Next** and RealPlayer Setup will complete the installation. Now choose whether you want RealPlayer to be your universal player (this means RealPlayer will be used to play all types of media, from MP3 to CDs). If not, select which media types you wish to play using RealPlayer.

RealPlayer will launch automatically to complete the setup process. The RealPlayer Radio page shows links to a variety of different types of audio content.

Using the plug-in

You can use RealPlayer to see or hear RealMedia clips on various websites (like www.cbc.ca or www.bbc.co.uk), but the player itself also has channels that you can access.

Turn off to speed up

Multimedia files can often be very large, which means that a Web page with lots of multimedia elements, such as sound and animation, can take a long time to open. If you would rather not have these elements present when you are using the Web, you can instruct your browser not to download them. Go to the **Start** menu and right-click on **Internet**. Click on

Internet Properties then on the **Advanced** tab. In the Multimedia section you will see that some items have ticked boxes beside them. Choose the features you want to keep and those you want to disable. If you want to disable sounds and images, for example, click in the boxes to remove the ticks. Click on **Apply**, then on **OK**. Next time you access a Web page, it will appear without sound or images.

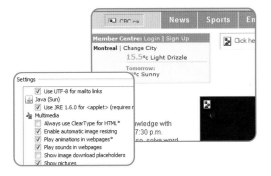

Chat with others online

Use the World Wide Web to make new friends and contacts

One of the most exciting things about the Internet is that it brings people together. People who share similar interests can keep in touch via e-mail and by subscribing to mailing lists; others who want to chat in "real time" (messages appear on the other person's computer screen as you type),

can use instant messenger programs to "talk." A growing section of the Internet, called Usenet, is made up of thousands of discussion groups. Here, people post messages that can be replied to, thereby initiating a discussion. Obtain a list of the main discussion groups from your Internet Service Provider (ISP).

Find out which of your friends are regularly online and use Windows Live Messenger. Gather their e-mail addresses to add to your Messenger contacts.

BEFORE YOU START

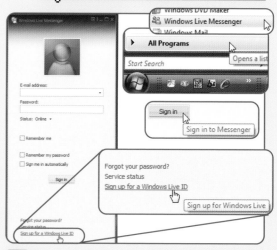

1 Go to the **Start** menu, select **All Programs**, then **Windows Live Messenger**. If you don't have a Windows Live ID, click on the **Sign up for a Windows Live ID** link at the bottom of the window, and follow the step-by-step instructions (see below right). When you next open Windows Live Messenger, click on **Sign in** to begin chatting.

There are other instant messenger programs available, such as Yahoo Messenger and AOL Messenger. You can also search the Internet for sites such as www.tucows.com, from which you can download messenger software that is compatible with MSN, Yahoo and AOL.

OTHER PROGRAMS

Bright idea
Windows Live Messenger can automatically update your address book whenever your contacts change their details. Just subscribe to Windows Live Contacts to make sure that you never lose touch!

2 Once Messenger is set up, your Messenger window appears onscreen. To close the window, make it larger or minimize it, use the buttons on the top right-hand corner. To open the window, double-click on the Messenger icon in the taskbar at the bottom right of your screen.

3 To add a contact, select **Add a contact** from the **Contacts** menu. Enter your contact's details in the "Instant Messaging Address" box along with an invitation message and other relevant details, such as a nickname, and click on **Add contact**. Your contact will receive a message and, if they accept, you will be connected.

4 To send a message, double-click on your contact. A conversation window opens. Type your message in the bottom section and click **Send**. Leave the window open and the reply appears under your message. Close the window and the reply pops up at the bottom right of your computer screen – click on it to continue your chat.

Sign up to Messenger

To sign up for Messenger, you may need to install the program. At Step 1 (above left), you will see a window with **Download it FREE now!**. Click on this and then on **Save** to download Windows Live Messenger to your PC. When prompted, click on **Run**. A Security Warning window will appear. Click on **Run** again to start the Installation Wizard. Follow the prompts and finally click on **Finish**.

Keyword

Emoticons These are small pictures or icons, which can be added to messages to show emotions, such as laughter. In the conversation window, click on **Emoticons** and then click on an emoticon in the drop-down menu.

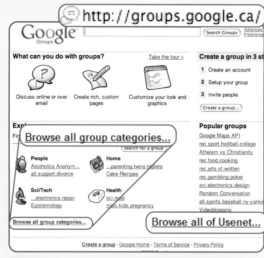

5 To have a three-way conversation, click on **Invite someone to this conversation**. Choose and click on a Messenger contact in the next dialogue box, then click on **OK**. When you finish chatting, simply close the window. When you want to chat again just click on the Messenger icon at the bottom-right of your screen.

6 Discussion groups – unlike chat – do not operate in "real time." You post a message and check back to see if anyone posts a response. To find a group, type http://groups.google.ca into your Web browser's address box and press **Return**. Click on **Browse all group categories...** to start, then on **Browse all of Usenet...**.

7 To find Canadian groups, scroll down the directory until you get to **can.** and select a category from the list of groups (here **can.rec.boating**). A list of "thread" subjects is now listed. To start a new discussion, click on **+ new post**.

Sharing Folders by Messenger

With Windows Live Messenger you can share files on your PC with someone else, which can be a great alternative to sending large files by e-mail. Simply drag a file – a photo, for example – onto a contact's name, and a Sharing Folder will automatically be created. You can add as many files as you like. Now you and that person can access all the files in the folder at any time, even if one of you is offline.

Watch out
When you are communicating with others over the Internet, never divulge personal information such as your address and phone number to anyone unless you know them or feel sure you can trust them.

Google Accounts — Create an account

Do you not have a Google Account?

Create an account now

Create an account

Your Google Account gives you access to Google Groups and other Google services. If you Account, you can sign in here.

I accept. Create my account.

e.g. myname@example.com. This will be used to sign-i account.

Choose a password: •••••••• — Password stren

Minimum of 6 characters in length.

Re-enter password: ••••••••

☑ Remember me on this computer.

Creating a Google Account will enable Search History. S a feature that will provide you with a more personalised Google that includes more relevant search results and recommendations. Learn More

8 You will then be required to register. Click on **Create an account now**, then fill in your e-mail address and a password, and read the terms and conditions. If you are happy to go ahead, click on **I accept. Create my account**. An e-mail will be sent to you. Click on the link in the e-mail to verify your e-mail address and account.

Discussions

View: Topic list, **Topic summary**

Description: Discussions on recreational boating

☆ **Engine Problems**
I have a Doral Prestancia 270 with twin 4.3 liter Mercruisers. Re and the synchronizer at zero now and again the synchronizer wi When this happens there is a change in the sound of the motors
By **Cogeco News** - Aug 18 - 2 new of 2 messages

☆ **can.rec.boating FAQ and charter**
=========================== ==================
=========================== ==================
boating Author: Pat Drummond Why a Canadian boating newsgr
By **Pat Drummond** - Aug 18 - 1 new of 1 message

☆ can.rec.boating FAQ and c

Post message   **Cancel**

9 Return to "can.rec.boating" and click on **+ new post**. Type a subject and message in the panels that appear. When you have finished, click on **Post message** and then on **Return to can.rec.boating**. You may have to wait a short time before it appears on the site. Keep checking back to see when your message, and replies to it, appear.

Engine Problems
I have a Doral Prestancia 270 with twin 4.3 liter Mercruisers. Recently a strange problem has develope and the synchronizer at zero now and again the synchronizer will show the port engine down by 200 to When this happens there is a change in the sound of the motors... more »
By Cogeco News - Aug 18 - 2 new of 2 messages

can.rec.boating FAQ and charter   CHARTE
===   Newsgro
boating: Author: Pat Drummond Why a Canadian boating newsgroup?... more »
By Pat Drummond - Aug 18 - 1 new of 1 message

can.rec.boating FAQ and charter   CHARTE
===   Newsgro
boating Author: Pat Drummond Why a Canadian boating newsgroup... more »

fiona-green

Skirting / Coving - best way to fix / paint

☆ 5 messages - Collapse all

tester View profile

Add Cc | Add Followup-

Hi,

I know you usually attach skirting / coving and then it possible / advisable to paint the edges before att reason I ask is I want to get the best finish in terms straight lines when painting.

Along with this it would mean the walls / ceiling are before attaching the named items - will the coving surfaces properly?

On Mar 5, 9:04 pm, tester <n...@bt
> Hi,
>
> I know you usually attach skirting
> it possible / advisable to paint the
> reason I ask is I want to get the be
> straight lines when painting.
>
> Along with this it would mean the
> before attaching the named items
> surfaces properly?

You could prepare and paint the skir to fix to the walls/ceiling.

Send   **Discard**

10 To reply to a posting, click on it. In the next window, all the replies from other users are displayed. Click on them to read them and then, if you like, add your own message by clicking on **Reply**. You must have logged in before you can post your own reply.

Shopping on the Internet

Buying **what you want is** just **a question of** point and click

Online shopping is now becoming an everyday activity. Users have access to a far wider range of goods than can be bought in local shops. Many people prefer online shopping because of the convenience – no parking or queues, the "shops" are open 24 hours a day, seven days a week, and goods are delivered to the door.

The prices of goods offered over the Internet are extremely competitive. Even after paying for delivery they can work out cheaper than shopping by conventional means.

In this project we show you how to buy a book and a piece of computer hardware. Use the steps as a general guide to buying any goods online.

Have a good idea of what you want to buy before you go online – it is easy to get distracted and buy things you don't need.

▶ BEFORE YOU START

1 Connect to the Internet. In your Web browser's address box type in the address of an Internet shopping Web site (in this case, www.amazon.ca). Press **Return** and then wait for the site's home page to appear on screen.

© Amazon.com. Inc. or its affiliates. All rights reserved.

Popular shopping sites

Addresses for popular shopping sites include:
- www.amazon.ca (books and music)
- www.cdnow.com (music)
- www.tigerdirect.ca (computer equipment)
- www.ftd.com (flowers)
- www.expedia.ca (tickets and travel)
- www.futureshop.ca (electronics)

Bright idea
When you buy over the Internet make a note of information such as the date of purchase, item, cost, contact phone number or e-mail address. This makes follow-up queries easy.

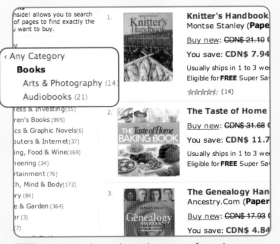

*When you click on the **Add to Shopping Basket** button you are not committed to buy at this point. You are simply collecting items.*

2 Navigate through to the type of product you are looking for. For example, if you want to buy a book, click on the Books tab at the top of the screen on Amazon's home page. The books page lists many different categories. Narrow your search by selecting a category in the Browse panel.

3 The most popular titles and types of book appear at the top of the list of entries for each category. As with other major authors, there are hundreds of titles available on the subject of Shakespeare – these are grouped together into subcategories to make searching easier.

4 For information on any book, such as reviews or its price, click on the title. If you want to purchase a book, click on the title then on the **Add to Shopping Basket** button. To make the purchase, click on **Proceed to Checkout** or carry on shopping to look for further items.

Making a quick search
On the Amazon home page you will see a search box near the top of the page. If you're searching for a book, type in the author, title, or subject of the book and in the box to the left, click on the arrow and select "Books" from the drop-down list. Then click on **Go!** A list of relevant books appears, which you can browse through before choosing whether you would like to buy any.

Shopping Basket
You can see the items in your Shopping Basket by clicking on the **View Basket** icon at the top of the Amazon site. This page lists all the items you have selected to buy. If you decide not to buy something in your basket, click on the **Delete** button next to the item. If you would like to continue browsing, click on the browser's **Back** button.

Bright idea
If you are reluctant to send financial details over the Internet, look for an option to fax, telephone or mail your order.

Using the Internet to buy computer hardware can save you money. We used the Yahoo! search engine, at www.yahoo.ca.

COMPUTER HARDWARE

5 Enter your e-mail address and select either "I am a new customer" or "I am a returning customer" option, as appropriate. Then click on **Sign in using our secure server**. Fill in your details and follow the onscreen instructions to complete your purchase. You can cancel the transaction up to the last minute.

6 Type www.yahoo.ca in your browser's address box, then press **Return**. When the page appears, click on **Shopping** in the left menu. Once the Shopping page appears, enter the item you want in the "Search" box at the top. You can also pick a category from the drop-down menu

Reproduced with permission of Yahoo! Inc. ® 2008 by Yahoo! Inc. YAHOO! and the YAHOO! logo are trademarks of Yahoo! Inc.

7 Yahoo! will list all the products it can find that match your description, displaying the prices and the stores that sell the product. Scroll down the list and when you see an item that interests you, click on the **See It** button to visit the online shop selling it.

Secure shopping

Never give out your credit or debit card details on the Internet unless the seller uses a secure server for payments. In Internet Explorer 7, the way to tell this is to look for the padlock icon displayed in the Security Status Bar, located at the right of your Web browser's address box. The Security Status Bar is not normally displayed unless you are about to enter a site where special security issues exist. Click on the padlock icon to view a security report for the site you are about to enter. The background colour of the address box may also change to indicate potential security issues:

White (default) – no information is available.
White (with padlock icon) – communication is encrypted and is therefore secure.
Green – the site has been checked and its identity approved.
Yellow – proceed with caution as this site appears to be misrepresenting its identity.
Red – do not use this site. Red indicates a known problem, such as expired or revoked encryption. These sites have been reported to Microsoft.
In all cases, avoid entering sensitive data until you are sure that the website is the one you intended to visit.

Watch out

The Internet makes it easy to buy things from overseas. However, while some goods can seem cheaper, they may not be suitable – for example, European voltage is different from North American. Also, duties and delivery charges can eat up the savings.

8 Check the details and specifications carefully to make sure that the product is the one you want. If everything seems right, click on the **Add to Cart** button (some websites have Buy Now buttons instead).

9 Once you have added everything you need to your shopping cart, click on **Checkout** (this button may be called Order or Buy now). Follow the instructions to add your customer details, then click on **Submit Your Order Now**. Check your details, then proceed to the credit info.

10 The final step is to enter your card details in the panel on the right. Check for a padlock symbol to ensure that the vendor is using encryption (see page 108), and click on the **Submit Your Order Now** button. You will usually receive confirmation via e-mail. Then simply wait for your goods to be delivered.

Compare prices

There's no need to visit a lot of websites to be sure that you're getting good value. Comparison shopping sites, such as PriceCanada.com, do the legwork for you, checking the price of an item at many different online stores.

Find and buy an antique

Use the Internet to seek out new items for your collection

The Internet is an excellent source of information for collectors of almost anything, from records and model cars to paintings and antiques.

For keen collectors of antiques the World Wide Web opens up a completely new way of shopping and dealing, and many auction houses now run "virtual auctions" online. Collectors can also find a wealth of detail on their favourite craftspeople, designers and painters. And they can share information with other enthusiasts, arrange sales and purchases, or simply enjoy chatting about their hobby with people all over the world.

Make a list of the categories or keywords to search by. If one search doesn't yield many sites you can search again without wasting time.

⬆ BEFORE YOU START

http://www.google.ca/

Google Canada

antiques

(Google Search) (I'm Feeling Lucky)
Search: ○ the web ◉ pages from Canada

Advanced Se
Preferences
Language To

Google.ca offered in: Français

Advertising Programs - Business Solutions - About Google - Go to Google.com

©2008 · Privacy

1 Connect to the Internet. In your Web browser's address box, type in the address of a search engine and press the **Return** key. Type a keyword in the search engine's search box (here, "antiques") and click on **Find**.

Popular search engines
Addresses for popular search engines include:
- www.google.ca
- www.lycos.ca
- www.yahoo.ca
- www.excite.com
- www.altavista.ca
- www.dogpile.com

Bright idea

If you are bidding online in a foreign currency, make sure you know the latest exchange rate. You will usually pay at the rate on the closing date for bids. Check with the auctioneer.

Close-up

eBay and many other online retailers use PayPal for sending and receiving payments. PayPal is a secure method of payment, offering fraud protection, and it's quick, easy and free to use.

Close-up

With Internet Explorer you can search and browse multiple websites within a single window. Type keywords into the search bar at the top of the window. Then switch between sites using the tabs at the top of the browser window.

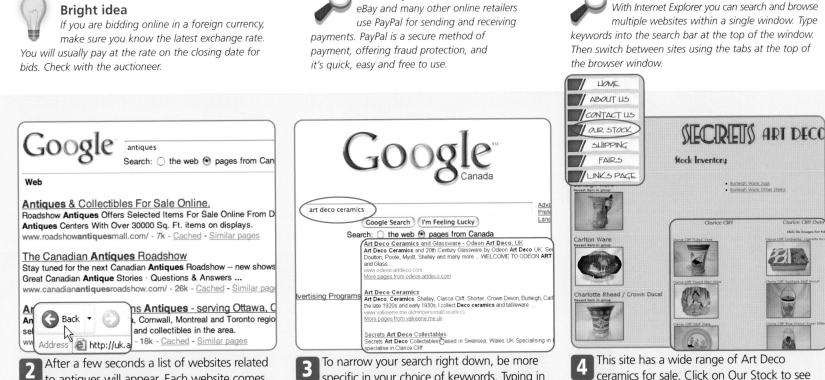

2 After a few seconds a list of websites related to antiques will appear. Each website comes with a brief description of what it offers. To view a website, click on its name. To return to the list of sites found by the search engine, click on your Web browser's **Back** button.

3 To narrow your search right down, be more specific in your choice of keywords. Typing in "art deco ceramics" will reduce the number of relevant websites considerably. The sites on offer could include book publishers, dealers, dedicated enthusiasts and experts. We've chosen a site called "Secrets Art Deco Collectables."

4 This site has a wide range of Art Deco ceramics for sale. Click on Our Stock to see the items on offer. You can view items by a particular artist – for example, Clarice Cliff – by clicking on the picture under the relevant heading.

Virtual auctions

Online auctions such as www.ebay.ca operate along similar lines to traditional auctions. A seller places an item on the site, often with a photograph. Bidding continues up to a set closing time. When bidding closes, the highest bidder wins. Winning bidder and seller then contact each other to arrange payment and delivery. Fraud is rare, but you should still take precautions. Always pay by a secure payment method, such as PayPal (see above). Also check the feedback that eBay users give on each other – this is a quick way to find out if someone has a bad reputation.

Surfing the Internet

You can browse websites – or "surf the Net" – in several ways. You can open any site by typing its address in the browser's address box and pressing **Return**, or by clicking on its link in another site. Alternatively, you can use the browser's toolbar buttons to move backward and forward through pages and sites.

111

Watch out
If you join in an online discussion, never give your home telephone number or home address to others in the group, and always follow forum rules.

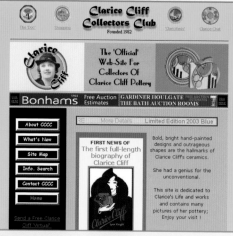

5 If you want information relating to a specific artist, type the name into the search engine's search box, enclosed in quotation marks, for example "Clarice Cliff". Google will look for the two words as a phrase, and only show sites that match it precisely.

6 There are some excellent resources on the Web for Clarice Cliff fans. The site at www.claricecliff.com is designed for collectors, and provides lots of useful information, as well as being a forum for chat and discussion.

7 Other sites operate as virtual showrooms, allowing you to browse through a large selection of items and buy any that interest you. If you want to revisit a page, click on the browser's **Back** button, or use your browser's **History** button to show all the pages you have visited recently.

Picture search

Google is one of the most popular search engines because of its speed and high success rate. You can also use Google to search for images.

Click on the Images link, then in the search box type keywords to describe what you are looking for. Google will return a page of thumbnail images – click on one to see an enlarged view.

*You can access the Internet from the Taskbar in Windows Vista. Right-click on the Taskbar, select **Toolbars** from the pop-up menu, followed by **Address**. Type in a Web address in the address box that appears, then press **Return**.*

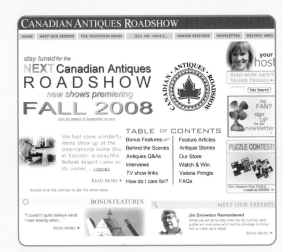

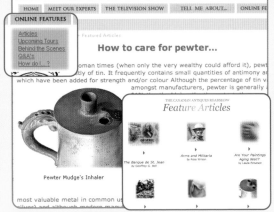

8 The web is literally crawling with information for and by antiques enthusiasts. A terrific online resource is the website of CBC TV's Candadian Antiques Roadshow. The site features information about the show, and lots more (see www.canadianantiquesroadshow.com).

9 The site's Feature Articles explore a specific piece, spotlight a designer or describe the best way to care for your antiques. To get to the articles, click on the **Online Features** menu item, then select **Articles** in the drop-down menu. Now click on your choice of topic from the list in the main part of the page

10 You can also read up on your chosen field by clicking on **Tell Me About...** and choosing from the list on the page. The site's experts won't evaluate your item for you, but sometimes they can tell you a little bit about it. To ask a question, look under **Helpful Info** for contact information.

Using search engines
Each search engine has its own way of allowing you to narrow or broaden your searches for information. Look for pointers to special help sections on a search engine's home page that will teach you about searching successfully.

World wide diary

Share your thoughts and experiences with the world via a weblog

If you would like to get creative, share your thoughts on issues you care about, make new friends, and perhaps even earn a little money, then a weblog could be for you. A weblog – or "blog" – is essentially an online diary or journal, on a hobby or any topic that interests you. It's fun, free and doesn't need any technical expertise.

All you need to do is come up with an idea for your blog – you can aim to be entertaining, light-hearted or authoritative, it's all up to you. Once you have your intentions clear in your mind, you can just follow the steps in this project and, before long, you will have joined the millions of people already in the blogging world.

Plan the theme of your blog, and work out what would be appropriate to include. You should always be careful in choosing your content.

BEFORE YOU START

1 Explore the blog world for advice on how to start. Search for blog topics that interest you at Google (http://blogsearch.google.com) and Blog Catalog (www.blogcatalog.com) or explore lists of popular blogs on a blog tracker site like Daypop (www.daypop.com/blogrank).

Blogging for free

Dedicated "blog hosting" websites provide a home for your online diary where visitors can read your musings, browse photos, watch videos, and even contribute their own thoughts. There are many blogging sites where you can sign up for free (see "Choosing where to blog," right), and most offer simple ways for you to update the content of your blog – by e-mail, for example – while travelling. Blogs are indexed, too, so potential visitors with similar interests can find your blog more easily.

Bright idea

Choosing the right name for your blog can be important in attracting readers. Think about who you want to appeal to – whether your blog will be humorous or businesslike, for example – and try to create a name that reflects this.

Permissions

Everyone
Everyone
Messenger
Messenger and friends
Messenger, friends, and friends of your friends
Custom...

Windows Live™ Spaces

Spaces | Interests | Friends | Photos | Blog | Customise | Safety | About Spaces

Welcome to Windows Live Spaces

Want to create a blog at Windows Live Spaces? It's easy to join the Spaces community, create a free blog, make new friends and start sharing! Become part of the MSN blog community! Live Spaces makes it easy to create a blog and share your life, and there's always something new to discover. Bring your stories to life with Spaces.

MSN Alerts   comedy

Go to your space   Create your space

Create your Windows Live Space

With your own space, you can share your thoughts and interests with just everyone. You can set up your own blog, profile, friends list, photo albums

* Required field

Enter a title for your space

* Title: Bird's Eye View

Enter a name to include in your Spaces web address

ⓘ The name that you typed is available.

*http:// birdseyeview-blog   .spaces.live.com/

Check availability

Your use of Windows Live Spaces is subject to the Wind

Create

You've created your space

Your space is located at:
http://birdseyeview-blog.spaces.live.com/

Your permissions are currently set to **Everyone** (Change Permissions)

Permissions allow you to decide who can view your space and your profile informat

- Everyone: Provides access to anyone on the Web. Permissions for your space Everyone if you want to syndicate your space, have your space displayed in t modules, notify ping servers, or allow trackbacks on your blog.
- Messenger: Provides access only to people in your Messenger allow list.
- Messenger & friends: Provides access only to people in your Messenger allow list.
- Messenger, friends & friends of your friends: Provides access only to people c allow list, your friends list, your mutual friends, and their mutual friends.
- Custom: Customize your permissions list by selecting which groups of people

Note: Because your space is associated with your Windows Live ID, people who kn your Windows Live ID will be able to search for and locate your space.

Please be advised that spaces that do not conf content reported to authorities.

Go to your space

---

2 Setting up and running a blog can be tricky so, as a first-time "blogger," use a service such as Windows Live Spaces. Go to http://spaces.live.com/ and click on **Create your space**. Complete the registration form and choose a login password (or you can use your existing Microsoft Passport password, if you have one).

3 You need an imaginative name for your blog, rather than just "Brian's Blog," for example. The blog shown here is about wildlife, so it's called "Bird's Eye View." Pick a variation for your Web address, here "birdseyeview-blog," and click on **Check availability** to make sure no one else is using it. If all is OK, click on **Create**.

4 At first, your Spaces blog can be viewed by everyone. If you would like to be selective about who views your blog, click on the **Change Permissions** link. Select one of the viewing options from the drop-down menu and click on **Save** to finish. Now click on **Go to your space** to continue setting up your blog.

Choosing where to blog

Windows Live Spaces is used in this project to build a blog, but there are plenty of free alternatives if you'd like to experiment. Blogger (far right), www.blogger.com, is a well-established Spaces competitor; BlogDrive, www.blogdrive.com, allows multiple authors to work on one blog; and Bloglegion (middle right), www.bloglegion.com, lets you add photo albums, podcasting and "friends" lists to your blog pages.

Watch out
Visitors to Internet sites have very little patience – you only have a few seconds to grab their attention. Try breaking up your text with headings and one or two different fonts to help readers scan your blog entries – but don't go overboard!

5 In the Blog pane click on **Add**. Enter a title and type your first story in the box: a simple welcome message and details about your blog. Use the toolbar to style your entry – you can make text bold, italic or underlined, add emoticons (facial expression icons) and more. Hover your cursor over a button to see what it does.

6 Click on **Publish entry** and then **Preview Entry** at the top to see how your blog will appear. This is a good start, but adding some digital photos would help give the blog more colour. To create a photo album that can be accessed from the main blog page, click on **Add album**.

7 Enter an album title and click on **Add Photos**. If you are warned that "Windows Live Photo Upload Control" is needed, click on the yellow bar at the top of the window, select **Install ActiveX Control** and then **Install**. You can then browse images on your hard drive. Tick the box next to any you'd like to share and click on **Upload Now**.

Get paid to blog

Blogging is about fun, not profit, but some successful blogs can make at least a little cash by including ads. If you are interested in using ads, you can try an advertising program such as Google AdSense (right), at www.google.com/adsense, which is supported directly by the well-known blog-creation site Blogger (www.blogger.com).

Quality over quantity

It's important to update your blog at least weekly, ideally every one or two days, to prevent your audience losing interest and moving elsewhere. But frequency isn't the whole story and it's really important to concentrate on the quality of your content. If you write interesting and informative pieces then readers will stick around, even if they only visit every couple of weeks or so.

Bright idea
There is nothing more annoying than writing your entry, only for the upload to fail. Try writing each entry in a Word file – where you can save it as you go – then copy and paste it into your blog program.

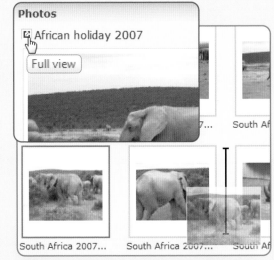

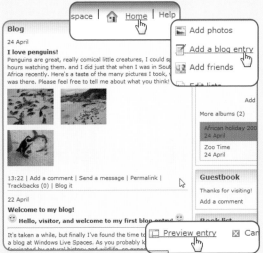

8 It may take a little while for your photos to upload. Once they have, drag and drop the thumbnail images in the photo editing window if you wish to reorder them, then click on **Save and close**. Your photo album appears as a small slide-show whenever people view your blog. Click on the **Full view** button to see full-size images.

9 To use images in blog entries, click on **Home**, **Add a blog entry** and then **Add Photos**. Browse for some images, tick your selections and select **Upload Now**. You will only see the image name, but visitors to your blog will see the full image. Type in any comments, then click **Publish Entry** and **Preview entry** to take a look.

10 Windows Live Messenger Spaces lets you create "Lists" on anything you choose, such as favourite books, films or holiday destinations. Think of a topic, click **Edit your space**, **Edit list**, then click **Add Item** and type in a name and description for the items you want to list. Then click **Save**.

Finding readers

Once you have great content, you need to find people to read it. Start by telling your friends and online contacts about the blog. Include the "URL" (the Web address) in your e-mails, and spread the word in Web forums. You can also submit your blog's URL to online blog directories, such as www.blogcatalog.com or www.bloghub.com.

Close-up
Make sure you check your spelling – it can be very annoying for visitors if your blog is full of mistakes, and they are unlikely to visit again.

Bright idea
A blog's success is measured in terms of visitor numbers. To increase your popularity, include links to other like-minded blogs – if their authors return the favour, you could receive visitors from their sites.

11 By adding links to associated sites, lists can be useful for your readers. Use www.google.ca to find suitable websites. Add each item by clicking on **Edit** and entering the Web address. When you've finished, click on **Edit list information** and change the name from "Custom List." Click **Save**, then **Exit edit mode** to view the finished list.

12 To give your site a more individual look, click on **Edit your space** then **Customize**. Select **Themes** to choose a new colour scheme and **Modules** to remove features you don't want or to reorganize others by dragging and dropping. Try out the options and click on **Close** when you have finished. Click on **Save** to record your changes.

13 Spaces blogs can be updated via e-mail, so you can also post entries from a mobile phone that has e-mail. Click on **Options**, **E-mail Publishing** then tick **Turn on e-mail publishing**. Type in your e-mail address, choose a password, then decide whether to save entries as drafts (until you get to your PC) or publish them immediately.

Encourage feedback

It's easy to get visitors to a blog, at least once, but if they're going to stick around then you need to make them feel involved. Do this by posting questions to your readers, asking them for their own thoughts, experiences or ideas. Let them use the Spaces Comments feature to discuss the blog with you and other readers – you'll create a community spirit that keeps people coming back.

Stay out of trouble

Blogs are all about free speech but you still need to be careful what you write. If you disagree with someone, by all means say why, but don't libel them by making accusations that you couldn't back up in court. Don't copy text or graphics from other sites and pass them off as your own. Also be aware of any other restrictions imposed by your blogging service (see http://spaces.live.com/coc.aspx for the Spaces Code of Conduct).

Watch out

If you publish your e-mail address on your blog, you will receive spam – unwanted junk e-mail. Try to beat the automatic e-mail readers by breaking it over two lines – a human will work it out, an automatic reader might not!

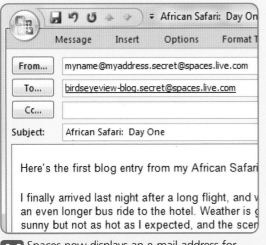

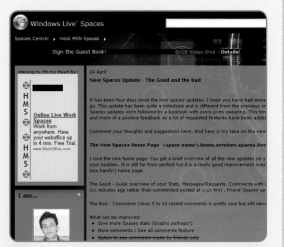

14 Spaces now displays an e-mail address for updating your blog. Add this to the address book on your mobile phone. Any e-mails sent from your nominated e-mail account to that address will go straight to the blog. This is handy, but be aware that anyone who discovers the e-mail address will have update access to your blog, too.

15 By now you have a great-looking blog, so the next step is to attract visitors. Try to find blogs you like on the same topic as yours in a directory such as Bloghub, www.bloghub.com, then link to them (see Step 11) or write a blog entry about them. Send an e-mail to the author, who may then link back to you, sending some visitors your way.

16 Now that you've seen how to set up and run your own blog, you can pick up advanced tips on blogging by visiting the Hack MSN Spaces blog, http://spaces.live.com/d3vmax. For more general advice on blogging, you could take a look at www.bloggerforum.com, www.bloggertips.com and www.bloggingpro.com.

Advertise your updates

To alert your audience to blog updates as you upload them, try out Real Simple Syndication (RSS). To turn this on in Windows Live Spaces, check your blog is set to "Everyone" by going to **Options** and then **Permissions**. Now click on **Space settings** and then tick the **Syndicate** box. To explore the Live Alerts system further, visit http://alerts.live.com.

Do research on the Net

Use today's technology to learn about our yesterdays

The World Wide Web is a great tool for historical research. Whatever your field of interest, there are bound to be sites, discussion groups and library resources dedicated to that topic.

If, for example, you are interested in the First World War, you will find thousands of resources on the Web. Some will be pages produced by amateur historians, some will be educational sites aimed at children and some will be highly academic.

The first step is to do a search. Here we use a search engine called AllTheWeb, but you can use any one you like and pick your own path through the wealth of information on the War to End All Wars.

Make a note of which direction you want your search to take. Be as specific as possible to limit the number of hits. For example, search for "Somme" rather than "battles."

BEFORE YOU START

alltheweb
∘·∘ find it all ∘·∘

Back · · Search Favo
Address http://www.alltheweb.com/search?cat=web&cs=utf8&q=

| Web | News | Pictures | Video | Audio |

SEARCH

Results in: ● Any Language ○ English

Privacy Policy :: Submit Site :: About Us :: Help

Copyright © 2005 Overture Services, Inc.

1 Connect to the Internet as usual. In your Web browser's address box type in the address of a search engine then click on **Go** or press **Enter**. The search engine's home page will appear. Type a keyword or words into the search box and then click on the **Search** button.

Popular history sites

Sites with information on war history include:
- www.history.com (general history site)
- www.encyclopedia.com (free online encyclopedia)
- www.worldwar1.com (reference works and discussions)
- www.bbc.co.uk/history/worldwars (many war articles)
- www.histori.ca (Canadian history site)
- www.warmuseum.ca (Canadian War Museum website)

Keyword

Home page *This is the opening page for any website. It will tell you what the site includes and provide links to the various parts of the site.*

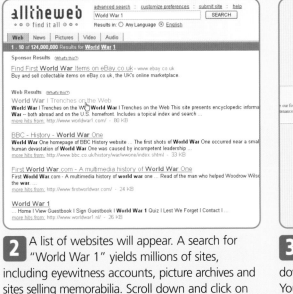

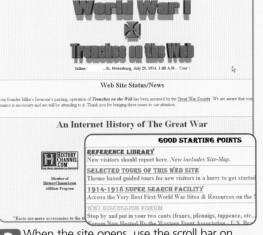

2 A list of websites will appear. A search for "World War 1" yields millions of sites, including eyewitness accounts, picture archives and sites selling memorabilia. Scroll down and click on **World War I Trenches on the Web**.

3 When the site opens, use the scroll bar on the right-hand side of your window to move down the home page a considerable way.
You will find a list with the heading "Good Starting Points." Click on **Reference Library**. This is a good place to begin your research.

4 Through the Reference Library you can access huge amounts of data, including biographies, maps, artwork and even sound recordings of the period. Click on one of the buttons at the foot of the home page to access an area of your choice.

Remember to use your Web browser's Back and Forward

buttons to revisit Web sites and pages you have opened since going online.

Bright idea
When you come across interesting sites, bookmark them (see page 96). This way you can revisit them quickly, without having to search for them again or remember their address.

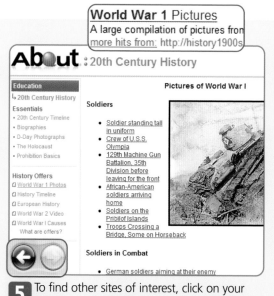

World War 1 Pictures
A large compilation of pictures from
more hits from: http://history1900s

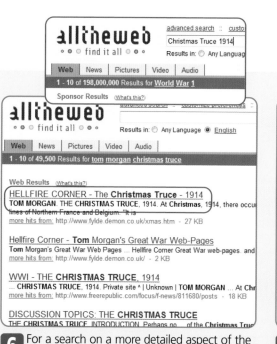

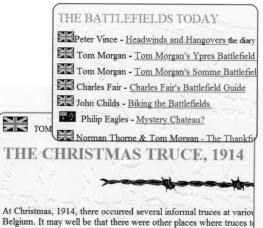

THE BATTLEFIELDS TODAY

Peter Vince - Headwinds and Hangovers the diary
Tom Morgan - Tom Morgan's Ypres Battlefield
Tom Morgan - Tom Morgan's Somme Battlefiel
Charles Fair - Charles Fair's Battlefield Guide
John Childs - Biking the Battlefields
Philip Eagles - Mystery Chateau?
Norman Thorpe & Tom Morgan - The Thankfi

THE CHRISTMAS TRUCE, 1914

At Christmas, 1914, there occurred several informal truces at variou Belgium. It may well be that there were other places where truces to by the amount of direct, eyewitness testimony which has so far bee reports (and even a few photographs) to convince us that something and that it was not entirely an isolated happening.

The image of opposing soldiers, shaking hands with each other on c next, is a powerful one, and one which is part and parcel of rememb of open-handed chivalry before the squalor and horror of the next t

This page gives a very general summary of the main events of some quoted in full at the end for those who would like to read them.

5 To find other sites of interest, click on your Web browser's **Back** button to return to the AllTheWeb site. Click on another site such as **World War 1 Pictures** to view a wide selection of images from this period.

6 For a search on a more detailed aspect of the Great War, return to the AllTheWeb site. Enter a more specific search term and select a page from the results returned. Below the title of each page is a series of excerpts from that page, which will give an idea of its contents.

7 Once you have read the page you have selected, you can click through the links on the site to access the main contents page where you can find other information. When you have finished, you can use your browser's **Back** button to return to your original search results.

Saving pictures

To save an image onto your hard disk, right-click on the image and select **Save Picture As** from the pop-up menu that appears. Click on the arrow beside the "Save in" box, scroll through and select a folder in which you want to save the image. Give the image a name in the "File name" box then click on **Save**.

8 Some of the most impressive resources on First World War history can be found at www.bbc.co.uk/history/worldwars. The BBC's website contains a detailed timeline of the war's events and fascinating features. One is an animated map showing how the Western Front developed.

9 The map uses the Flash plug-in for Internet Explorer – you will be asked if you would like to install it if you have not already done so. Once the map has downloaded you can follow the evolution of the trenches, with animations showing the key battles.

10 The BBC site also covers the human side of the war, with stories about individuals from the major fighting powers. The options in the left-hand panel allow you to choose different ways to browse through the site's extensive contents, for example, by topic, by time, or by people.

Printing a Web page

To print out a Web page for future reference, go to the **File** menu on your browser's menu bar at the top of the screen and click on **Print**. In the Options tab of the Print dialogue box you can choose how to print out Web pages with frames (separate elements that may not all print out at the same time).

File	Edit	View	Favorites	Tools	Help

New Tab — Ctrl+T
New Window — Ctrl+N
Open... — Ctrl+O
Edit with Microsoft Office Word
Save — Ctrl+S
Save As...
Close Tab — Ctrl+W
Page Setup...
Print... — Ctrl+P
Print Preview...
Send

Primary-school learning

Help **your** **children** expand **their** knowledge **through** the Net

Make a daily study plan so you can work out exactly which subjects to study and when, to make more efficient use of your time online.

The World Wide Web is, among many other things, a learning resource. It is full of material that can enhance children's understanding of their school subjects and of the world around them. There are thousands of educational sites, along with related sites that both parents and children will find useful. This project shows you a selection – some are bright and breezy interactive sites, others contain resources for literacy and learning.

Using the Internet for education is fun, and it equips elementary-school children with learning skills they are likely to use throughout their school years, and beyond.

BEFORE YOU START

1 Connect to the Internet. In the browser's address box type in a search engine address – here, http://kids.yahoo.com, an engine specially designed for children. Press the **Return** key. When the home page loads, type a keyword into the search box and click on **Search**.

Searching by category

In addition to a search box, some search engines let you search by category. You narrow your search by clicking on subdivisions that have been made already. This is useful for children who might misspell keywords.

Close-up
Keep a record of a Web site's address by adding it to your Web browser's Favorites (or Bookmarks) file (see page 96). Once entered, all you need do to view the site is click on the entry in the list instead of typing in the Web address every time.

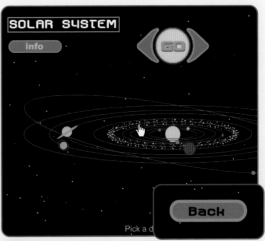

*Click on the **Back** button to revisit sites and pages already viewed since you have been online.*

1. **Arty** the Part Time Astronaut - join **Arty** and Gre each of the nine planets.
http://www.artyastro.com
More sites about: Astronomy and Space > Solar Sys

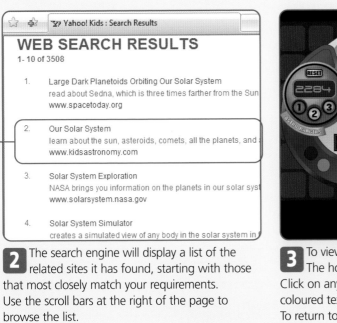

⭐ ✿ ✌ Yahoo! Kids : Search Results

WEB SEARCH RESULTS
1- 10 of 3508

1. Large Dark Planetoids Orbiting Our Solar System
   read about Sedna, which is three times farther from the Sun
   www.spacetoday.org

2. Our Solar System
   learn about the sun, asteroids, comets, all the planets, and
   www.kidsastronomy.com

3. Solar System Exploration
   NASA brings you information on the planets in our solar syst
   www.solarsystem.nasa.gov

4. Solar System Simulator
   creates a simulated view of any body in the solar system in

2 The search engine will display a list of the related sites it has found, starting with those that most closely match your requirements. Use the scroll bars at the right of the page to browse the list.

Most search engines provide a brief description of the contents of a Web site. This helps you to decide whether the site is likely to be useful or not.

3 To view a website, click on its underlined title. The home page of that site will then appear. Click on any buttons or links (indicated by different coloured text and underlining) to explore the site. To return to the list of other sites, click on the **Back** button.

4 Arty the Part Time Astronaut is a site that uses exciting animations and graphics to explain how the Solar System works. To view some of the features you will need the Flash plug-in, an add-on to your browser. Most PCs will have the plug-in preinstalled; if not you will be asked if you want to download it.

Useful educational sites
You may find these Web sites particularly useful for children under 13:
- www.owlkids.com (contains sections dedicated to toddlers, kids between 6 and 9, and those aged 9 to 13)
- www.quia.com/web/ (fun and games for all ages)
- kids.nationalgeographic.com (great online learning resource)

Bright idea
*If you have a dialup connection you can teach children how to read long web pages offline to keep your phone free. If you're using Internet Explorer, go to the **File** menu and click on **Work Offline**.*

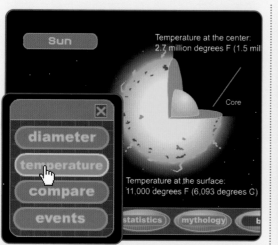

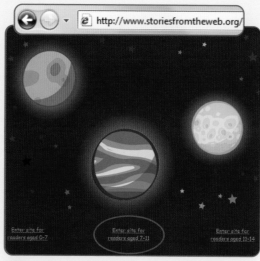

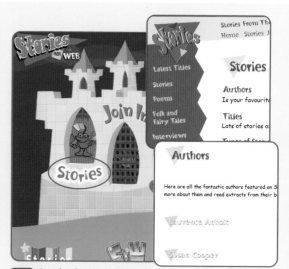

5 Remember to explore links to other areas within the same site or to related sites. This can take a lot of time, so if you have a dialup connection, keep an eye on the clock. Or, sign up for a broadband service for unlimited time online.

1 Reading and storytelling are key parts of primary school learning. Stories From The Web (www.storiesfromtheweb.org) is an eye-catching site, with stories, clubs and interactive elements. Click on an age group link to enter the site.

2 On the home page, click on **Stories**. The site organizes stories by Authors, Poetry, Titles and Types of Story – clicking on a section header gives you more options to choose from. Here we clicked on **Authors**, then **Laurence Anholt**.

*When you find a page that contains useful information, you may want to print it. Click on the text first, then go to the **File** menu and click on **Print**.*

POLLY the most p[...]

As soon as Polly wakes [...] morning, she starts to [...]
"Poems in the bedroom, [...] the shower,
Poems in the kitchen, ho[...] hour.

File	Edit	View	Favorites	T

New Tab
New Window
Open...
Edit with Microsoft Office Wo[...]
Save
Save As...
Close Tab

Page Setup...
Print...
Print Preview...

As you read stories on the *Stories From The Web* site, an animated page counter at the top right of the screen will help you keep track of how far you have got.

Well-organized websites such as the one below will give you a guarantee that their pages and the sites they contain links to are child-friendly and safe.

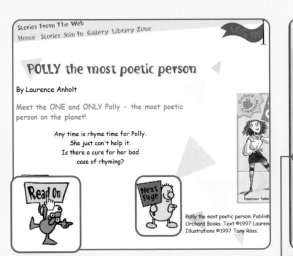

POLLY the most poetic person

By Laurence Anholt

Meet the ONE and ONLY Polly - the most poetic person on the planet!

Any time is rhyme time for Polly.
She just can't help it.
Is there a cure for her bad
case of rhyming?

3 The stories appear onscreen, page by page. You have to click on the **Read On** button to start and then on the **Next Page** button to turn the pages – a page counter in the corner tells you how many pages the book has.

4 Perhaps the best thing about this site is that it encourages children to write their own stories, review new ones and send in suggestions of their favourites. Click on **Join In**, then click on a category in the panel on the left of the page to try out the site's interactive elements.

5 Learning is easier when it's fun. The MaMaMedia site (www.mamamedia.com) contains lots of animation, colour and energy. This is a site your children are sure to enjoy, perhaps as a break from homework.

The Activities section includes a Send a Postcard feature. This allows youngsters to select a special picture from the site's image library to send as an e-mail to a friend.

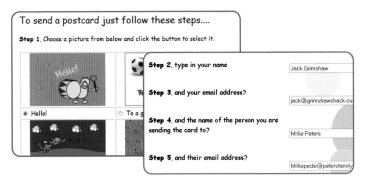

To send a postcard just follow these steps....

Step 1, Choose a picture from below and click the button to select it.

Hello!

Step 2, type in your name — Jack Grimshaw

Step 3, and your email address? — jack@grimshawshack.ou

Step 4, and the name of the person you are sending the card to? — Millie Peters

Step 5, and their email address? — Milliepede@petersfamily

Keyword

E-mail *Electronic mail (e-mail) is a form of high-speed communication that is supported by the Internet. Messages can be sent across the phone lines to people on the other side of the world in seconds.*

Close-up

Links to other web pages and sites usually appear underlined and in a different colour from the main body of text on a page. A mouse pointer will always change to a pointing hand when it passes over a link. Just click once on a link to open it.

6 Another search engine specifically geared towards children is Ask Kids (www.askkids.com). A child can type in a question and the site will help him or her to find the answer by listing websites that might contain relevant information.

7 E-mail can also be used for learning. Epals (www.epals.com) is a Net-based organization that links schoolchildren from around the world via e-mail. It can bring together pupils of a similar age who are studying similar types of subjects.

8 The Web is a treasure trove of information and resources on child literacy. The International Reading Association and National Coucil of Teachers of English maintain the site readwritethink.org as a resource for teachers and families who want to improve students' reading and language arts skills.

Navigating between windows

Sometimes, when you click on a link to another site, a new window opens in front of the original window. If you want to return to the original site, you have to make the original window "active."

To make the original window active, minimize or close the new window and then click on the original window (clicking on the **Back** button in the new window will not work).

Watch out
To prevent children accessing unsuitable material on the Internet, consider buying a Web-screening program, such as Net Nanny or Cyber Patrol (see page 99).

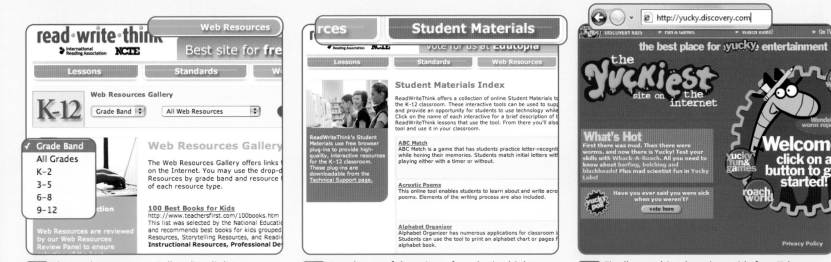

9 The Web Resources Gallery lists links to various helpful sites and tools, organized by grades from kindergarten straight through to grade 12. To get there, click on the **Web Resources** menu item, then select your child's grade from the drop-down menu.

10 Another useful section of readwritethink.org is the Student Materials area. Simply click on the **Student Materials** menu item to find these resources.

11 Finally, combine learning with fun. Take a look at The Yuckiest Site on the Internet (http://yucky.discovery.com), a child-friendly interactive science site that provides education and entertainment.

High-school learning

Gather material to help you study for your exams

The Internet is a valuable aid to learning and study. In addition to helping with research for everyday school work, students can find lots of useful material that relates to college or university preparation.

Certain sites offer the chance to browse past examination papers, take part in question-and-answer sessions, and chat with other students online. And when it comes to preparing for exams, students can get help setting up revision timetables.

But not all Web-based learning is geared towards specific exams. Language students can hone their skills by reading online foreign-language magazines, and you should be able to find resources for all areas of study.

First make a list of the subject areas you wish to study, then make a note of appropriate keywords and phrases to search by.

BEFORE YOU START

Google™
Canada

Google Search   I'm Feeling Lucky
Search: ⦿ the web ○ pages from Canada

Advanced S
Preferences
Language T

Google.ca offered in: Français

Advertising Programs - Business Solutions - About Google - Go to Google.com

©2008 · Privacy

1 Connect to the Internet. In your Web browser's address box, type the address of a search engine (here, www.google.ca), then press the **Return** key. After a few seconds the home page will load and appear onscreen.

Close-up
Although the full address for websites includes "http://" before the "www...," you don't need to type this into the address box. For most websites, you can simply start the address with "www."

The Google search engine highlights every occurrence of your keywords to help you make your choice of websites.

Watch out
When you do a word search, be as specific as you can. Simply searching for "scholarships" might yield unsuitable results, such as those for schools or cities you aren't going to. See page 94 for search advice.

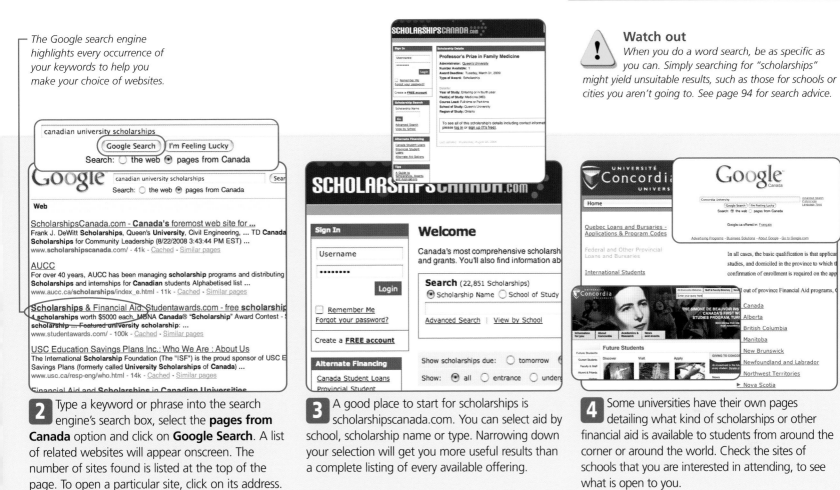

2 Type a keyword or phrase into the search engine's search box, select the **pages from Canada** option and click on **Google Search**. A list of related websites will appear onscreen. The number of sites found is listed at the top of the page. To open a particular site, click on its address.

3 A good place to start for scholarships is scholarshipscanada.com. You can select aid by school, scholarship name or type. Narrowing down your selection will get you more useful results than a complete listing of every available offering.

4 Some universities have their own pages detailing what kind of scholarships or other financial aid is available to students from around the corner or around the world. Check the sites of schools that you are interested in attending, to see what is open to you.

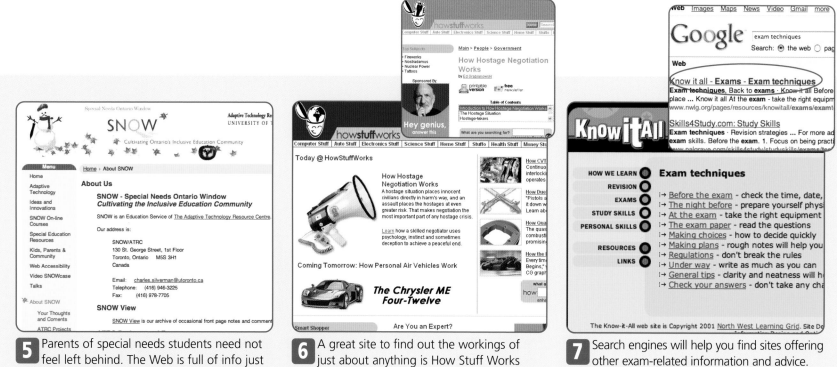

5 Parents of special needs students need not feel left behind. The Web is full of info just for them. The Special Needs Ontario Window (www.snow.utoronto.ca) is based in Ontario, but it has many resources that parents anywhere can adapt to their own child's situation.

6 A great site to find out the workings of just about anything is How Stuff Works (www.howstuffworks.com). It covers a range of subjects, from car engines to tornadoes, and offers an extensive question-and-answer section.

7 Search engines will help you find sites offering other exam-related information and advice. For example, type "exam techniques" into your search engine and look through some of the sites it comes up with. Here, "Know It All" provides advice on planning revision, stress management and exam techniques.

Keep yourself posted

It's not just links to other websites that are underlined on web pages – links to e-mail addresses are as well. Look out for free subscriptions to educational newsletters that you can receive via e-mail.

Attention parents!

Chatting online can be addictive. If you allow your children to chat to other students on the Web, it's sensible to limit the time they spend doing so, just as you would do when they are on the telephone.

There are online timer programs that help you keep tabs on time spent chatting online. You can set an alarm to go off when your alloted time has been reached. Try Computer Time by Software TIme (www.softwaretime.com).

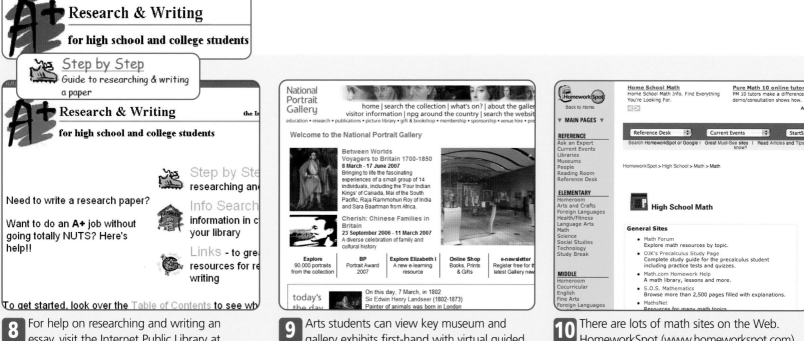

8 For help on researching and writing an essay, visit the Internet Public Library at www.ipl.org/div/teen/aplus. This useful site gives practical step-by-step information on planning, researching and writing an essay or project, even down to creating a revision timetable.

9 Arts students can view key museum and gallery exhibits first-hand with virtual guided tours. Visit the Museum of Modern Art in New York (www.moma.org) or the UK's National Portrait Gallery, London (www.npg.org.uk) for seminal works of art.

10 There are lots of math sites on the Web. HomeworkSpot (www.homeworkspot.com) offers a number of options to aid students. Math lessons, a forum, study pages, quick references and a lot more are available online to help solve tricky issues.

Don't lose your focus

It's easy to become sidetracked when going through search results. Be disciplined about assessing each page quickly and deciding whether a site is likely to contain useful information about the subject you are researching. If it does, save the site as a bookmark or a favourite (see page 96). Then click on the **Back** button to return to the results page.

Useful educational sites

You may find these websites particularly useful for children aged 11 to 16:

● www.dictionary.com (online spelling and grammar guide)
● www.statcan.ca/english/edu/index.htm (online education resources by Statistics Canada)
● www.plato.com (general educational resource)

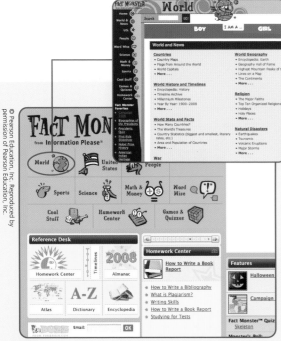

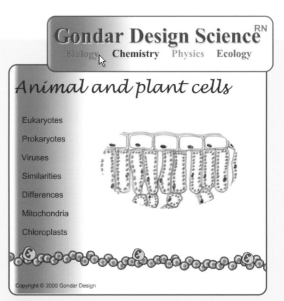

11 Factmonster.com is a good source of information for students at any level. Simply pick a subject from the index page to see a selection of related topics. Another great site for students is the Independent Learning Centre (ilc.org), which is for Ontario students, but which also has excellent resources for students anywhere.

12 The site's homework section has plenty of help for students, divided along subject and skillset lines. The Homework Center also has links to other sources, listed under the heading "School Tools."

13 Search engines can also help you find sites that are written by academics or teachers but are not necessarily linked to larger sites. For example, www.purchon.com is a site run by a teacher for pupils at his school, but is useful for anyone studying biology, chemistry, physics or ecology.

Search a site

Many websites have their own search engines to help you locate a specific topic within the site. Type in a keyword for the subject area you'd like more information on and wait for a list of results to be displayed.

Losing a link

websites come and go on the Internet all the time. You might sometimes click on a link and get a message saying that the page either no longer exists or that "A connection with the server cannot be established" (this often means the page no longer exists). So be prepared for the occasional disappointment.

⚠️ **Watch out**
Students using the Internet to study should always check with their teachers to make sure that what they are looking at is relevant to their particular course.

If you find educational CD-ROMs or DVDs expensive, remember that you can borrow them from public libraries.

 Bright idea
For further information and suggestions on how to write and design an eye-catching Curriculum Vitae, turn to page 154.

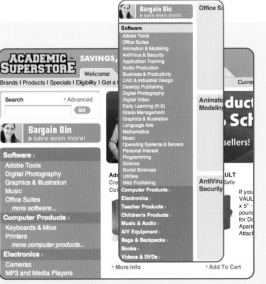

14 The Canadian Virtual University website is a wealth of information about Canadian universities that offer online degree programs. Online courses are a great way for people with limited time or mobility to get a recognized university degree.

15 You can also use the Internet to find and buy additional educational resources. For example, The Academic Superstore (www.academic superstore.com) sells educational and academic software for students from K-12 to university.

16 Prospective job-seekers can seek advice on writing their Curriculum Vitae (a.k.a. "Resumé"). Visit the CV Tips website (www.cvtips.com) for guidance.

Work offline

If you have a dialup connection and find you're becoming engrossed in a single detailed web page, remember that you can work offline and free up your phone line. With Internet Explorer, for example, go to the **File** menu and click on **Work Offline**.

Games on the Internet

You'll never lack a playing partner when you're online

The Internet is an unrivalled source of entertainment as well as information. In fact, when it comes to computer games, the Internet is in a league of its own, as it not only provides the games, but the players too.

Many online games are adventure or action-based, but there are plenty of gaming sites catering to more diverse tastes. There are, for example, a large number of chess-related services, some of which allow you to play against opponents from around the world in "real time" – that is, live over the Internet. Another option for some types of games is to play via e-mail, which lets you play at your leisure. You can also download games to play from your own computer.

For security reasons, when playing against others online, never divulge any personal details such as your telephone number.

PLAYING GAMES BY E-MAIL

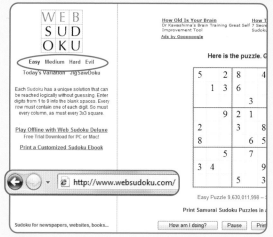

1 There are plenty of websites offering free access to online games. If you like playing Sudoku, for example, go to www.sudoku.com. There are thousands of grids to choose from and you can select your playing level – Easy, Medium, Hard or, for the very advanced player, Evil.

Bright idea
Online advertisements can be an irritation. However, it's easy to resize the window and block them out. Just click on the bottom right-hand corner of your browser window and drag the corner up and in until the ad has been hidden.

Watch out

When downloading from some sites, don't click on any "Warning" boxes that say you have won a prize. A new window will open, taking you to a different site. It's very unlikely that a prize will be waiting for you.

2 Enter your answers by clicking on an empty square and typing in a number. You can click on **How am I doing?** at any time to check your progress. You can also view your statistics and set preferences by clicking on **Options**. Make your choices and then click on **Save options** to close.

3 For a wide choice of online games, try www.shockwave.com. For an example of a word game, click on **Online games** in the top bar and then on **Word games** on the left-hand side. Next, click on **Text Twist** and then on **Play online**.

4 A new window will open and the game will load. Once the game has loaded, click on **Click to start**. You can then click and drag the circled letters to the boxes above. Each time you finish a word, click on **Enter** – and then start again until the time runs out.

Game playing preparation

A good way to prepare for an online game is to click on the various information links or tabs in the game's main window. For information about Text Twist, for example, click on the tabs to read the rules, pick up useful tricks and tips, read reviews and learn about how to share the game.

GAME INFO   REVIEWS   SHARE THIS GAME

Text Twist®

How many words can you spell from a jumbled group of letters before time runs out? That's the task in Text Twist®, a deceptively challenging word game.

Go on and do the Twist!

Instructions

Please note: This is not a Shock UNLIMITED game. It's available purchase only.

How to Play:
Click on the balls to form a w[...] press the ENTER button. If the[...] in the dictionary for the game[...] show up on the left-hand side[...] game. Use the TWIST button[...] you get stuck to help you see[...] words. You may also use the[...] keyboard to enter words.

For more detailed instructi[...]

*Many game sites require regular users to sign up. To sign up to Shockwave, click on **Join now – it's FREE**, fill in your account details, then click on **Sign Up Today!***

Watch out

Using a high-speed broadband connection can make online gaming faster and more fun. However, make sure you protect your system with a "firewall" – software or hardware that stops other Internet users accessing files on your PC.

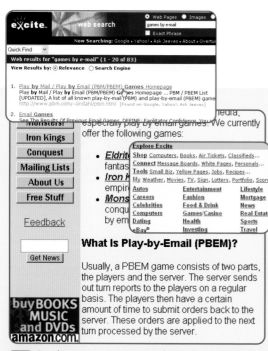

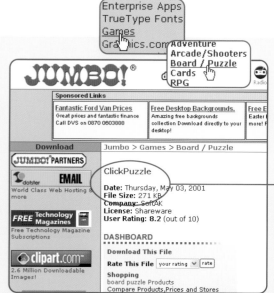

5 On the Internet you can also access strategy and fantasy games that work by sending your moves to your opponent(s) by e-mail. To find one of these, go to www.excite.com and type "games by e-mail" in the Search box. Select a site from the search results listed.

6 The Jumbo site has a vast selection of programs – some of which are games – that users can download. In your Web browser's address box type in www.jumbo.com then press **Return**.

7 To see the games available click on **Games** in the Download column. Click on **Board/Puzzle** in the Games panel, then scroll down and click on a game that interests you. A screen appears with information about the game, with the option to download it.

Software for free...

● **Shareware** is software that is distributed free for a limited period. When the licence expires you should buy the program if you want to continue using it.

● **Freeware**, as the name suggests, is software that's distributed free of charge and can be used indefinitely. However, it often comes without any user support.

● **Demo/Sample software** is a reduced version of a commercial program. You use it to decide whether you want to buy the complete program.

File sizes

When you download a game file from the Internet you will usually be told the size of the file. A file of a couple of hundred kilobytes should take just seconds to download, but a file of several megabytes could take an hour or more. Games that contain lots of sophisticated graphics take the longest to download.

Watch out

*Some games are free to download, but may still come with some restrictions. Read any licensing agreements before you play. Tick the "I agree" box and then click on **Next** to continue with your install.*

15% of clickp.exe Completed

Saving:
clickp.exe from mirror1.softakgames.com

Estimated time left 6 sec (124 KB of 852 KB copied)
Download to: C:\Documents and Setting...\clickp.exe
Transfer rate: 113 KB/Sec

☑ Close this dialog box when download completes

Open   Open Folder

Bright idea

Avoid deleting downloaded files after the programs have been installed. If possible, back them up onto a separate storage device, such as a CD. The installation programs may be needed again at a later date.

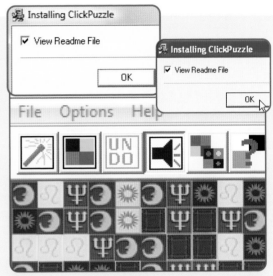

Installing ClickPuzzle

☑ View Readme File

OK

Installing ClickPuzzle

☑ View Readme File

OK

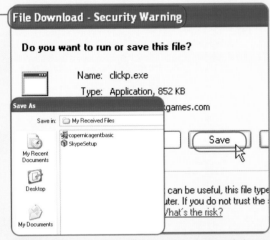

File Download - Security Warning

Do you want to run or save this file?

Name: clickp.exe
Type: Application, 852 KB

Save As

Save in: My Received Files

- copernicagentbasic
- SkypeSetup

My Recent Documents

Desktop

My Documents

Save

Open File - Security Warning

The publisher could not be verif... ...you want run this software?

Name: clickp.exe
Publisher: **Unknown Publisher**
Type: Application
From: C:\Documents and Settings\Tony\Desktop\My R...

Run   Cance...

Installing ClickPuzzle

Installation was completed successfully
100%

OK

File   Options   Help

8 Click on the download icon and then click on **Save** to download the game. (A security warning box may appear, see below.) In the Save As dialogue box select a place in which to save the file and click on **Save**. It's a good idea to save it to your Desktop. Once it has downloaded, click on **Close** in the File Download window.

9 To install the file onto your hard disk, close your Internet connection and double-click on the icon of the downloaded file on your Desktop. Read the Licence Agreement (see above left) and click on **Start** in the Installing window. Click on **OK** when the installation is complete.

10 In the next Installing window you will see an option saying "View Readme File." Want more information on the file you're downloading? Tick the box and click on **OK**. To play your game, go to the **Start** menu. Click on **All Programs** and select your game in the drop-down menu.

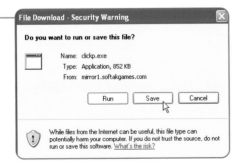

File Download - Security Warning

Do you want to run or save this file?

Name: clickp.exe
Type: Application, 852 KB
From: mirror1.softakgames.com

Run   Save   Cancel

While files from the Internet can be useful, this file type can potentially harm your computer. If you do not trust the source, do not run or save this software. What's the risk?

Keeping secure

On some PCs a "File Download – Security Warning" dialogue box appears, warning the user that the action they are about to perform may be dangerous. If you are not confident that the file you are downloading is from a safe and reputable source, click on **Cancel** to abort the process.

Remove a game

To delete a game from your computer, go to the **Start** menu and select **Control Panel**, then **Uninstall a program**. Highlight the program you wish to delete – here "ClickPuzzle" – and click on **Uninstall/Change**. Then just then follow the prompts.

Network

Connect To

Control Panel

Default Programs

Organize   Views   Uninstall/Change

Name
- Adobe Acrobat 7.0 Standard
- Adobe Flash Player 9 ActiveX
- Adobe Photoshop Elements 4.0
- Adobe Reader 7.0.9
- Business Contact Manager for Outlook 2007
- ClickPuzzle
- Copernic Agent Basic

Add or Remove Programs

Currently installed pro...

Chess is a popular game on the Web. You play against a computer or a person in real time. If you have a dialup connection, set a time limit on moves to free up your phone line.

PLAYING CHESS ONLINE

Bright idea
Before you begin playing a game of chess, print out and study a copy of the game rules and any tips you are given for online chess etiquette.

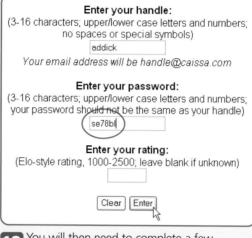

Enter your handle:
(3-16 characters; upper/lower case letters and numbers; no spaces or special symbols)

addick

Your email address will be handle@caissa.com

Enter your password:
(3-16 characters; upper/lower case letters and numbers; your password should not be the same as your handle)

se78bl

Enter your rating:
(Elo-style rating, 1000-2500; leave blank if unknown)

Clear | Enter

Member Info

Required inform...

Please fill out the f...
confidence by Cais...

Browser Setup

There...
that C...
in you...
Caiss...

Java Test

The purpose of this test is to determ... the Java programming language. T...

Welcome

Your account number is **#12013**. Please include this number in an correspondence you submit. If you forget it, your account number is available online in your Member Workspace.

Your free trial membership lasts for 14 days from today's dat that you use this time with no obligation other than to make sure tha service and that your Internet connection/Web browser is compatib enough (we recommend using Netscape Navigator or Microsoft Int Explorer with at least a 28.8kbps connection).

We will give you notice of the trial membership's impending conclu week before this date and request that you submit your subscriptio would like to subscribe at that time, there will be detailed instructio pay. If you do not wish to subscribe, do nothing and your account w automatically. Also keep in mind that you can subscribe at any time trial membership by going to the Member Wo... "Subscription Payment."

CONTINUE

11 A good site for playing chess online is www.caissa.com. Type this in your browser's address box and press **Return**. When the home page loads, click on **New members signup here**. The next page explains how the site works. Click on **Sign Me Up!** for a trial membership.

12 You will then need to complete a few questions. Type in a "handle" (the name by which you want to be known when playing) and a password, and then click on **Enter**. Make sure you make your password easy to remember, as you will need it to log on to the site in future.

13 Fill in your details in the Member Info window and click on **Enter**. Adjust your browser setup following the instructions for your version of Internet Explorer (or whichever browser you use) and click on **Continue**. Next, complete the Java test, after which you will be given an account number. Then, click on **Continue**.

Try before you buy

Some Web-based chess services are free, but others, including Caissa's site (above), are membership services for which you have to pay a fee. Free trials help you to decide whether it's worth paying for these services or not.

Online etiquette

When playing games online remember that you are often playing against other people – not a computer – and so the usual rules of social etiquette apply.

For example, you should not leave your computer without a mutual agreement to stop playing. One of the Caissa site's particular rules is that you should never prolong a game that you are clearly going to lose.

New Member Orientation

You have been configured to use the **Mars Chess Engine** for playing Games. Instructions on how to use this interface are documented be in mind that you can custom-configure your interface (Board Size, B etc.) in the Caissa Configuration Options.

14 In the New Member Orientation window read through the website's rules and then click on **Main Menu**. To play, click on **Live Game Room** and then on **Play A Live Game**. To play a practice game against the computer, scroll down to the bottom of the screen and click on **Play Caissa**.

15 Select your preferences in the Configuration options box and click on **Continue**. Then click on **OK** in the Live Game Pairing window. To start the game, move your pieces by clicking and dragging them. After each of your moves, you will see Caissa make a move. If you are clearly beaten, click on **Resign**.

16 When you are ready to play a person, go to the Live Game Room (click on your browser's **Back** button), and click on the **Challenge** button under "Play a Live Game." Select a player and click on **Issue Challenge** to begin your game.

Added insight

If you prefer to learn how the system works before you play a game, watch one first. Click on the **Watch** button under "Play a Live Game," which you can find on the website's Live Game Room page (see above).

Live Game Room

Watch A Live Game

40 Active Games, **0** Tournament Games, **2** Games On Hold

White	Rating	Black	Rating	Speed
Slacker	1600/0	Caissa	1699	30/60
RandyH	1200/0	LawAndOrder	1740	30/15
FYA	1519	NH90	1600	G/2
Drozd2	1252	tengns1	1402	30/30

PRACTICAL HOME

This section will guide you, **step by step**, through **39 practical projects** over a range of subjects. Each task is self-contained – you require **no prior experience** of the program used. Suggestions are also made of ways you can bring the projects together to undertake more **ambitious events**, such as organizing a reunion.

PROJECTS

Design a letterhead

Create your personal stationery with an individual look

In the age of e-mail and online chat, the importance of letters is often overlooked. However, we all still need to send letters from time to time – whether formal instructions to your lawyer or insurer, or a chatty letter giving an old friend your latest news. Whoever you are writing to, a well-designed letterhead giving your name and contact details will save you time in starting your letters as, once you have created your letterhead, you can save it as a template. This means that you can use it each time you write a letter and if any of your details change, you can easily alter them on the template.

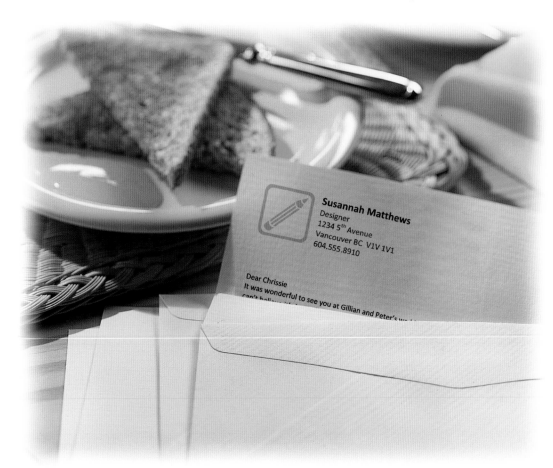

> Decide what you are going to use your letterhead for. If it is for letters to family and friends, you can be creative with your choice of fonts.
>
> **BEFORE YOU START**

1 Go to the **Start** menu, click on **All Programs** and select **Microsoft Office Word 2007**. Click on the **Microsoft Office** button in the top left corner of your screen and select **Print** then **Print Preview** from the menu that appears.

> To create a letterhead in Microsoft Works, open Microsoft Works and then click on the **Programs** button. Choose **Works Word Processor** from the Quick Launch menu on the right.
>
> **OTHER PROGRAMS**

Bright idea
If you have an e-mail address or Web site, remember to include them in your letterhead.

2 Click on the Page Setup dialogue box launcher and in the **Margins** tab set the Top, Bottom, Left and Right margins. In the Headers and Footers section of the **Layout** tab, set the "From edge" distance between the header and the top of the page. Click on **OK**. From the far right of the Ribbon, click on **Close Print Preview**.

3 You are going to create your letterhead within the Header section of your document. Go to the **Insert** tab and, from the "Header and Footer" group, click on **Header** and then select **Blank** from the drop-down list of styles. Type your name, address and telephone number in the "[Type text]" prompt area.

4 Now highlight your name, click on the **Home** tab, then on the Font dialogue box launcher and select a font, style and size, hovering the mouse pointer over these to see them in the Preview window. Then click on **OK**. Style your address using the same method.

Using Word's Templates

Word 2007 has lots of templates that you can use to create personalized letterheads. Click on the **Microsoft Office** button and select **New**. Scroll down the list of templates and select **Stationery**, then in the pane on the right click on **Speciality paper**. Choose a style from the selection of thumbnail images and click on **Download**. Highlight the text and type in your details.

Works template

Microsoft Works also has a templates feature. Open Microsoft Works and click on the **Templates** button and then, from the list on the left, choose **Letters & Labels**. Next, click on the **Letters** icon and choose a template style, then click on **Use this style**. Type in your details as you follow the onscreen instructions. To save your letterhead as a template, go to the **File** menu and select **Save As**. In the dialogue box click on the **Template** button in the bottom right-hand corner. Then type in a name for your template and click **OK**.

145

Keyword

Handles The term describes the four round and four square symbols that appear on the corners and sides of an object when selected (see Step 6). Click and drag outwards or inwards to resize an object.

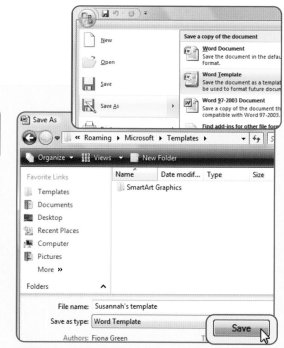

5 You can also add a Clip Art image to your letterhead. To make space, highlight your letterhead, then click and drag the left indent marker on the ruler. Go to the "Insert" group and click on **Clip Art**. Type a keyword in the "Search for" box in the Clip Art pane and click on **Go**. Click on an image and select **Insert** in the pop-up menu.

6 Go to the "Arrange" group and click on **Text Wrapping**, then select **Square**. Click on the image and drag it to reposition it on the left of the text. Resize the image by clicking and dragging on one of the corner handles. Click on **Close Header and Footer** on the far right of the Ribbon.

7 When you are happy with your design, save it as a template that you can use again and again. Click on the **Microsoft Office Button** and select **Save As**, then choose **Word Template** from the options on the right. Give the template a name, select a suitable folder to save it in (for example, the Templates folder) and click on **Save**.

Use your toolbar

The toolbar buttons at the top of the screen help you style your text quickly. Highlight the text and then click on the relevant button to make it bold, to italicize it or to underline it. You can change your text's position by clicking on the left, centre or right alignment buttons.

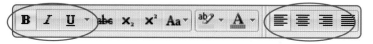

Change your picture or Clip Art

If you would like to change the artwork you originally chose for your letterhead, first double-click on the picture or Clip Art image. Next, go to the "Adjust" group and click on the **Format** tab and select **Change Picture**. You can now browse pictures or Clip Art and select the new image. Click on **Insert** and, if necessary, click and drag on the handles to resize it (see Step 6, above).

Bright idea
*Save yourself time by using automatic dating for your letters. Click where you want the date to appear in your document, go to the **Insert** tab and click on **Date and Time**. In the dialogue box click on your preferred style and then click on **OK**.*

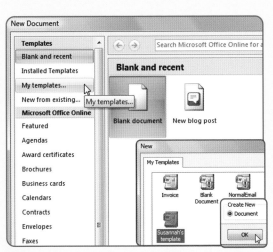

8 To use your template, click on the **Microsoft Office** button and select **New**. Under Templates in the left pane click on **My templates**. The New dialogue box appears. Look for your new template, here "Susannah's template." Click on it and then on **OK** to create a new document.

9 The cursor will flash below your letterhead. Use the **Return** key to create a few blank lines and then type your letter. To save it, click on the **Microsoft Office** button and select **Save As**, then click on **Word Document** from the options on the right.

10 When the Save As dialogue box appears, click on **Documents**. At this point you can select a subfolder or create a new folder if you wish. Type in a name for your document and click on **Save**. This letter will now be saved, and your letterhead template can be used again and again.

Changing your template

Click on the **Microsoft Office** button and select **Open**. Under "Favorite links" select **Templates** and then, in the right-hand pane, double-click on your template. Make your changes and then save it.

In Works, choose **Works Word Processor** in the Task Launcher. Click on your letterhead in the list of templates, make your changes, go to the **File** menu and select **Save As**. Double-click on the old file in the Templates folder to replace it with the new one. Click on **Yes** in the Dialogue box to confirm your choice.

*To see line spaces and other "hidden" elements, go to the Home tab and click on the **Show/Hide** button.*

Microsoft Office

- Microsoft Office Excel 20
- Microsoft Office Outloo
- Microsoft Office PowerP
- Microsoft Office Publish
- Microsoft Office Word 2007
- Microsoft Office Tools
- Microsoft SQL Server 2005

Home   In
Office Button
Past

◀ **Back**

Start Search

New
Open
Save

1 Go to the **Start** menu, click on **All Programs** and select **Microsoft Office Word 2007**. Click on the **Microsoft Office** button in the top left corner of your screen and select **New** from the menu that appears.

Send a formal letter

Give your business correspondence a professional look

Writing a formal letter can sometimes seem quite daunting, but Word 2007 includes many ready-made templates that make it straightforward. Simply pick a template design, type in your details and relevant information and restyle the document as appropriate.

It is usual to include the name, company position and address of the person you are writing to. It's also a good idea to include an official reference. For example, if you are writing to your bank, you could give your account number. When replying to a letter, see whether a reference is included, and repeat it in yours.

Watch out
You are in danger of losing your work if you do not save it frequently. Make a habit of saving your letter every few minutes.

Close-up
To save time and keep the document accurate, Microsoft Word 2007 automatically inserts the date into templates, if appropriate.

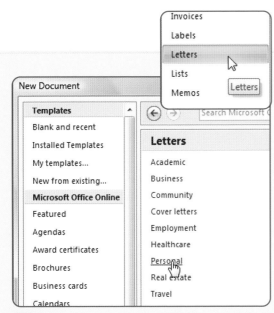

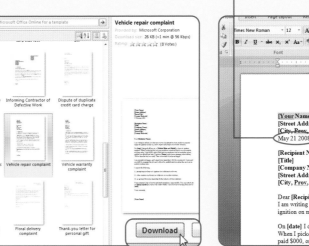

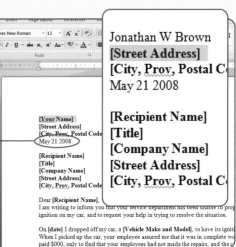

2 You will see a long list of different templates, organized into two groups – "Templates" (those already installed) and "Microsoft Office Online." Scroll down the list to find a relevant category, here "Letters." Click on **Letters** and then, in the pane on the right, click on **Personal**.

3 In the middle panel you will now see thumbnail images of different types of pre-formed letter templates. Click on an image to preview a larger version in the panel on the right. Select a style, here "Vehicle repair complaint," and click on **Download**.

4 The downloaded letter will have bracketed bold "prompt" areas within it. Click inside the square brackets to highlight the prompt, and type your own details. Other areas of the letter will also need to be modified, so highlight these as you go through and add your own details.

Quick Access Toolbar

The Quick Access Toolbar is a customizable toolbar that contains a set of commands, independent of the tab currently selected. Initially it shows three commands (Save, Undo and Redo), plus a Customize button (to add further commands). To add a command, click on **Customize Quick Access Toolbar**. You can then select a command from the list or click on **More Commands**. Click on **Add** and then on **OK**. Alternatively, right-click on a command on the Ribbon then click on **Add to Quick Access Toolbar**. If you would like the Quick Access Toolbar nearer to your work, it can be moved below the Ribbon. Click on the **Customize** button and select **Show Below the Ribbon**.

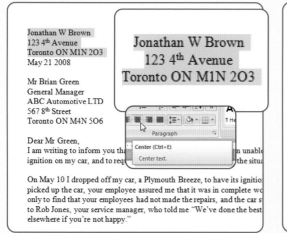

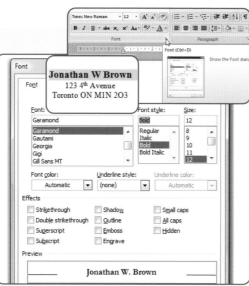

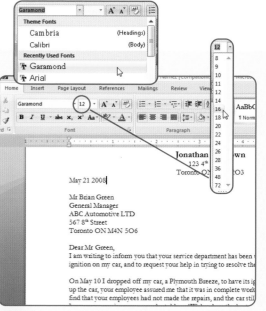

5 You can personalize your letter by positioning your own details in the centre of the page. Highlight your name and address, then go to the **Home** tab at the top left of your screen, and click on the **Center** button.

6 To style your letter, first highlight your name at the top. Next, click on the **Home** tab and click on the Font dialogue box launcher. Select a font, style and size – you can see how it looks by clicking on a style and then viewing it in the Preview window. Make your selection and then click on **OK**.

7 Continue to style the remainder of your text, using the tools outlined in step 6. You can apply different styles to paragraphs, sentences or even individual words – just highlight the area you would like to style. For speed, you can use the font and font size shortcuts on the Ribbon as shown.

Select a font

If you know the name of the font you want to use, type its first letter into the Font box. All the fonts beginning with that letter will then appear at the top of the font window. This saves you scrolling through all the fonts on your PC.

Change the scale

If you would like to magnify your document to see it in more detail, you can do so without adjusting the type size. The scale can easily be changed by clicking on the "+" or "-" zoom buttons found on the status bar at the bottom of your window. Alternatively, click on the **View** tab at the top of the window, then click on **Zoom**, select one of the options, then click OK.

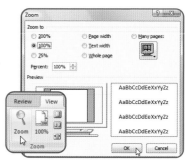

Bright idea
It is often easier to spot mistakes on a printed page than on screen so after printing your letter read it through carefully to check for errors.

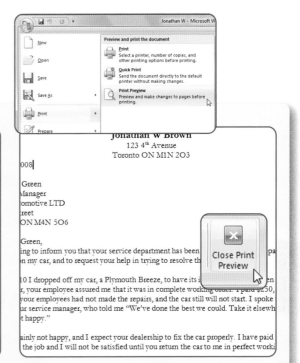

8 To check for spelling mistakes, click on the **Review** tab, go to the "Proofing" group and click on the **Spelling & Grammar** button. If you only want to check a section of the document, highlight the relevant text before clicking on the button.

9 If Word questions a spelling, click on **Ignore** or **Change** depending whether the word is misspelled. If you can't think of the exact word you want, you could use the Thesaurus. Click on the **Review** tab and, in the "Proofing" group, click on **Thesaurus** to find words with similar meanings.

10 To see how your letter will look, click on the **Microsoft Office** button, move your mouse over **Print** and select **Print Preview**. If you need to make a change, click on **Close Print Preview** to return to your letter. To print, click on the **Microsoft Office** button, then **Print** and **OK**.

Make your point

If you are making a number of important points in your letter and want to emphasize them, type each one on a new line. Highlight the whole section, click on the Paragraph dialogue box launcher and choose an option to increase the line spacing. Finally, click on the **Bullets** button to pick out each of your points.

- prompt repair of my car's ignition
- a free courtesy car for my use w
- an apology from your dealership

Improve your service as

If you are the chief organizer of a tennis club, bridge club or community theatre company, your PC can make light work of the daily administration

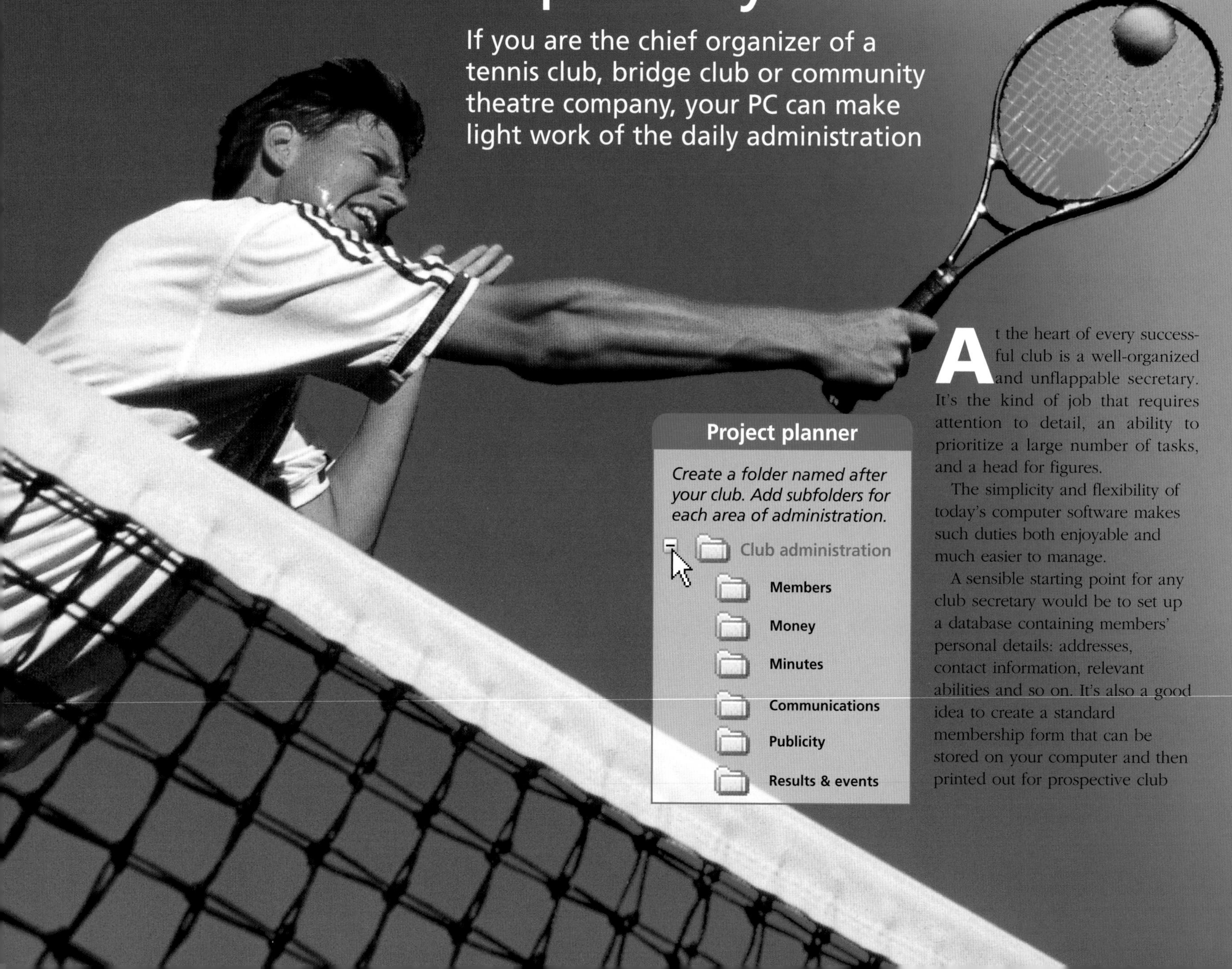

Project planner

Create a folder named after your club. Add subfolders for each area of administration.

- 📁 Club administration
  - 📁 Members
  - 📁 Money
  - 📁 Minutes
  - 📁 Communications
  - 📁 Publicity
  - 📁 Results & events

At the heart of every successful club is a well-organized and unflappable secretary. It's the kind of job that requires attention to detail, an ability to prioritize a large number of tasks, and a head for figures.

The simplicity and flexibility of today's computer software makes such duties both enjoyable and much easier to manage.

A sensible starting point for any club secretary would be to set up a database containing members' personal details: addresses, contact information, relevant abilities and so on. It's also a good idea to create a standard membership form that can be stored on your computer and then printed out for prospective club

a club secretary

members to complete. Once you have a database set up, it's a simple task to produce address labels for your club correspondence.

Using a second database, the secretary of a sports club can produce tables to show schedules, results and club rankings.

Keeping club accounts and tracking membership fees are simple tasks once you set up a spreadsheet. You can use it for recruitment-based fiscal planning.

For communications with other organizations, create your own club stationery. You could design a club logo using Paint or another graphics program. The logo could then be used on club newsletters or, with the help of an

outside supplier, on merchandise such as club ties and keyrings. You might like to consider compiling a pictorial club history on your computer. Somebody could write a short account that can be published for members' interest.

And don't forget that many members will be online. If you compile an e-mail address book, you can send information on rankings, schedules and social events to everyone at once.

With the wide availability of online banking, monitoring your club accounts could not be simpler. And, provided the software is compatible, you can download information straight from your bank to your spreadsheets and pay the bills online.

Start the ball rolling

- Compile and collect all membership details and transfer them to your database
- Transfer a copy of the club's accounts to a spreadsheet on your computer
- Set up an online bank account
- Produce a club logo for all communications
- Arrange for all league or club information to be sent via e-mail to online members

Ideas and inspirations

Customize the following projects and ideas to suit the needs of your club. That way, you'll spend less time on administration, and far more time enjoying the club's benefits. Once you've set up the basic documents you need, maintaining them should be a quick and easy matter.

166 **Membership database**
Compile a handy reference document to keep a record of all your members' details.

272 **Club accounts**
Keep track of income and outlays, and budget for projects, such as buying new equipment.

170 **Produce address labels**
Print off address labels for all your club members to make correspondence quick and easy.

190 **Create a greeting card**
Send your members (or prospective members) cards for Christmas or to publicize a club event.

224 **Design your own poster**
Design your own logo or artwork for stationery, club posters or Internet use.

Write an eye-catching CV

Make the most of your experience and achievements

Your curriculum vitae – or resumé – is intended to make a favourable impression on potential employers. As well as giving details of all the companies you have worked for and how long you were employed by each, they explain what your responsibilities were and what skills you have developed.

Keep your resumé brief and to the point. If possible, try to fit it on a single page. Select a clear, easy-to-read font and don't be tempted to make the font size too small in an effort to squeeze everything in. Also, keep your CV's design simple, with well-defined sections that make it easy to extract information.

> To make sure all your dates of employment are correct, collect your old ROE forms and refer to them as you type in your details.

BEFORE YOU START

1 Go to the **Start** menu, click on **All Programs** and select **Microsoft Office Word 2007**. Click on the Microsoft Office button in the top left corner of your screen and select **New** from the menu that appears.

> You can also create your CV in Microsoft Works. Open Works then click on the **Templates** button. Choose **Letters & Labels** from the list on the left, then click on **Resume (CV)**.

OTHER PROGRAMS

Watch out

You are in danger of losing your work if you do not save it frequently. Make a habit of saving the changes to your CV every few minutes.

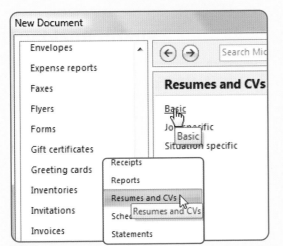

2 You will see a long list of templates, split into two groups, "Templates" (those already installed) and "Microsoft Office Online." Scroll down the list to find a relevant category, here "Resumes and CVs." Click on **Resumes and CVs** and then, in the pane on the right, click on **Basic**.

3 In the middle panel you will now see a selection of thumbnail images of different types of pre-formed CV templates. Click on an image to preview a larger version in the panel on the right. Select a style, here "Chronological CV (traditional theme)" and click on **Download** (bottom right).

4 Your downloaded CV will have bracketed bold [Prompt] areas within it. Click inside the [brackets] to highlight the prompt, and type your details as appropriate. Use the "Tab" key to move to the next area of the CV and add your own information.

Using Works

Microsoft Works also has some useful templates to help you create a CV. Open Works, and click on the **Templates** button at the top, then **Letters & Labels** in the left-hand column and choose **Resume (CV)** from the list of tasks. Select a style then click on **Use this style** and enter your details where prompted.

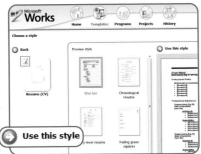

Bright idea

When you write your cover letter, use the same fonts as in your CV. Not only will your letter and CV complement each other, but they will also have a professional appearance. A potential employer may well form the impression that you pay attention to detail.

Make sure you have the correct spellings of all the dishes on the menu, and a list of names of the guests you have invited.

BEFORE YOU START

Page Setup

| Margins | Paper | Layout |

Margins

Top:	2.5 cm	Bottom:	2.5 cm
Left:	2.5 cm	Right:	2.5 cm
Gutter:	0 cm	Gutter position:	Left

Orientation

Portrait   Landscape

Pages

Multiple pages: Normal

1 To make a menu, go to the **Start** menu, select **All Programs**, then **Microsoft Word 2007**. Go to the **Page Layout** tab, click on the **Margins** button and then **Custom Margins**. With the Margins tab selected, set the margins to **2.5 cm** and the orientation to **Landscape**, then click on **OK**. Create two columns (see above right).

Design a dinner party menu and place cards

Impress your guests with specially designed table decorations

Great food and good company are the key ingredients of a dinner party, but to make the evening really special, you need to pay attention to detail. One way to set just the right tone for your party is by designing and printing your own menus and place cards. Whether the mood is formal, fun, festive or themed, you will be able to find fitting fonts, colours and clip art graphics on your computer.

You can style text and add clip art in Microsoft Works but it is easier to size the place cards and to position text precisely in Microsoft Word. However, you can still produce an attractive design using Works.

OTHER PROGRAMS

To set columns, go to the **Page Layout** group and click on **Columns**. Select **Two** from the drop-down menu of options.

If you can't see your Return symbols click on the **Show/Hide** toolbar button in the Paragraph group. (In Microsoft Works, go to the **View** menu and click on **All Characters**.)

2 Go to the **Insert** tab and click on **Table**, then on **Insert Table**. Set the columns and rows to **1** and set the width to **11.5 cm**. Click on **OK**. Next, right-click inside the table and select **Table Properties**. Click on the **Row** tab and set the height to **400 pt** and **At Least**. Click on **OK**.

3 Type your text into the table, adding a line space between the details of each course. Highlight the text and click on the **Center** button from the "Paragraph" group. Next, click on the **Font** dialogue box launcher and choose a font, style and size for your text and then click on **OK**.

4 To adjust the spacing between the details of each course, highlight the first Return symbol and click on the **Paragraph** dialogue box launcher. In the Spacing section, click on the arrows to the right of the "Before" and "After" boxes until you are happy with the result. Click on **OK**, and then repeat with the other blank lines.

Checking your spelling

Any words that your computer doesn't recognize will appear on the screen with a wavy red line underneath. To check the spelling of these words, click on the **Review** tab and then the **Spelling & Grammar** button in the "Proofing" group. However, just because a computer doesn't recognize a word, it doesn't mean it doesn't exist. It's best to double-check in a dictionary.

Using Works templates

Microsoft Works includes templates for several types of menu, with a variety of eye-catching styles to choose from.

To use a template, open the Works Task Launcher, click on **Templates** then, on the left, **Home & Money**. Choose **Menus** from the list of tasks and select a style, then click on **Use this style** to open the template. Choose your design and follow the onscreen instructions.

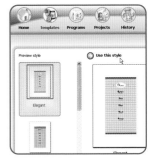

Create a family newsletter

Keep in touch with distant friends and relatives

A regular newsletter is a great way to keep family members in touch with each other. The first step is to ask your relatives whether they would like to contribute any news, such as a new job or a recently passed exam. They may even like to send in favourite recipes or poems they have written. Set a deadline and suggest they send their contributions to you by e-mail – this will save you from having to type in their text.

Once all the material has arrived, write your own stories to incorporate them. Finally, decide what you are going to call the family newsletter. It's tempting to use your surname in the heading, but remember that not all family members share the same name.

Prioritize your contributions. If there isn't enough space for all your news in the current edition of the newsletter, save some for the next.

BEFORE YOU START

1 Go to the **Start** menu, click on **All Programs** and select **Microsoft Office Word 2007**. Click on the Microsoft Office button in the top left corner of your screen and select **New** from the menu that appears.

*You can also create a newsletter using Microsoft Works. Open Works then click on the **Programs** button. Choose **Works Word Processor** from the Quick Launch menu on the right.*

OTHER PROGRAMS

Watch your language

Word templates downloaded from Microsoft's online resource may well have been generated in the United States. To change the language setting to English (Canada), click on the language setting box at the bottom of your window. The Language dialogue box appears. Click on **English (Canada)**, then on **OK**.

2 In the New Document dialogue box you will see a long list of different template styles, organized into two groups: "Templates" (those already installed) and "Microsoft Office Online." Scroll down the list to find a relevant category, here "Newsletters." Click on **Newsletters**.

3 In the middle panel you will now see a selection of thumbnail images of different types of pre-formed newsletter templates. Click on an image to preview a larger version in the panel on the right. Select a style, here "Family newsletter," and click on **Download** at the bottom right of the window.

4 Your downloaded newsletter template will appear with text and pictures positioned for you to replace with your own. This template style is already pre-formatted into two columns containing text and picture boxes ready for you to start creating your newsletter.

Using Works Templates

Open Microsoft Works and click on the **Templates** button. From the list on the left, choose **Newsletters & Flyers**. Click on the **Newsletters** icon and choose a template style, then click on **Use this style**. Type in your own details as you follow the onscreen instructions.

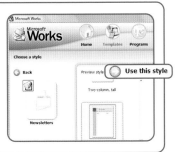

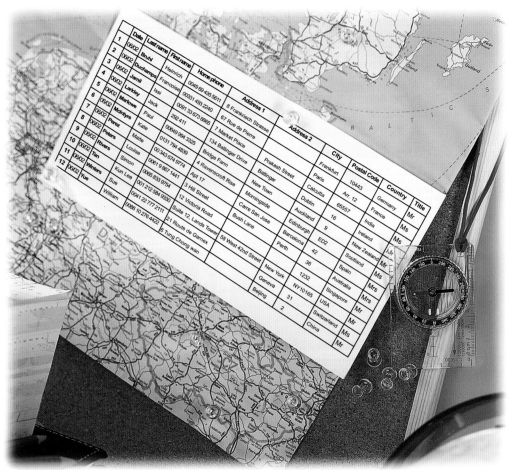

	Date	Last name	First name	Home phone	Address 1	Address 2	City	Postal Code	Country	Title
1	0602	Bruhl	Heinrich	0049 69 435 5611	8 Frankriech Strasse		Frankfurt	10443	Germany	Mr
2	0602	Duchamps	Francoise	0033 1 489 2240	67 Rue de Pierre		Paris	Art. 12	France	Ms
3	0602	Jamil	Issi	0091 489 2240	7 Market Place		Calcutta	65557	India	Ms
4	0602	Larkley	Jack	0091 33 673 8965	134 Ballinger Drive		Dublin	16	Ireland	Ms
5	0602	Marlowe	Paul	292 411	Bridge Farm	Prakesh Street	Auckland	9	New Zealand	Mr
6	0602	Perez	Kate	0049 994 3325	4 Ravenscroft Rise	Ballinger	Edinburgh	ED2	Scotland	Mr
7	0602	Peters	Maite	0131 794 4839	Apt 17	New Town	Barcelona	42	Spain	Ms
8	0602	Rivers	Louise	00 343 674 9774	3 Hill Street	Morningside	Perth	36	Australia	Mrs
9	0602	Tan	Simon	0061 9 857 1441	12 Victoria Road	Carre San Jose	New York	1232	Singapore	Mrs
10	0602	Winters	Kim Lee	0065 833 9764	Suite 12, Lands Tower	Bush Lane	Geneva	NY10165	USA	Mr
11	0602	Yue	Sue	001 212 584 9330	21 Route de Gamex		Beijing	31	Switzerland	Mr
12	0602		William	0041 22 777 2111	6 Tung Chong wan			2	China	Ms
				0086 10 276 4422		58 West 42nd Street				Mr

Make an address list

It can be easy to keep in touch with friends and contacts

One of the most useful things you can do with a database is make an address list. There are many advantages to doing this on your PC. You can easily update it when people move house or change their name; you can sort addresses; you can even create group e-mail lists so that you can send all your friends the same e-mails at once. You can also search your database for individual words (if, say, you can remember that someone was called Jim but you have forgotten his last name). And you can always print it out if you need to.

1 Go to the **Start** menu, select **All Programs** and then click on **Microsoft Works Task Launcher**. Click on the Programs button at the top and select **Address Book** in the list that appears on the left. To launch the application, click on the **Address Book** icon on the right.

> You can also create an address list in Outlook. Open Outlook and click on the **Contacts** icon in the left pane of the window. Press **Ctrl** and "N" at the same time to open a new data entry form.

► OTHER PROGRAMS

Keyword

Field *This is a category of information in a database – for example, "Name," "Street Address" and "Phone" are all individual fields.*

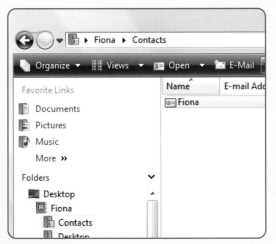

2 You will now be presented with your Contacts folder. If this is the first time you have added a contact, it will be empty except for an entry for you. This is known as "My Contact" and is automatically set by the software.

3 Make sure your Contacts folder is highlighted and then click on the **New Contact** button. In the Name and E-mail tab, type in your contact's first and last names – these then automatically appear in the Full Name field – and add their e-mail address in the relevant box.

4 There are several other tabs where further information can be added. Click on each tab and fill in as much information as you want to record. Click on **OK** when you have finished. With your Contacts folder highlighted on the left, your new entry appears in the list on the right.

Adding e-mail addresses

Make sure you include e-mail addresses wherever possible as they can be used in Windows Mail. You can set up Windows Mail to automatically add addresses to your Contacts list whenever you reply to an e-mail. To do this, launch Windows Mail. In the **Tools** menu, click on **Options**, and then on the **Send** tab. Check the box **Automatically put people I reply to in my Contacts list**.

Make address labels

Save time and effort by printing your own labels

Computers come into their own when there are repetitive or time-consuming tasks to be done. Writing addresses on envelopes – at Christmas or for a charity mailout – is one such task. Why not use your PC to create and print stylish address labels?

It will spare you the tedium of writing them out by hand, and give your envelopes a truly professional look.

You can create labels with a wide variety of designs, text styles and sizes, and you can save them to use over and over again.

You must have the addresses you want to print compiled on a database. To do this, see Make an address list on page 166. You also need to buy sheets of sticky labels.

BEFORE YOU START

1 Go to the **Start** menu, select **All Programs** and then click on **Microsoft Works Task Launcher**. When it has launched, click on **Works Word Processor** in the Quick Launch menu on the right, which will open a blank Word Processor document.

*You can also create address labels in Microsoft Word. Go to the **Mailings** tab and click on the **Start Mail Merge** button and follow the prompts.*

OTHER PROGRAMS

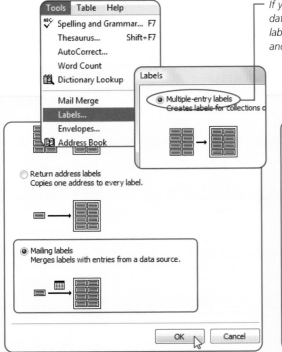

*If you don't have an address book database and just want to print single labels, click on **Multiple-entry labels** and follow the on-screen instructions.*

2 Go to the **Tools** menu at the top of the screen and click on **Labels**. The Labels dialogue box appears, where you can select **Mailing labels**. This enables you to merge the addresses you have stored in your Address Book into your labels document. Click on **OK**.

3 In the Label Settings dialogue box, click on the arrow at the side of the "Label products" box and select the brand and type of your labels. Then, scroll through the Product Number menu and click on the product reference from your labels" box. Next, click on **New Document**.

4 In the Open Data Source dialogue box, click on **Merge from the Address Book**. The Insert Fields dialogue box appears. Click on the first field you would like to use – here **Title** – and then click on **Insert**.

Close-up
Address labels come in a variety of sizes, each with their own reference number. You can buy labels that fill a whole letter-sized page, for example, or specialized labels to put on CDs, videos or DVDs. One of the most common address labels is the 5160, with 30 labels to a letter-sized page.

Searching for a database

The Open Data Source dialogue box also gives you the option of merging information from other databases you have created.

Click on **Merge information from another type of file** to locate a different data source. Next, scroll down the "Look in" window to locate your file. You should also scroll down the "Files of type" window to make sure that your file type is displayed. Finally, click on **Open**.

Make a home

Let your computer take care of the

Project planner

Create a folder named after your business. Add subfolders for each of its various aspects.

- Business
  - Clients
  - Suppliers
  - Finance
  - Product development
  - Publicity

Millions of people around the world have seized the opportunity to start their own business. There is a real thrill to be had from having a go at your own idea, from being your own boss and taking your financial destiny into your own hands.

But with this opportunity come new responsibilities: for accounting, correspondence, and publicity; for dealing with suppliers, your bank manager and the taxman, and – perhaps most importantly – for finding your next client. In fact, most of your time could very easily be taken up with anything

business work
details while you take care of the profits

other than realizing your original business idea.

Your PC can reduce the time spent on many of these tasks. It can even help you to research your business idea before you invest heavily in it.

For correspondence and publicity you could design a logo based on clip art or use a drawing program. It's often easiest to design your stationery and produce correspondence from a template, and keep a record of all your communications either on your computer's hard disk or backed-up on CDs or DVDs.

You can use your PC's database program to create a client database and, from that, customer name and address labels.

Make sure that you never miss an appointment by running your

business agenda from your Desktop. If you use a car for work, you can calculate your operating costs to claim them as business expenses. And your spreadsheet program will make dealing with your accounts less of a headache.

With your PC you can design your own business cards, or you can reach a much wider audience by advertising on your blog.

You can also use the Internet to correspond by e-mail, compare competitors' prices and services, and surf the Web for trade leads – some companies even post supply requirements on government sites set up to encourage trade.

Before long, your computer will establish itself as your most productive and versatile employee, leaving you more time to enjoy your work.

Minding your own business

- Research the market for your business
- Research prices and costs for your product and those of competitors
- Prepare a business plan
- Arrange and prepare start-up finances
- Seek an accountant's advice on running a business
- Officially register as a business

Ideas and inspirations

Below are some suggestions for limiting the time you spend taking care of your business and maximizing its efficiency. The projects can be adapted depending on your own circumstances. If you have business partners, you may wish to divide the tasks between yourselves.

252 **Do your own accounts**
Organize your income, expenditures and overheads; project future expenditures and profit.

176 **Create a business card**
Increase the profile of your business and ensure customers have your contact details.

166 **Compile a client database**
Make sure you don't lose track of anyone by storing their details in an updatable record.

180 **Set up a business agenda**
Keep track of your appointments and timetable a variety of tasks in an onscreen agenda.

Also worth considering...

Use pictures as well as words to sell your product and to get the message home to potential clients.

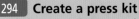

294 **Create a press kit**
With the same techniques used to produce a baby book you could design a mailout or brochure.

Form a pressure group to

Whether you're campaigning to save the rainforests or your local

Project planner

Create a folder named after your group. Add subfolders to it for each mini-project.

Pressure group
- Research
- Contacts
- Communication
- Membership
- Publicity
- Money

Across an enormous range of concerns – from the global movement to preserve the rainforests to local campaigns petitioning for lower speed limits – the number of people involved in lobbying official bodies has never been greater.

Whether you are starting a new group or opening a local branch of an existing one, it is important to recruit and organize committed members, accrue campaign

donations and maintain momentum. Many pressure groups are run by volunteers on slender resources. Your computer can help to make the best use of both.

Increasingly, pressure groups are turning to the Internet to formulate and publicize their campaigns. Researching topics online is an obvious starting point. Many educational facilities and research centres release reports via the Net, and the introduction of more

make a difference

park, your PC can get the message across

"open government" in some countries has led to the publication on the Web of a vast quantity of official statistics and information, which can aid a campaign.

Newsgroups also offer fertile ground for pressure groups. There are issue-specific bulletin boards and forums, where information is traded and debates instigated by interested parties, such as members of other groups and contributors with expert knowledge. Any pressure group would do well to post its details and aims on suitable sites, both to attract members and donations and to collect new information.

A blog is a cheap and effective way to publicize a cause, and is a medium with a truly global reach. The real cost of maintaining a blog is minimal once it has been set up.

Beyond research and publicity, your computer can be used to manage your organization or branch. You can set up a membership database in Microsoft Works, use a spreadsheet package to manage the group accounts, and produce newsletters and press releases using a word-processing program. You can also create a mailing list, an e-mail list and print address labels. Consider producing questionnaires or petitions using your database's Form Design feature, and lobby local politicians via e-mail.

Form your plan of action

- Arrange venue/date/agenda for launching group
- Publicize launch meeting
- Arrange a visiting speaker
- Appoint officers and detail responsibilities
- Organize street publicity, collect shoppers' signatures and recruit new members
- Plan local demonstrations/publicity campaign
- Design and produce publicity material and flyers

Ideas and inspirations

Adapt the following projects and ideas to enhance your pressure group's profile, attract new members and make the most of your existing members' time and your group's resources. You may even think of other ways to apply your new skills and your computer's capabilities.

94 **Internet research**
Find the facts to formulate your argument, or simply keep up to date with affiliated groups.

166 **Make an address list**
Create a handy, easy-to-manage reference file for all your membership and contact details.

162 **Create a newsletter**
Keep your members updated about ongoing developments with a brief publication.

114 **Create a Web blog**
Use a blog to publicize your cause and gain the support of others around the world.

272 **Accounts**
Set up a spreadsheet to keep track of membership fees, donations and expenditures.

Also worth considering...

Once your pressure group is up and running, make regular mailouts easy to manage.

170 **Make address labels**
Use your membership database as the basis for time-saving printed stationery.

Using clip art images

Give a touch of creativity to your work by adding illustrations

Clip art images are predesigned graphic illustrations or pictures that you can incorporate into any document to give it a professional look. A gallery of such images is included free with Word and Works.

You can search the image gallery by typing in keywords like "Christmas," "Children" or "Travel." The images can be used as logos, bor-

ders, dividers, or just as decorative devices. You can also alter the look of an image – cropping it, framing it and colouring it as you wish.

It's not always easy to get the best results on the first attempt, so don't be afraid to experiment with clip art. Before long, you'll be making your own greeting cards, wrapping paper, invitations and address labels.

Watch out

Keep your program CDs handy. The Clip Art Gallery contains thumbnails of many thousands of images. The full-sized version may be on an extra CD-ROM, which you will be asked to insert when you place the image in your document.

1 To insert clip art into a Word document, place the cursor where you want the image to go. Next, go to the **Insert** tab and, in the "Illustrations" group, click on **Clip Art**. A column appears down the right-hand side of the screen with a Clip Art search facility at the top.

A clip art gallery comes as standard with Word and Works. You can also buy clip art on CD-ROM, download it from the Internet or scan in your own designs to use as clip art.

OTHER SOURCES

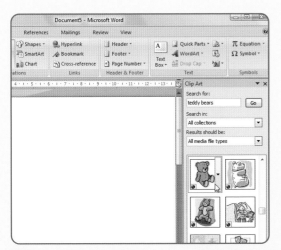

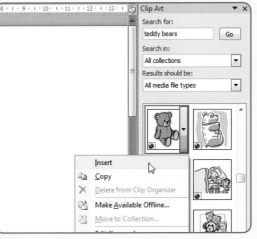

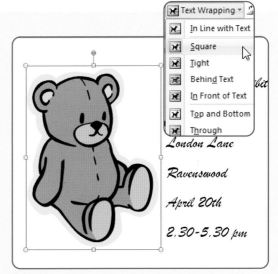

2 To find an image, type a keyword into the "Search for" box then click on **Go**. Any images matching your criteria will then be displayed. When you hover the cursor over an image that interests you, a toolbar appears. Click on the toolbar and a pop-up menu is displayed.

3 To insert the image into your document, click on the **Insert** option in the pop-up menu. To resize it (while keeping it in proportion), click on one of the round corner handles and drag it inwards or outwards to the required size.

4 Next, click on your image and then on the **Format** tab. Click on **Text Wrapping** in the "Arrange" group and then select "Square." Any text you type into your document will now appear to the right of the image. To move the image, click on it and drag it to the correct position.

Clip art online

To download online clip art, you must first log on to the Internet. Then go to the **Insert** tab and, in the "Illustrations" group, click on **Clip Art**. Next, click on **Clip art on Office Online** at the bottom of the column on the right-hand side of the screen. A browser window will open where you can search for images. If you like one, click on the **Copy to clipboard** button (see right).

Using text in Works

Microsoft Works offers you three options when positioning text around an image. With the image selected, go to the **Format** menu, choose **Object** and select the **Wrapping** tab. **In line with text** places the bottom of the image in line with the text it precedes. The **Square** option makes text wrap in a straight-sided box around the image. **Tight** makes the lines of text follow the shape of the image.

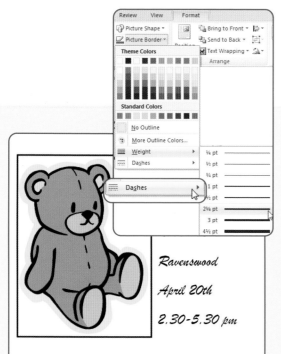

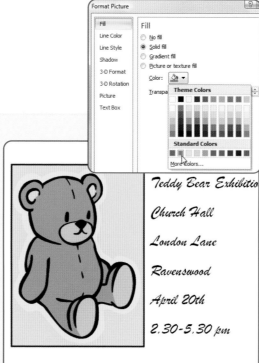

5 To add a frame to the image, double-click on it and then click on **Picture Border** in the "Picture Styles" group. Click on **Weight** and select a line width. You can also give your line a dashed effect by clicking on **Dashes** and choosing a style. Do not be afraid to experiment – you can keep changing styles until you find one you like.

6 To give your image a background colour, right-click on it and select **Format Picture**. Click on **Fill**, then on **Solid fill**. Click on the **Color** selector and choose a colour. Then move the Transparency slider to lighten or darken the colour. To remove your background colour and frame, select **Fill**, **No Fill** and **Line Color**, **No Line**.

7 If you want to shape text closely around the image, click on the **Page Layout** tab and, in the "Arrange" group, click on **Text Wrapping** and then on **Tight**. To adjust the wrap, click on **Edit Wrap Points** from the same menu. Click on the points that appear and drag them in or out.

Using images with text

If you want to use text with clip art on a page of type, you need to decide how to position the text and images together. Double-click on the image and, from the **Format** tab, click on **Text Wrapping**. The drop-down menu displays a number of options. Experiment with your layout by clicking on each in turn and seeing how this affects the position of your text and picture on the screen. At the bottom of the menu, click on **More Layout Options** to open the Advanced Layout dialogue box. Here you will need to click on **OK** for each selection and then click on **More Layout Options** to experiment with the next option.

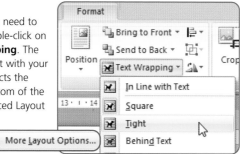

Bright idea
*In Word you can customize clip art. To change a colour, for example, right-click on the image and click on **Edit Picture**. Click on an area to edit, then right-click and select **Format AutoShape**. In the Format AutoShape dialogue box, under the "Colors and Lines" tab in the "Fill" panel, click on the **Color** selector and choose a different colour. Click on **OK**.*

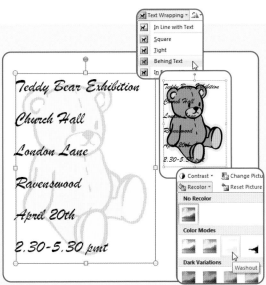

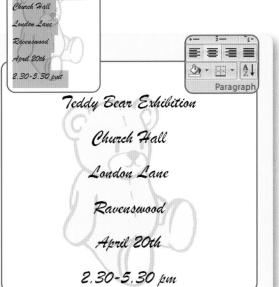

8 You can crop your image – that is, remove part of it. Click on the **Crop** button in the "Size" group and then on the image. Drag a handle into the image to crop out the areas you don't want, then click on the **Crop** button again. To restore the image, just click on the **Crop** button and pull the handle back out.

9 If you select **Behind Text** from the Text Wrapping menu, the text will appear on top of the image. This can look messy but you can make the text stand out by reducing the vibrancy of the image. Double-click on the image and then, in the "Adjust" group, click on **Recolor** and then on **Washout** under "Color Modes."

10 To centre your text on top of the image, highlight the text and click on the **Center** button in the "Paragraph" group. Finally, drag the image to sit behind the text.

Changing the image
You can alter the way your clip art looks by clicking on the **Recolor** button on the "Adjust" group:
● **No Recolor** gives a normal image – this is the default setting
● **Color Modes** provides options for Grayscale, Sepia, Washout and Black and White
● **Dark Variations** gives dark colour options
● **Light Variations** gives light colour options

*You can also make adjustments by clicking on the **Brightness** and **Contrast** buttons.*

Design a greeting card

Send a personal message with your own special occasion cards

Making your own greeting cards allows you to combine a personal message with an appropriate – even unique – choice of image, and ensures that you always have the right card for any occasion.

On a Christmas card, for example, you could insert a series of photographs showing things that you and your family have done over the past year. And for birthday cards you could scan in and use pictures your children have painted (see page 194).

Anyone who receives personalized cards such as these will greatly appreciate all the thought and effort that has gone into producing them.

Look at your printer manual to find out the maximum thickness, or weight, of paper your printer can take. Consider mounting paper onto card stock to give it strength.

BEFORE YOU START

1 Go to the **Start** menu, select **All Programs** and click on **Microsoft Office Word 2007**. To name and save your document click on the **Microsoft Office** button and select **Save As**. Select a suitable location, type in a file name, then click on **Save**.

*You can create greeting cards in Microsoft Works. Open Works then click on the **Programs** button. Choose **Works Word Processor** from the Quick Launch menu on the right.*

OTHER PROGRAMS

*To view your entire page, first go to the **View** tab and click on **Zoom**. When the Zoom dialogue box appears select **Whole page** and click on **OK**.*

*If the ruler does not appear in your document, go to the **View** tab and click on **Ruler**.*

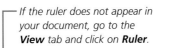

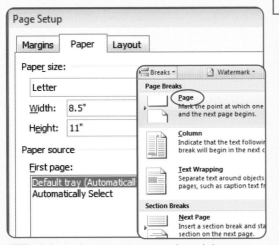

2 Click on the **Page Layout** tab and then on the **Page Setup** dialogue box launcher. Under the **Margins** tab, click on the **Landscape** icon. Under the **Paper** tab choose **Letter** from the "Paper size" menu. Click on **OK**. To create separate pages for the inside and outside of the card, click on **Breaks** and then, under "Page Breaks," select **Page**.

3 Scroll up to the first page and create a fold line. Go to the **Insert** tab and click on the **Shapes** button in the "Illustrations" group. Next, click on the **More** button and select the **Line** tool. Click on the left-hand ruler and drag to create a vertical line that splits the page in half. The area on the right of the line will be the front of your card.

4 Now select an image. Go to the **Insert** tab, and, in the "Illustrations" group, click on **Clip Art**. A column appears on the right of your screen with a search facility at the top. Type in some key search words and click on **Go**. To use an image, hover your cursor over it, click on the bar and then click on **Insert**. See page 186 for more on clip art.

Mounting your design

If your printer can't cope with card, mount your paper print-outs onto coloured card. Choose a colour that matches one of the colours in your image. Cut the card (ideally using a guillotine for a smooth edge) slightly larger than your image, or trim the image to leave a border. Finally, ensure that you have envelopes large enough to hold your cards.

*Click on the "More" option (the arrow) on the **Shapes** button to reveal a menu of drawing lines, shapes and arrow options.*

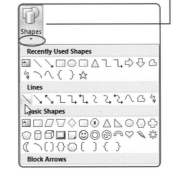

Repositioning clip art

To drag and drop your clip art around your document, first click on your clip art image. Go to the **Format** tab and from the "Arrange" group click **Text Wrapping**, and then **In Front of Text**. When inserting WordArt (see Step 7), click on your WordArt and follow the same procedure as above.

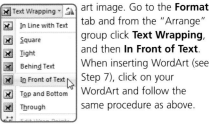

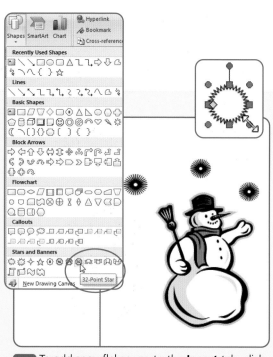

Keyword

WordArt *This describes the Microsoft library of text formats that you can customize. All you need to do is select a form of WordArt then type in your text. You can colour the text and style it however you wish.*

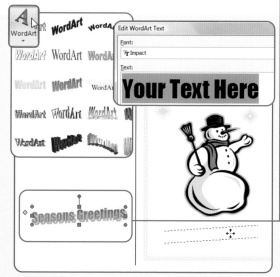

Click and drag your WordArt into position. To resize it, click and drag on one of its corner handles.

5 To add snowflakes, go to the **Insert** tab, click on the **Shapes** button in the "Illustrations" group and select **Stars and Banners**. Click on the shape you like, then click and drag to draw it on the page. You can resize the shape with the blue handles, or alter its shape with the yellow one. To rotate the image, use the green handle.

6 To add colour to your snowflakes, right-click on one of the flakes and select **Format AutoShape** from the pop-up menu. In the dialogue box the Colors and Lines tab is selected. Click on the arrow beside the "Color" box in the "Fill" section and choose a colour. Click on **OK**.

7 Now add a message to the front of the card. Go to the **Insert** tab and select **WordArt** from the "Text" group. In the WordArt Gallery click on a style, then on **OK**. The Edit WordArt Text box appears, inviting you to type "Your Text Here." Type the message you would like and then select a font, size and style. Click on **OK**.

Create a frame

It is easy to create a border that runs around the front of your card. Go to the **Insert** tab and click on the **Shapes** button. Then, in the "Basic Shapes" section, click on **Rectangle**. Click and drag on the document to create a frame of the appropriate size.

Right-click in the box and select **Format AutoShape**. In the **Colors and Lines** tab set "Fill Color" to **No Color**, then select a line colour, weight and style. Click on the **Fill Effects** button and, in the **Pattern** tab, choose a pattern, foreground and background colour, then click **OK**. Click on **OK** again.

Colouring WordArt

To change the colour of WordArt, select and then right-click on the WordArt. Next, select **Format WordArt**. In the "Fill" section of the **Colors and Lines** panel choose a colour for the text. In the "Line" section, select a colour and style for the text outline. Click on **OK**.

To change a WordArt message, right-click on it and select **Edit Text** from the menu. Type in your new text and click on **OK**. To alter its format, click on the "More" arrow in the WordArt Styles group, and double-click on the style you'd like.

Use the alignment buttons to position text within your text box.

Before you print, remove the fold lines you have used as guides. Click on each of them and press the **Delete** key.

8 Scroll down to the second page and draw a fold line as in Step 3. Go to the **Insert** tab, select **Text Box**, then **Draw Text Box** and click and drag to draw a box on the right-hand side of the page. Type in your text, highlight it, then go to the **Home** tab and click on the **Font** dialogue box launcher. Make your font choices and click on **OK**.

9 To give the text box a background colour, right-click on the edge of the box and select **Format Text Box**. In the "Fill" section of the dialogue box, click on **Fill Effects**. Click on the **Gradient** tab and then select the colours, shading style and variant that best suit your image. Click on **OK**.

10 Now click on the **Microsoft Office** button and select **Print**, then **Print Preview**. If you are happy with your card, click on **Print** in the "Print" group. Print page 1 only and then place the paper or card back in the printer (you will need to experiment with orientation) and print page 2 on the reverse.

If you give your text box a background colour (see Step 9), remove the border around it before you print. Right-click on the edge of the box and select **Format Text Box**. In the "Line" section of the dialogue box, click on the arrow beside the Color box and select **No Color**. Click on **OK**.

Wishing you joy and success in the New Year

Add your own images

Scan **in your** favourite photographs **to** liven up your documents

There is no limit to the variety of images you can use in your documents. If you have a scanner, you can transfer photographs, or pictures from newspapers or books, to your own computer.

A scanner takes a digital copy of an image that you can manipulate in any way you wish before placing it in a newsletter, invitation or card (just remember that the use of published material is covered by copyright laws).

It is possible to scan images using Windows Vista using more than one method. In this project, we'll show you two ways of achieving similar results – choose whichever works the best for you and then fine-tune the scanned image to use however you wish.

The following steps apply to one type of scanner. As products vary, some screens may look different when using other hardware.

BEFORE YOU START

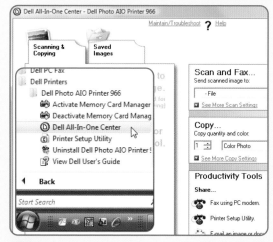

1 To begin using your scanner go to the **Start** menu and select your scanning software (here Dell All-In-One Center). When the software has launched, click on the **Scanning & Copying** tab to access the scanning functions.

 Watch out
Most printed material is covered by copyright laws. Unless you are copying it purely for your own use and not for distribution, it is not available for you to use freely. As a general rule, if you are designing a newsletter or poster, you will be breaching copyright laws if you use images from published sources without the copyright owner's permission.

Keyword
AIO stands for "All in One" – this is one machine that incorporates a printer, scanner, copier and fax. They are ideal for use at home.

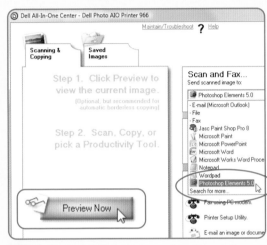

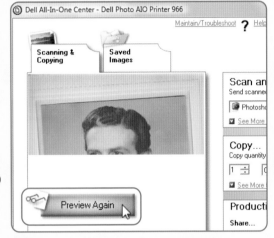

2 If this is the first time you have used the scanning facility of your AIO, click on the drop-down menu and select an application to edit your images (here Photoshop Elements 5.0). Place the image to be scanned on the bed of the scanner and click on **Preview Now**.

3 The scanner now peforms a quick, low-resolution pass over your image so you can decide how you would like to crop it. As the scanner passes over your image it gradually displays onscreen. If the image is crooked don't worry, just reposition it and click on **Preview Again**.

4 When the scan has finished, your image will have a dotted border around it with square black handles in each corner and on each side. Click and drag on these – the mouse pointer changes to a white double-headed arrow – to "crop" out any areas you don't want to include in the final scanned image. Click on **Scan Now**.

Push-button scanning

Many modern printer/scanners have buttons that you can press to launch an automatic scan of a picture. This Dell AIO device has a set of button options, including one that will scan a document at a resolution suitable for sending in an e-mail message. Other button options launch processes such as scanning an image for a Web site or sending a scanned image direct to a printer. The exact way these work depends on your hardware and software.

For more control over your scanned image, some models come with software, called a TWAIN driver, that works within an image editing program such as Photoshop Elements 5.0.

▶ ADVANCED SCANNING

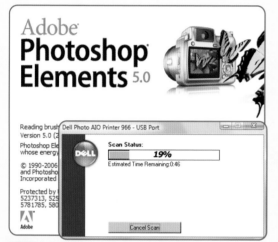

5 The scanner will now make the scan and a "Scan Status" window will appear to display the progress. When it has finished, your pre-selected image editing software (see Step 2) will automatically launch. (For more on Photoshop Elements 5.0, see pages 200–209.)

6 Your scanned image will now automatically open in your editing software. From here you can make adjustments to the image using the toolbar on the left, add a caption or simply save the image to your computer's hard drive. For more on using your images, see page 199.

1 Open your scanner's image editing program (here Photoshop Elements 5.0) and choose **Edit & Enhance Photos** from the Welcome screen. Then, in the **File** menu, click on **Import** then on **TWAIN-Dell Photo AIO Printer 966**. The TWAIN utility will launch.

Scanning a printed image

If you are scanning an image from a newspaper, you may find the scan appears slightly distorted. This arises from the hexagonal pattern of ink dots that printing produces.

You may find a "de-screen" setting within your scanning controls that contains different settings in "lpi" (lines per inch). For glossy, printed material select 133-200 lpi; for newspapers select 65-120 lpi. If you don't have these settings try to improve the scan by reducing the sharpness setting (see Step 4 on page 197 for how to access Advanced Scan Settings).

Bright idea
Experiment with different settings until you get the look you want. You can greatly increase the image's impact by editing it to suit your own material – it doesn't have to look like the original.

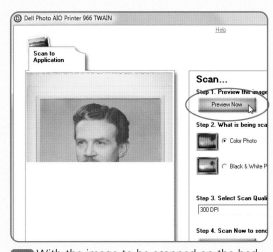

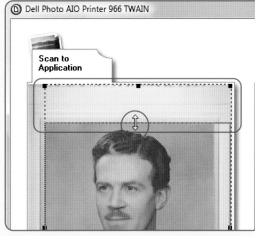

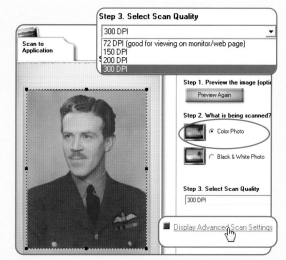

2 With the image to be scanned on the bed of the scanner, click on **Preview Now**. The scanner now peforms a quick, low-resolution pass over your image so you can decide how you wish to crop it. As the scanner passes over your image it gradually displays onscreen, in the "Scan to Application" panel.

3 When the preview finishes your image will have a dotted border around it with square black handles in each corner and on each side. Click and drag on these – the mouse pointer changes to a white double-headed arrow – to "crop" out any areas you don't want to include in the final scanned image.

4 In the "What is being scanned?" panel select the type of image to be scanned (here Color Photo). In the "Select Scan Quality" panel choose one of the four presets in the drop-down menu. For a greater selection of definitions click on the **Display Advanced Scan Settings** link at the bottom of the "Scan" panel.

What is TWAIN?

Although it looks like yet another computer acronym, TWAIN does not in fact stand for anything. The name was coined at a time when it was very difficult to get scanners and computers to communicate with each other and is taken from the line "...and never the twain shall meet..." in *The Ballad of East and West*, by Rudyard Kipling.

Conserving space

The amount of space your file uses relates both to the resolution at which the image has been scanned and to its dimensions (height and width). By increasing the resolution of this scan from 72dpi to 300dpi, the amount of memory and hard drive space it uses increases by more than ten times.

Ensure the Bitmap (.bmp) file format is selected in the File Format box. This means the scanned file can be imported into Word, Works and Paint, the Windows accessory program.

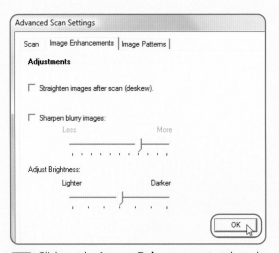

5 Click on the **Image Enhancements** tab and use the slider to adjust the brightness if your original image is under- or over-exposed. You can also adjust the sharpness or straighten a wonky image. Click on **OK** and then click on the **Scan Now** button.

6 You will hear the scanning head passing across your image, more slowly than it did when you previewed the image. You will also see a progress bar showing how much of the scan has been completed. When finished, your image will be shown in your image editing software. To stop this process at any time, click on **Cancel Scan**.

7 Now save your scan. Select **Save As** from the **File** menu and choose a name and location for your scanned image. To use or edit it in other programs, save it as a Windows bitmap (shown by a .bmp at the end of the filename). Click on **Save**. The BMP Options dialogue box will appear. To use the default settings, click on **OK**.

Create a background

You can use a scanned photo as the background picture on your Desktop if you saved it as a .gif or .jpg file. Open the folder containing the image, right-click on it and select **Set as Desktop Background**. To adjust the Desktop appearance right-click on it and choose **Personalize** then click on **Desktop background**. You can then select one of the presets to alter the look.

Now try placing your scan into a document to make, say, a card, a mini-magazine or a newsletter.

▶ **NEW PROGRAM**

*To crop the image, click on the **Crop** tool in the "Size" group, then click and drag on one of the black "line" handles. The mouse pointer changes to a small black cross. To resize the image, click on it, then on one of the white "round" or "square" handles; the mouse pointer changes to white double-headed arrow. Now drag the handle to a new position.*

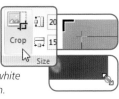

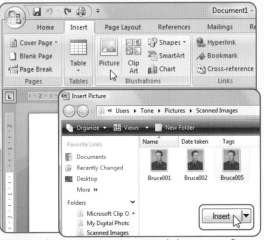

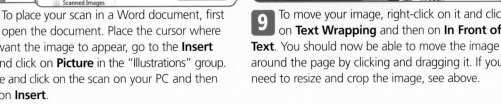

8 To place your scan in a Word document, first open the document. Place the cursor where you want the image to appear, go to the **Insert** tab and click on **Picture** in the "Illustrations" group. Locate and click on the scan on your PC and then click on **Insert**.

9 To move your image, right-click on it and click on **Text Wrapping** and then on **In Front of Text**. You should now be able to move the image around the page by clicking and dragging it. If you need to resize and crop the image, see above.

10 To add text, go to the **Insert** tab and select **Text Box** from the "Text" group. The cursor will change to a large cross. Draw two boxes – one for the heading and one for a caption. Size them in the same way you did for the picture. Now click on the boxes and type in your text.

Using photos in Works

Inserting a photograph in Works is very similar to the procedure in Word. Go to the **Insert** menu, click on **Picture**, then on **From File**. Navigate to the folder containing your photograph, click on it and then on **Insert**. The picture will appear in the document. You can resize the picture by clicking and dragging on one of the handles at the corners and the sides of the image. To keep the photograph in proportion, hold down the shift key as you drag a corner handle. Unlike Word, however, you cannot crop or adjust the colours of pictures in Works.

Work with digital images

Put your photos on your PC and start sharing right away

The benefits of digital photography are now very well known – and most people have experienced the ease of using a digital camera. The days of waiting until a roll of film has been finished and then taking it to be developed are gone. While some may miss the surprise of finding what was on the film, there are many advantages to the immediacy offered by digital photography.

The best thing is, of course, that you can see whether your photograph has come out well. If not, there is nothing to lose by trying again for the perfect shot. Next, by downloading it onto your PC you can print it right away – a dedicated photo-printer can give great results. You can also e-mail the image file around the world, sharing photos with friends and relatives at amazing speed.

Install Adobe Photoshop Elements 5.0. It is a straightforward process – just follow the onscreen instructions and you will soon be ready to go.

BEFORE YOU START

1 Switch on your camera and connect it to your computer using the USB cable that came with the camera. Adobe Photoshop Elements 5.0 may launch automatically, in which case go to Step 5. If not, go to the **Start** menu, click on **All Programs** and select **Adobe Photoshop Elements 5.0**.

Your camera may have been supplied with custom software from the manufacturer – this should allow you to perform all the basic print and edit functions.

OTHER PROGRAMS

*You can always return to the welcome screen by going to the **Editor** bar and selecting **Window** and then **Welcome**.*

Watch out
To download from your camera, it must be switched on and in "view" mode. If it is switched off or in "camera" mode, it will not appear in Photoshop Element's list of available devices.

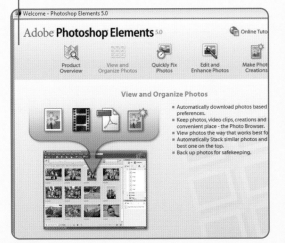

2 From the Photoshop Elements welcome screen, click on **View and Organize Photos**. The program will then load fully, showing you the most recent picture taken on your camera.

3 Before downloading, you can amend some of the "import settings," such as naming the folder the images will be stored in. Click on the Create Subfolder(s) drop-down menu and select **Custom Name** and then type the name of your new folder into the box below. To start the image download process, click on **Get Photos**.

4 The Photo Downloader will launch and start copying your photos to the folder you created in Step 3. A dialogue box will appear, showing you the progress of the download.

Understanding digital 'film'

With a traditional camera, your pictures are stored on a roll of film. A digital camera stores images on electronic memory cards. These come in a range of shapes, sizes and storage capacities, depending on the make and model of camera.

Secure Digital (SD) is common in compact cameras, while professional cameras often use Compact Flash cards. Sony products use a proprietary type of card called Memory Stick. Cameras built into mobile phones often use tiny cards known as Mini-SD. It makes little difference what format your camera uses, but you can only insert the correct type of card.

All these cards are based on a technology called "flash memory" that keeps images stored even when the camera is turned off. So, having filled up the card, you can take it out and leave it to one side while you take more pictures using another card, then transfer the pictures to your PC when you're ready.

You could keep all your photos stored on cards, but it's best to copy them to your PC and then store them on recordable CDs or DVDs. You can then reuse your memory cards to take more pictures.

Watch out

Attaching digital photos to e-mail messages is simple but it can make your e-mails enormous. If you are e-mailing photos you should first save them in a compressed format (see Size matters, page 203).

5 When the files have been copied to the folder you chose, the Files Successfully Copied box will appear. Click on **OK**. By default, Photoshop Elements 5 will automatically fix any pictures with red eye. When this process has finished, these images will be ready for editing in Photoshop Elements' Editor mode (see page 204).

6 You can choose the size of the images shown on your screen by using the slider at the bottom right of the screen or by clicking on the four small squares to see thumbnails of every image. Use the icon to the right of the slider to view single images, and the far right icon to view the images full screen.

7 Printing your photos right away is a great advantage of digital cameras. Click on **File** and then on **Print** to launch the Print Photos dialogue box.

Send photos by e-mail

Photoshop Elements allows you to select and attach images to an e-mail. Double-click on the first image you would like to send, then click on the **Share your photos via Email** button at the top of the screen and select **E-mail**. You will now need to select your e-mail program, here Microsoft Outlook. If you would like to send more than one photo, click on **Add** in the Attach to Email dialogue box. Here you can also add the recipient if their details are in your e-mail Contacts list (see page 91), and enter any message you would like to send. Click on **Next**. Over the next two screens you can add a caption and amend the design by clicking on the options in the left-hand panels. Click on **Next** when you are happy with the look. Finally, an e-mail box will appear – add your recipient's e-mail address if you haven't already, and click on **Send**.

Shortcut
Photoshop Elements has a useful shortcuts bar at the top of the window. You can click on the icons to Print, Capture, Share Online and Share via Email.

Bright idea
Save money by refilling the plastic cartridges that hold the ink for your printer. You can take your used cartridges to a refilling service or buy your own kit.

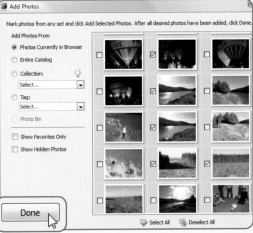

8 The Print Photos dialogue box will show a page with the last photo you selected already placed. Check the settings for Printer, Type of Print and Print Size. If you need to change the paper size or orientation, click on **Page Setup** to access these settings. To print more than one picture on a sheet, click on **Add**.

9 Scroll through the thumbnail images and click in the boxes next to the pictures you would like to include. Click on **Done** when you have finished. If you change your mind about a picture, click on it in the left-hand pane and then click on **Remove**.

10 Photoshop Elements will automatically place the images on the page, rotating images and running onto extra pages if necessary. Click on the right arrow at the bottom to see additional pages. When you are happy with your layouts, click on **Print** to get immediate copies of your pictures.

Size matters

When e-mailing photos you should first save them in a compressed format such as JPEG. To do this, choose **Save As** from the **File** menu, rename the image and from the "Format" drop-down list choose **JPEG**. Then click on **Save**. In the JPEG Options dialogue box select from one of the four image options to determine the size and quality of the image. Then click **OK**.

Letting the experts do it

You don't have to print out your pics yourself. There are lots of companies that offer photo printing services, including stores like Shopper's Drug Mart/Pharmaprix and Black's/Astral Photo. You can take your digital camera's memory card into a store and pick up the prints later. Or you can upload pictures to the Net and get quality prints on photographic paper by mail. You can even order enlargements or special items such as mugs or T-shirts with your pictures on them.

Editing digital images

Make your pictures perfect with just a few tweaks

Using an image-editing program, you can make almost any imaginable alteration to a photo. First of all, you need to have the picture stored as a digital file. It could come from your digital camera, or the picture may have been taken on traditional film – you can have your photos put on CD when you have your film processed, or use a scanner to copy prints onto your PC (see page 194).

Once you have opened an image file in your editing program, you can alter it in a variety of ways. For example, you can turn the photo around or "crop" it, cutting out parts of the picture you do not want. In this feature, we will show you how to correct "red eye" and restore a healthy tone to the subjects of your photos – you'll be amazed at how quickly you can create great pictures.

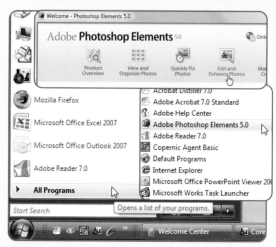

Download the images you would like to edit from your camera (see page 200), or scan a printed photo to create a digital file (see page 194).

BEFORE YOU START

1 Automatic flash often causes "red eye" and spoils pictures. To remove it, first go to the **Start** menu, click on **All Programs** and select **Adobe Photoshop Elements 5.0**. From the Photoshop Elements' welcome screen, click on **Edit and Enhance Photos**.

Other image-editing programs will perform the same tasks – options include Corel Paint Shop Pro, Microsoft Digital Image Suite and the full version of Adobe Photoshop.

OTHER PROGRAMS

Keyword
Red eye *When you photograph a person using the flash, light reflected from the back of the eye glows red, known as "red eye." Many cameras have an option to reduce red eye but it is also quickly remedied in image-editing software.*

Shortcut
*If you would like a closer look at an image, double-click on the thumbnail. To return to the screen displaying all images, click on **Back**.*

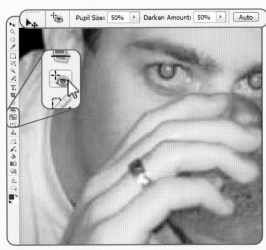

2 Next, go to the **File** menu, click **Open** and locate the photo you want to edit. When the image appears, click on the **Zoom Tool** in the toolbox on the left, and then click and drag around the eyes. This part of the image will then enlarge so that you can focus on the area with red eye you want to correct.

3 Click on the **Red Eye Removal Tool** in the toolbox on the left. The options at the top of the screen change so that you can alter the size of the pupil and the amount by which you would like to darken it. If you're not sure, leave these settings on the program's automatic setup.

4 Next, click on an area of red eye in the picture, or click and drag over the affected area. Photoshop Elements will automatically correct the problem. Repeat this process until you are satisfied with the result.

Finding your stored photos

If you're not sure where an image is stored, click on **View and Organize Photos** on Photoshop Elements' welcome screen. When the program has fully launched, click on the thumbnail icon at the bottom right-hand corner of the screen to see all the files that have been downloaded into Photoshop Elements. Find the image you would like to edit and click on it. Next, click on the **Edit** button at the top of the screen and select **Go to Full Edit**. The Editor mode will then launch, with your selected image onscreen, ready for you to start work.

Bright idea
*If you want to experiment without losing your original image, use **Save As** from the **File** menu to create a new file – you just need to choose a slightly different name to store it under.*

5 Click on **File** and then **Save** to save your adjusted image. If this is the first time you have saved this image, you will be asked to rename the file and you can choose where to store it – click on the **Save in** drop-down menu at the top of the dialogue box and find an appropriate folder. Click on **Save**.

6 Digital photos can sometimes make the subject look quite washed out. You can adjust the tones in Photoshop Elements to restore a healthier look. First, open the photo in Photoshop Elements' Editor mode.

7 Click on **Enhance** from the menu bar at the top of the screen, and select **Adjust Color** and then **Adjust Color for Skin Tone**.

Size matters

The resolution of an image is usually given in "dots per inch" (dpi). The term "300dpi" means 300 dots across and down each inch. "Dots" here means pixels. Don't confuse these with the dpi ratings of printers, which refer to the dozens of ink dots needed to print each pixel. Digital cameras are rated in megapixels, referring to the total number of pixels in millions. For a photo to print at 8 x 6 inches with a resolution of 300dpi, you need 8x300x6x300 = 4,320,000 pixels – just over 4 megapixels.

Storing a "true colour" digital picture requires 24 bits multiplied by the number of pixels – this uses up a lot of space. To save space, you can reduce the number of pixels by setting your digital camera to a lower resolution or by changing the file format to a format such as JPEG, where the data is compressed but some colour information is discarded. Essentially, you must balance image quality against file size – but remember that once data is lost, you can't get it back.

Watch out
*It's easy to overdo the changes when adjusting skin tone. If you do, click on the **Reset** button in the Adjust Color for Skin Tone dialogue box to return to the original image and start again.*

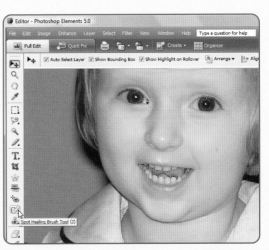

8 Move the mouse over to the face on the image (you may need to click on and drag the Adjust Color for Skin Tone dialogue box out of the way). Once the mouse is in the right area, an eyedropper icon will appear. Click once and Photoshop Elements will automatically adjust the skin tone.

9 If you would like to adjust the tones further, drag the sliders for **Tan** and **Blush** along to change the skin (see below), and drag the **Ambient Light** slider to alter the light in the image. When you are happy with the result, click on **OK** and then save the altered image as in Step 5.

10 Great photos can sometimes be spoiled by an unfortunate skin blemish. You can quickly remedy these complaints with Photoshop Elements. Open an image that needs correcting in the Editor mode, and click on the **Spot Healing Brush** tool in the toolbar on the left.

Adjusting skin tones

The Adjust Color for Skin Tone command will automatically alter the colours used in a photo to make the best of natural skin tones. To use this tool in Photoshop Elements, you just need to select it from the toolbar and then click on an area of skin. If you wish, you can manually adjust the brown (tan) and red (blush) colours separately to achieve the final colour you want. When you're finished, click on **OK**. To cancel your changes and start again, click on **Reset**.

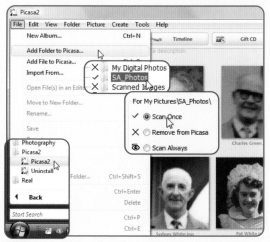

To create a photo album your pictures need to be digital images. Scan them yourself (see page 194) or download them from a digital camera (see page 200).

▶ BEFORE YOU START

1 Click on the **Start** button, choose **All Programs** and then select **Picasa2**. Browse to the folder that contains the photos you want to use, here "SA_Photos." If you can't see the folder, click on the **File** menu and choose **Add Folder to Picasa**. In the dialogue box, click on your folder, tick **Scan Once**, then click on **OK**.

Build an online album

It's easy to create a photo album on the Web using Picasa

Many of us have large collections of photographs that never make it into an album. With friends and family living far away, sharing these pictures can often be difficult. But the arrival of digital photography has changed all that. Now it's possible to build an online album, where you upload your images to the Web for everyone to see. Google provides a free photo-management program called Picasa, where you can assemble a photo album from any collection of images. It can then be used as a stand-alone Web page, which can be placed in any Web space to which you have access. Once there, everyone can admire your photos using their Internet browser.

You can use Web editors such as FrontPage or Dreamweaver to build great websites. It is also possible to rent Web space from hundreds of providers around the world.

▶ OTHER PROGRAMS

Close-up
*If you do not already have Picasa on your PC, go to http://picasa.google.ca and click on **Download Picasa**. The software will download and be stored with other applications on your hard drive.*

Bright idea
Cropping your pictures so that the main subject of the photo is at the centre of the image makes for a more eye-catching display.

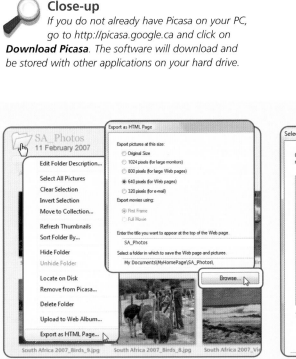

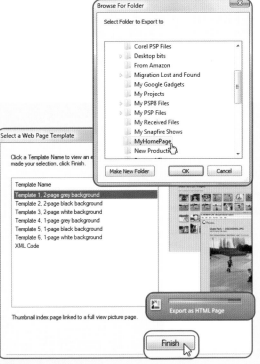

2 Scroll down the thumbnail images displayed in the main window to find your photos. Right-click on the folder icon and select **Export as HTML page...** from the drop-down menu. In the dialogue box select **640 pixels** under "Export pictures at this size" and type a title for the Web page, here "SA_Photos." Click the **Browse** button.

3 In the Browse For Folder dialogue box, click on the "MyHomePage" folder in "Documents." If it isn't there, click on **Documents** then on the **Make New Folder** button, type "MyHomePage" and click **OK**. Click on **Next** and choose a template from the panel on the left. Click on **Finish**. An "Export as HTML Page" bar displays the progress.

4 Your Web browser loads to display the album, so you can see how it will look when it's on the Web. Thumbnail images of the photos are displayed – you can click on a thumbnail to see the image at its full size (in this case, 640 pixels wide). In full-size view, you can use the navigation links at the top to move around the images.

Connecting a digital camera

Windows Vista makes it easy to get pictures from a digital camera. Most cameras come with a USB cable. Connect this to a vacant USB port on your computer, switch the camera on and it should be recognized and configured automatically. You will see a dialogue box asking what you want to do each time you connect. You can choose whether to print all of the pictures in the camera's memory, view them as an onscreen slide show or copy them across to a folder on your computer.

Album template options

Picasa offers two main types of template (see Step 3), with background colour variations in each. The first displays all the thumbnail images in a grid across the page. Click one and the thumbnails are replaced with the photo, shown full screen. The second option (right) creates a frame-based display, where thumbnails are in a narrow scrollable frame on the left, with the currently selected photo filling a large frame on the right. Either type will integrate within the frames of your homepage.

Create your own calendar

Make a **personal calendar** with a new **photo** for **every month**

With the widespread use of digital cameras, it is now incredibly easy to produce your own, personalized calendar. You don't even need to be creative – Microsoft Office Online supplies a number of templates that, using Excel, you can adapt to make a calendar that's exclusive to you and means a lot to your friends and family.

Most of the work is already done within the template. You just need to select 12 of your favourite images – anything from picturesque landscapes to snapshots of family or friends will work well. It's then up to you to choose any other personal touches you might like to add before printing and binding your own special record for the year.

Look through your photos and try to choose relevant images – one idea is to show family members with a birthday in the featured month.

▶ BEFORE YOU START

1 Go to the **Start** menu, select **All Programs** and click on **Microsoft Office** and then on **Microsoft Office Excel 2007**. Connect to the Internet and go to the Microsoft Office Online website (see page 215). Once you have signed in, click on **Templates**, and then on **Calendars**.

To create a more professional-looking calendar, try using the templates on websites such as www.kodakgallery.com or www.snapfish.com.

▶ OTHER PROGRAMS

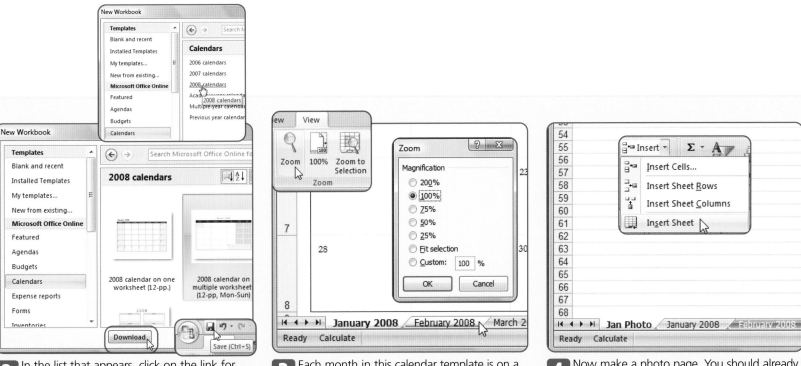

2 In the list that appears, click on the link for **2008 calendars**. Scroll down and select **2008 calendar on multiple worksheets (12-pp, Mon-Sun)**. Then click on the **Download** button; the file will automatically open in Excel. Click on the **Save** button on the Quick Access toolbar to save the new document.

3 Each month in this calendar template is on a separate worksheet. To view a particular month, just click on its tab at the bottom of the screen. If you cannot see the whole page, go to the **View** tab and click on **Zoom** to choose a different magnification. Click **OK**.

4 Now make a photo page. You should already be on the January 2008 worksheet – if not, click on its tab. From the **Home** tab, go to the "Cells" group and click on **Insert**, then choose **Insert Sheet** to add a new worksheet for your photo. Double-click on the **Sheet 1** tab and rename it "Jan Photo," and press **Return**.

Accessing Microsoft Office Online templates

It is easiest to access the Microsoft Office Online templates that fit this project from within Excel. Once the program has launched, click on the **Office** button and choose **Excel Options** at the bottom of the list. In the pane that opens, click on **Resources** in the left-hand bar, and then click on the **Go Online** button next to "go to Microsoft Office Online."

If this is the first time you have used an online Microsoft service, you will need to register and create a password. This username and password can then be used for all Microsoft sites. Once your registration has been accepted, or you have signed in, you can click on the **Templates** button in the top bar. From this project, you should then click on **Calendars** in the "Browse Templates" panel.

Create an invitation

Make a special occasion even better with your own design

Making your own invitation allows you to create a design that reflects the type of event you are organizing – and the type of person you are arranging it for. If it is going to be a lively party, use bright colours and fun fonts. If it is for a more sober dinner party, choose more subtle colours and traditional fonts.

Before designing your invitation, make a note of the relevant information guests will need, including the date, time, location of the event – and any dress requirements.

Decide what size you want your invitation to be. For convenience, it's a good idea to print two or four per sheet of letter-sized paper.

BEFORE YOU START

1 Go to the **Start** menu, select **All Programs** and click on **Microsoft Office Word 2007**. A new document appears. Save it by going to the **Office** button and clicking on **Save As**. Select a location, type in a file name, then click on **Save**.

*You can create an invitation in Microsoft Works. Open Works then click on the **Programs** button. Choose **Works Word Processor** from the Quick Launch menu on the right.*

OTHER PROGRAMS

CAROLINE'S
8TH BIRTHDAY PARTY
24 CHAPEL ROAD, BATH. S.
RSVP: LYNN 514.987.6543

CAROLINE'S
8TH BIRTHDAY PARTY
24 CHAPEL ROAD, BATH. SATURDAY 9TH DECEMBER @ 3.30PM
RSVP: LYNN 514.987.6543

2 Go to the **Page Layout** tab and click on the Page Setup dialogue box launcher. Click the **Paper** tab and make sure that Letter is selected in the "Paper size" box. Click the **Margins** tab and set the Top and Bottom margins to 0 inches. Click **OK**. A warning box comes up, click **Fix** then **OK**.

3 Type in your text. To style it, highlight the first part, click on the Font dialogue box launcher and under the **Font** tab, select a font, style, size, colour and effect, then click **OK**. Continue to style the rest of your text in a similar way.

4 Highlight all your text and click on the **Center** button, found in the "Paragraph" group. Alternatively, you can use the special effects facility, WordArt. This gallery contains a selection of text designs that you can edit and customize. Highlight the text you want to add an effect to and click on **Cut** in the "Clipboard" group.

Close-up
If you want to design a classic, traditional invitation, choose from the following fonts: Book Antiqua, Copperplate Gothic Light, Garamond, Monotype Corsiva or Palatino Linotype. For a more fun look, try Comic Sans MS, Curlz MT, Kristen ITC or Bradley Hand ITC.

Press the **Ctrl** key then, keeping it pressed down, press the "**V**" key to paste cut or copied text.

You can exaggerate the effect of the WordArt shape by clicking on the yellow diamond and dragging it across the screen.

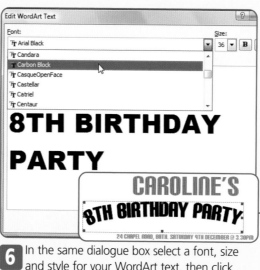

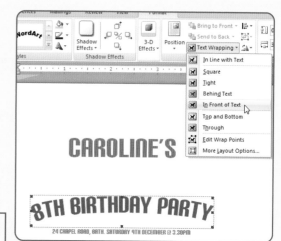

5 Go to the **Insert** tab and click on **WordArt** in the "Text" group. Then click on a style in the WordArt Gallery. The Edit WordArt Text dialogue box appears showing the words "Your Text Here" in the "Text" box. Hold down the **Ctrl** key then press the "**V**" key to paste in your text. Click **OK**.

6 In the same dialogue box select a font, size and style for your WordArt text, then click **OK**. Your text will now appear in the document in your chosen style. To select a colour, right-click on the WordArt box and click **Format WordArt**. In the dialogue box, select a colour from the "Color" drop-down list.

7 With your WordArt selected, click on the **Center** button in the "Paragraph" group. Now roughly space out your lines of text by pressing the Enter key on your keyboard. Select your WordArt again, then go to the **Format** tab and select **Text Wrapping**, then **In Front of Text**.

Letter spacing in WordArt

You can adjust the spacing between WordArt letters, or characters. With your WordArt selected, click on the **Spacing** button in the "Text" group, then click on your choice from the pop-up menu.

Colour in WordArt

You can change the colour of some WordArt. Right-click on the WordArt, and select **Format WordArt** from the drop-down menu. Under the Colors and Lines tab, choose a colour in the Fill section for the body of your text; and in the Line section choose a colour to outline the words.

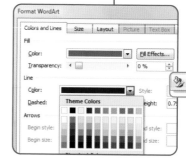

Bright idea
For a professional look, print your invitations on card. Not all printers can handle card stock, however, so you may need to store the document on a CD/DVD and take it to a print shop.

8 Select your WordArt again, then use the cursor keys on your keyboard to move it so it sits neatly between the first and third lines. To adjust the shape of your WordArt, click on it, then click on the **WordArt Shape** button in the "WordArt Styles" group. A palette pops up offering you a selection of effects. Click on your choice.

9 If you wish, you can add a photograph to your invitation. Position your cursor at the top of your page. Go to the **Insert** tab and click on **Picture** in the "Insert" group. In the dialogue box, navigate to your picture, click on it, then on **Insert**. Your text will automatically move down to create space for the new image.

10 Now go to the "Arrange" group and click on **Text Wrapping** and then on **Behind Text**. Your text will then automatically move back onto the first page and sit neatly in front of your picture. To print out the invitation, go to the **Office** button and select **Print** from the left pane.

Adding clip art

If you wish, you can add a Clip Art image to your invitation instead. Place the cursor where you want the clip art to appear, go to the **Insert** tab and click on the **Clip Art** button in the "Illustrations" group. The Clip Art panel appears on the right-hand side of the screen. Type in a search term and click **Go**. Scroll down the images and click on your choice, then click on **Insert** on the pop-up toolbar. To manipulate your image, see page 186.

Plan the perfect party for

Use your computer to help organize your celebration

An informal get-together at home is one thing, but it is quite a different matter to arrange the kind of special party your friends and relatives will be talking about for years.

Wedding anniversaries, landmark birthdays, marriages and christenings – these occasions do not come around very often, but when they do you want to be sure it all goes right. The preparations can take months and the planning will have to be meticulous. Venue, catering, entertainment, guests and accommodation – if people are coming a long way – must be booked and confirmed well in advance. You also need to plan the cost of it all.

One of the main areas in which your computer can help is in compiling a guest list. The

Project planner

Create a folder called "Party." Add subfolders to it for each mini-project.

📁 Party
- 📁 Guest list
- 📁 Invitations
- 📁 Letters to suppliers
- 📁 Budget
- 📁 Menus
- 📁 Reminders

a special occasion

and ensure you have a day to remember

Microsoft Works database will store the contact details of guests and of key suppliers, such as caterers. Use your PC's design capabilities to produce invitations, then address them instantly by making labels from your guest database. As people reply, input the information into the database for a record of confirmed numbers.

Using a database means you'll only have to compile the list once, and you can then use it to note additional details: the number of people in each group; who has small children; who is a vegetarian and so on. Now you can estimate the number of people attending,

and use a spreadsheet to prepare a budget. Allocate a sum for the cost of the venue and entertainment, and an amount per head for food. If you need to contact and select caterers, DJs and so on, send out letters written in your word-processing program giving your requirements and requesting quotes. Use the word-processing program to create menus and place cards, too.

Now set up a planning spreadsheet in the form of a "Celebration Countdown." Use it to schedule remaining tasks.

Once everything is in place, you can relax and start looking forward to the big day.

Pay attention to detail

- Compile guest list
- Book venue
- Organize caterer
- Design and send out invitations
- Book disc jockey and Master of Ceremonies
- Compile "Celebration Countdown"
- Write and send reminders/directions

Ideas and inspirations

These suggestions will get you started on organizing your event. All the projects can be adapted depending on the nature of your occasion. For example, on your invitation you could include your e-mail address so guests can respond by computer.

166 Guest list and address labels
Set up a guest list to keep track of who you invite and use labels to mail your invitations.

218 Create an invitation
A little imagination – and the versatility of Word and Works – will ensure a good response.

148 Send a formal letter
Use Word to produce businesslike letters to suppliers to check availability and prices.

272 Project-based budgeting
Compile a spreadsheet to help keep track of all your party's expenses.

312 Celebration countdown
In the same way you plan a holiday, create a spreadsheet to organize last-minute tasks.

Also worth considering...

Whether you have a caterer or are doing the food yourself, guests might like to see the menu.

158 Dinner party menu
If your party involves catering, you could save money by asking guests to select their choice in advance.

Design your own poster

Use graphics **and** text imaginatively **to get your event** noticed

When it comes to advertising an event, a colourful, eye-catching poster can really pull in the crowds. It's easy to make a poster for almost any event – from a company dinner to a rummage sale. And with a computer you don't even need to be artistic to design an effective poster.

When designing your poster, you should think about catching the attention of any passers-by. You also need to make sure that all the essential details of the event – the date, time, place and admission price – are clearly stated in an easily readable font and size. Soon everyone will know what's going on!

Check that all the information you want on your poster is correct, and think about which type of image will make the greatest impact.

BEFORE YOU START

1 Go to the **Start** menu, select **All Programs** and click on **Microsoft Office Word 2007**. To create your page, go to the **Page Layout** tab and click on the **Page Setup** dialogue box launcher. In the Page Setup dialogue box, type in measurements for the Top, Bottom, Left and Right margins (at least 1 cm). Click on **OK**.

*You can also design a poster in Microsoft Works. Open Works, click on the **Templates** button and select **Newsletters & Flyers** from the categories menu on the left. Click on **Event flyers** icon on the right, choose a style, then click on **Use this style**.*

OTHER PROGRAMS

Bright idea
There are certain fonts specifically designed for headlines. For example: Arial Black, Britannic Bold, Copperplate Gothic Bold and Impact. Try out any that have Black, Bold or Ultra in their name.

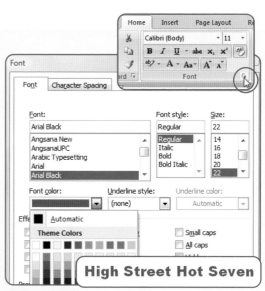

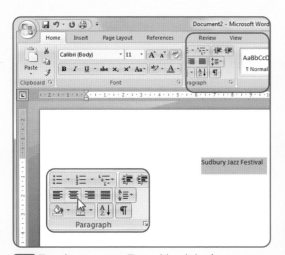

2 Type in your text. To position it in the centre of your document, highlight it and click on the **Center** toolbar button. To create WordArt, highlight the word or words you want to style, then go to the **Insert** tab and click on **WordArt** from the "Text" group.

3 You will be presented with the WordArt Gallery. Click on a style you like and then, in the Edit WordArt Text dialogue box, select a font and font size. Click on **OK**. Your heading will now appear as WordArt (it's actually a type of image) in your document.

4 Now style the remainder of your text. Highlight each section in turn, click on the **Font** dialogue box launcher and make your choice of fonts, sizes, styles and different text effects. Make sure you don't get carried away – a good poster should be clear and easy to read.

Using Word templates

Microsoft Office online has a collection of templates that might help you with your poster. If you choose to use one, make sure that the paper size and orientation are right for your printer – go to the Page Setup dialogue box and click on the **Paper** tab. Click on the arrow to the right of the "Paper size" box, scroll through and select your preferred size. To check or change the orientation, go to the **Margins** tab and select Portrait or Landscape.

Making the most of WordArt

Once you have created WordArt, you can format it further. Select your WordArt image then right-click on it and select **Format WordArt** from the drop-down menu. Click on the **Layout** tab where the default setting is "In line with text." When WordArt is set to this option you can move it down the screen by pressing the **Return** key; select one of the other options if you'd prefer to click and drag it. If you would like to adjust the size of your WordArt click and drag one of the handles, or distort it by clicking and dragging on the yellow diamond.

5 To add space between text, place your cursor at the end of each section and press the **Return** key. For finer adjustments, place your cursor in the line above where you want to add extra space and click on the **Paragraph** dialogue box launcher. In the Spacing section, click on the top arrow beside After to increase the space.

6 To add a clip art image, place your cursor where you want it to appear, go to the **Insert** tab and click on **Clip Art** in the "Illustrations" group. Type in the subject of your poster in the "Search for" box in the right-hand column and click on **Go**. Choose an image, click on it and then on **Insert** in the pop-up menu.

7 You can now move and resize your image as necessary, and add more images if you like. To make sure text flows around an image, double-click on it, go to the **Format** tab and click on **Text Wrapping** in the "Arrange" group. Choose **Tight** from the drop-down menu.

Importing images

If you want to use your own image from a CD-ROM or your scanned picture folder, go to the **Insert** tab and click on **Picture**. In the dialogue box scroll through and click on the location of your image. When you have located your image, click on it and then on **Insert**.

Watch out

If a clip art image is too large to fit where you want it, the image will drop onto the next page. Reduce its size by clicking and dragging its picture handles and then move it to your desired location.

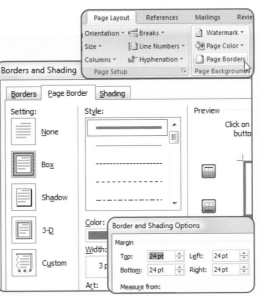

8 The "Tight" option keeps the text close to your image. "Square" allows you to position text neatly above, below and at either side of your image. With "Edit Wrap Points" you define the exact path the text takes around the picture by moving the wrap points. For more choices, select "More Layout Options."

9 To add a border, go to the **Page Layout** tab and click on **Page Borders** in the "Page Background" group. Choose a style, colour, width and setting. (If necessary, click on **Options** and, under Margin, set the size of the gap between the border and the edge of the page, and click on **OK**.) Click on **OK** to finish.

10 To view your poster, go to the **Microsoft Office button** and choose **Print** then **Print Preview**. If you need to make any alterations, click on the **Close Print Preview** button (on the far right of the ribbon), and edit as necessary. To print your poster, choose **Print** from the "Print" options.

Cropping images

If you do not want to use all of the clip art image in your poster, crop out the unwanted parts. From the **Format** tab click on the **Crop** tool in the "Size" group. Click and drag one of the picture handles in or out to cut or restore the sides of your image.

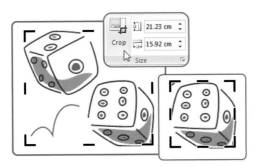

Make your fest a day

There's no aspect of a festival (except the weather) that

Project planner

Create a folder called "Festival." Add subfolders within it for smaller projects.

- 📁 **Festival**
  - 📁 **Correspondence**
  - 📁 **Publicity**
  - 📁 **Finance**
  - 📁 **Ideas**
  - 📁 **Timetable**
  - 📁 **Floor plan**

A successful festival is a matter of pre-planning and organization. The main thing is to coordinate everything so that it all comes together at the right moment. It is a serious job making certain that everyone has fun on the day.

There are so many things to think about that the first job is to delegate some of the work. Form a committee and assign roles: someone to deal with drumming up publicity in the press and on the radio; someone to approach businesses for sponsorship or material help; and someone to be festival treasurer (this is particularly important if yours is a fundraising or charitable event).

Now you have to decide on a venue, and on a beneficiary if you plan to donate the proceeds of the festival to charity. Someone on the committee should keep careful notes of the discussions, and these should be typed up and circulated soon after each committee

in a million

you can't plan on your computer

meeting. You may want to invite your local police, or someone from the town council to take part in the meetings.

By now, you will have set up a timetable database on which you record the tasks that need to be carried out and when. Tick tasks off as they are completed – that way you can use the sort facility to separate completed tasks from those yet to be done, and so plan a weekly schedule.

If you are seeking sponsorship or prize donations, you might like to create an event letterhead for your correspondence. You could send out regular e-mails to keep in touch with all the clubs and organizations taking part in the festival. Meanwhile, use your PC to plan the location of all the stalls on the site.

As the day approaches, you can use your PC to create flyers. By now you will know what the big attractions are and you can feature these on your publicity material (if you have asked a celebrity to open the event, make sure that their photograph is on the poster).

When the big day eventually arrives, just relax and enjoy it – by then you'll have earned it.

Event organizer

- Form an organizing committee. Arrange either monthly or weekly meetings
- Decide on a date and beneficiaries of the profits
- Provisionally book the venue
- Approach local businesses for sponsorship
- Contact the police or town council to ensure the date and venue are suitable
- Inform local press for advance and on-the-day coverage. Agree and implement publicity ideas

Ideas and inspirations

Listed here are a selection of projects you might want to use – or customize – to help you in the organization of a successful community event. Allocate as much work as possible to other people, but keep a record of all developments on your computer.

180 Timetable database
Leave nothing to chance – produce a helpful diary of "to do" tasks with your database.

144 Event letterhead
Correspond with stallholders and potential sponsors in a distinctive and memorable way.

224 Design your own poster
Publicize the date, time and venue of your event locally, together with details of its attractions.

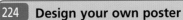

272 Accounts spreadsheet
Use a spreadsheet to keep track of all expenditure and income arising from your event.

302 Stall planner
Create a simple, overhead 2D plan of the venue and organize your space effectively.

Also worth considering...

If your timeline and responsibilities justify it, you may find the following project makes things easier.

162 Create a newsletter
Keep the key people involved in the event informed of developments and progress.

Create a party CD

Compile and record **your own** music compilation

Whatever the occasion, the right music can really get the party going. Using Windows Media Player you don't need to spend hours in music stores trying to find the perfect CD – you can create your own. Windows Media Player controls all the forms of entertainment you're likely to use on your PC, from playing music CDs to viewing DVDs. The Media Player comes into its own, however, if you have a CD recorder or "burner" within your PC. Using the recorder, you can back up your files cheaply and reliably, and it even allows you to create CDs with the mix of music that suits you. So get out the CDs you already own, and create a mix that will be a hit with all your guests.

> Go through your CD collection and choose music for your compilation. You don't need to choose the order you'd like them to play in.
>
> **BEFORE YOU START**

1 In the **Start** menu, click on **All Programs**, then on **Windows Media Player**. The program will open and, if it's the first time you've used it, start playing a sample of music. Open your CD drive and insert an audio CD. The CD should start playing automatically – to see track names and details, see below. Click on **Copy from CD**.

Naming tracks

Windows Media Player will automatically look up your CD against a database on the Internet and fill in the track title, artist, album title, length of play and even the songwriters for you.

Watch out
Respect copyright: it is illegal to copy and distribute the music on most CDs. You can make a single copy for your own use, but do not share files you copy with others.

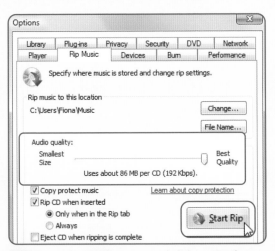

2 Go to the **Tools** menu and click on **Options**. Click on the **Rip Music** tab, set the slider to **Best Quality** (suitable for a CD) and click on **OK**. Select the tracks to copy by clicking in the boxes to their left, then click on **Start Rip**. The track will be copied to your hard drive. Eject the CD and repeat the "rip" for all the other tracks you want to copy.

3 Click on **Library**, then on **Create Playlist**. Name your playlist then click on **OK**. Click on the tracks in the left-hand column and drag them to your new playlist in the right-hand column. When you've finished, double-click on your new playlist to view it. You can change the order of tracks by clicking and dragging them up or down.

4 Insert a blank CD-R in your CD burner. With your playlist selected in the left pane click on **Burn 'playlist'** (here "Fiona's Party"). A status bar displays the copying progress of each track. When it's finished, your CD will be ejected and is ready to play.

Music formats

The CD that you create using Windows Media Player does not contain exact copies of the tracks on your original CDs. When it copies songs to your hard drive, the program encodes in a special space-saving format (called a .wma file), with a slight loss of quality. When you burn your CD, the files are reconverted, but the lost quality cannot be restored.

Shedding skins

Windows Media Player lets you radically alter its appearance. From the **View** menu select **Skin Chooser**. A list of different "skins" will appear, each replacing the standard buttons and sliders with a themed look. When you find a skin that you like, click on **Apply Skin** and the program will reclothe itself – maybe in rather a surreal way!

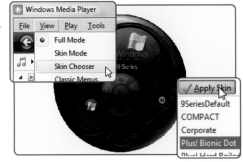

Digitize records and tapes

Learn how to digitize and clean up your old music collection

While they may hold some of your most treasured musical memories, cassette and vinyl recordings are delicate and don't last long. Unless you take great care, records get scratched, tapes stretch or get chewed and, before long, some of your old music can become unplayable.

It is possible, however, to record and even restore the quality of some records and tapes by transferring them to your PC. This not only means you can enjoy them for longer, but you can actually improve their sound quality by removing some of the annoying hisses, pops and crackles associated with tapes and LPs.

This project will help you breathe life into your old music collection. The memories linked to those tapes and LPs consigned to the attic will soon come flooding back!

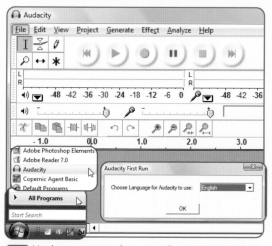

Download Audacity from http://audacity.sourceforge.net/ download. Select the appropriate system from the "Stable" box.

▶ **BEFORE YOU START**

1 Having connected your audio equipment (see page 233), click on the **Start** button, choose **All Programs** and then select **Audacity**. You may be asked to choose a language. Select **English** and click **OK**. The program will launch, displaying a grey control box. You can change the size of the box by clicking and dragging on the sides.

Other programs include Magix Audio at www.magix.com and LP Recorder at www.cfbsoftware.com. Some programs have free trials, while others must be bought.

 **OTHER PROGRAMS**

2 Now set up Audacity to record your tapes or records. Click on **Edit** and select **Preferences** at the bottom of the list. Click on the **Audio I/O** tab and, under "Playback" select **Speakers** in the "Device" drop-down box. Under "Recording," select **Line In** in the "Device" box.

3 You can choose whether you would like to record in stereo. Under the **Audio I/O** tab, select **2 (Stereo)** in the "Channels" drop-down box. If you would like to hear the music as it is being recorded, tick the box next to **Software Playthrough**. Click on **OK**.

4 Before you start recording your tape or record, set up a new Audacity project. Click on the **File** menu and select **Save Project As**. Add a filename and choose where you would like to save your project, and then click on **Save**.

Connecting your audio equipment

Your turntable or tape deck may have "Line-level" outputs (**1**), which carry a signal of sufficient strength to be recorded properly. If so, you can connect a cable directly to your PC's sound card – look for the "Line-in" port (**4**) on the back of your PC. If not, you'll need to connect first to an amplifier or preamp (**2**) using standard phono connectors, then connect a cable from your amplifier (**3**) to your PC (**4**). You'll need a cable with two phono plugs at one end (for the Audio Out connectors on the amp) and a single stereo mini-jack (for the sound card's Line-in port) at the other.

Watch out
*Make sure you use the **Pause** button between songs or sides – if you use the **Stop** button, you will create an additional Audacity track, making it difficult to edit later.*

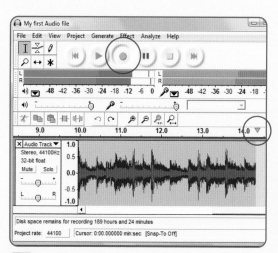

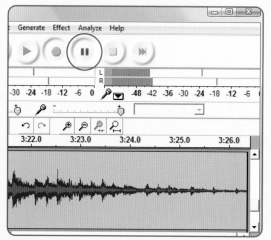

5 Now begin recording your tracks by clicking on the **Record** button (red circle) and starting your player. A red line with an arrow at the top starts to move across the screen, leaving a blue bar indicating the volume of the recording.

6 At the end of each track or, if recording a whole album, at the end of each side, click on the **Pause** button (two blue bars). When you are ready to add another track, or side, click on the **Pause** button again to continue recording.

7 When you have added all the material you want, click on the **Stop** button (yellow square). Go to the **File** menu and select **Save Project** to add your recording to the project you created in Step 4.

Clean up first

Before you start an electronic clean-up, remove any physical dirt you can see on the record or cassette tape as well as the player. Cassette player head cleaners are simple to use and effective. Consider replacing the needle on your turntable. If you're still unhappy, a better-quality connecting cable makes a big difference.

Vinyl records can be washed in warm water with a mild detergent. Try to avoid wetting the label too much. After washing the record, rinse it in warm running water and then dry thoroughly using a soft, lint-free cloth.

Make a test recording

Audacity's automatic settings will often do the job for you, but it's a good idea to make some test recordings first and get used to the functions available. After a preliminary listen, you may find that you need to adjust the input settings or tweak the treble and bass controls on your amplifier.

Watch out
If you have recorded in stereo, make sure that you click and drag over both bars or you will only cut one element of your recording.

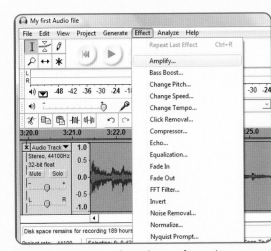

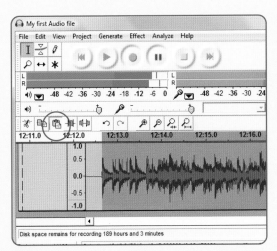

8 Depending on the volume of your input, you may find it helpful to amplify the project – this will make it easier to see where there are silent areas on your recording. Select all by holding down the **Ctrl** key and pressing **A**. Then go to the **Effect** menu and click on **Amplify**. In the dialogue box that appears, click on **OK**.

9 You may find that you have long gaps in your recording. To cut them out, first click on the **Selection Tool** on the toolbar. You can now click and hold down your left-mouse button and drag across the "silent" area to select it. Now click on the **Cut** button.

10 Go through your whole recording, repeating the process in Step 7 until all long silences have been removed. You can also reorder your recording if you want to by selecting the whole track and clicking on the **Cut** button. Select a new location on the Audacity timeline and then click on **Paste**.

Don't break the law

Always stay on the right side of the law by respecting the copyright of others. Making a single copy of a recording that you have paid for, for personal use only, is generally tolerated by record companies, although it's a bit of a grey area. Legislation is evolving at the moment, so it's best to check before you act.

Watch out
In Click Removal, do not make your Threshold and Spike width selections too sensitive as this could harm your recording as a whole.

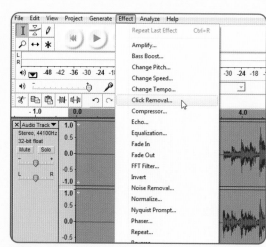

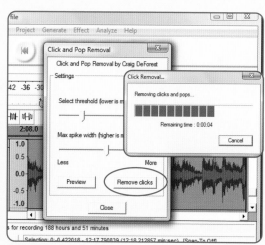

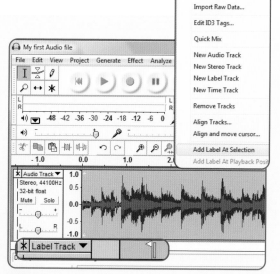

11 Audacity can also remove some of the background noise associated with tapes and records. Select your whole track by holding down the **Ctrl** key and pressing **A**. Go to the **Effect** menu and select **Click Removal**.

12 The "Threshold" slider will adjust the sensitivity of the noise detection, while the "Spike width" slider will change the length of the noise required before modifications are applied. Alter the settings, or leave them at the preset values, and then click on the **Remove clicks** button.

13 Your recording is currently one long track, so you may like to split it into individual songs. Click on the recording line at the point where the your first song starts. Go to the **Project** menu and select **Add Label At Selection**. A red flag appears with a small box ready for you to input text.

Noise removal

The "Remove Clicks" function in Audacity is particularly useful if you are recording from old LPs. A further function is "Noise Removal," although it will always remove some of the music with the noise. Make a selection by clicking and dragging – or select all by holding down the **Ctrl** key and pressing **A** – and then go to the **Effect** menu. Click on **Noise Removal**. In the dialogue box, click on **Remove Noise**. It is worth having a few trial runs to get used to how this function works, but it can really help to clean up older cassettes and LPs.

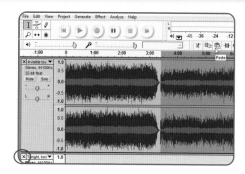

Joining tracks together

If you have stopped and restarted your recording, rather than using the Pause button, you will have created two Audacity tracks and won't be able to use the labelling function. To join the two Audacity tracks together, select the second track by clicking in its **Track Panel** (by the Mute and Solo buttons). Click on the **Cut** button. Now click in the white space at the end of the first track and click on the **Paste** button. Your first track now holds your whole recording. Delete the second track by clicking on the **[X]** at the top left of its Track Panel.

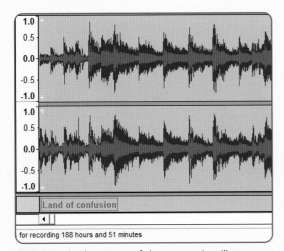

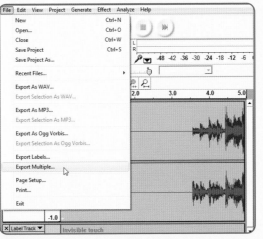

14 Type in the name of the song – it will appear underneath your first track. Now click at the start of your second track, and add a new label. Go through the entire recording, adding labels and naming the tracks as you go. If the label name doesn't appear, click on the box to select it and then try again.

15 When you have finished editing and naming your tracks, you need to export the recording as an audio file that you can either play on your computer or burn to a CD. To export all of your named tracks in one shot, click on the **File** menu and select **Export Multiple**.

16 In the Export Multiple dialogue box, select **WAV** from the "Export format" drop-down box. Click on **Choose** to select a location to save your files – it is probably best to select your Music folder. Click on **Export**. The Export Multiple confirmation box will tell you how many files have been exported. Click on **OK**.

Choosing file types

The most common formats for exporting music files are .wav, .aiff and .mp3. The best-quality files are .wav and .aiff but they will take up far more disk space than .mp3 – the file type used by small portable music players, such as iPods. If you intend to burn your recording to a CD, you should choose .wav when you export in Audacity. If you would like to use the files on your iPod, choose .mp3. As the project has been saved you can, of course, always export the file twice and get the most from both types of file.

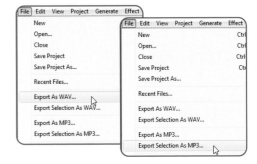

Shortcut
Media Player will automatically search the Internet for an album that matches yours – if it finds one, it will add the track information and even the original album cover.

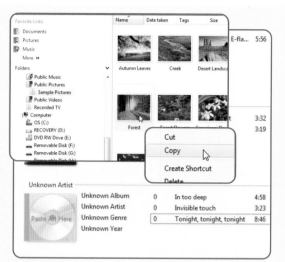

17 To test the success of your digital recording, go to the **Start** button, click on **All Programs** and select **Windows Media Player**. Click on the **Library** tab and select **Add to Library**. In the Add to Library dialogue box that appears, make sure that "My personal folders" is selected and click on **OK**.

18 Media Player now runs a check of your folders and will detect the exported files from Audacity. Click on **OK** in the dialogue box that appears and then scroll down the list of albums in the Library. Your new files should be at the bottom. Double-click on one to hear it play.

19 Media Player will have created an "album" of your exported tracks that you can customize. First, right-click on any of the track information and edit it if you need to. Now add an album cover of your choice – find an image you like (from your "Pictures" folder, for example) and then right-click on it. Select **Copy** from the pop-up menu.

Let Media Player entertain you

You can use your PC as more than a music player as Media Player can add moving art to your music. Click on the **Now Playing** tab and the screen will fill with imagery that moves in time to the music. To change the selection click on **Now Playing** again and hover over **Visualizations**. Click on one of the options next to **Alchemy**, **Bars and Waves** or **Battery** to change the appearance. Keep choosing until you find one you like, then sit back and relax!

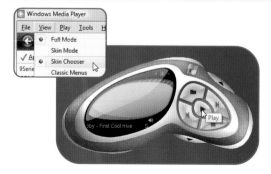

Windows Media skins

Give your Media Player a new look by applying a skin. You can select a skin from the standard set or download new ones from the Internet. To apply a skin, click **View** menu, then on **Skin Chooser**. In the skins list, click the skin you want and a preview of the skin appears. Click on **Apply Skin**. Now you can explore how the skin works and what it can do.

Bright idea
If you have recorded an old album that Media Player hasn't found, search the Internet for the original album cover and paste it onto the file you have created on your PC.

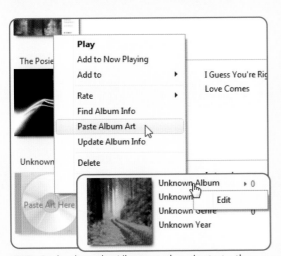

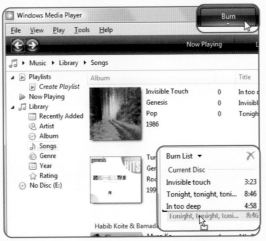

20 Go back to the Library and navigate to the new album. Right-click on it and select **Paste Album Art** from the menu. The new image will appear as your album cover. Right-click on the album name – currently "Unknown" – and select **Edit**. Add your own album name.

21 You can now assemble your recorded tracks in order to burn a CD. Click on **Burn** and a new column appears to the right of the Library. Click on each of your tracks in turn and drag them into the Burn List. If you would like to reorder the list, just click on the track and drag it to the new location before releasing the mouse key.

22 Insert a blank CD into your CD drive. Double-check your Burn list and ensure you have all the tracks you want and in the correct order. Click on the **Start Burn** button. The progress will be shown in the Status column and a "Burn complete" message will display when it has finished. Now you can enjoy your old music in its new format.

Create an album cover

Using the templates available from Microsoft Word, you can create a unique album cover for your new CD. Connect to the Internet and then launch Microsoft Word by going to the **Start** menu, clicking on **All Programs** and then on **Microsoft Office Word 2007**. Click on **Templates** and type **CD cover** in the Search bar. Scroll through the list and click on a template to choose it. Click on the **Download** button to save it to your desktop where you can open and then edit it.

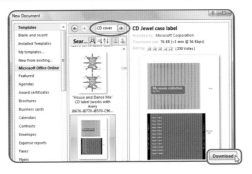

Create your own music

Start composing music in minutes with free software

Even if you don't have a musical bone in your body, you can use your home PC and a free music-creation program to compose a song that sounds as good as much of the music you hear on the radio.

In this project, we use a free demo version of Sony's ACID XPress music program. It helps its users – including those with no musical training – to compose music using a system of short, repeated recordings (known as "loops") of instruments or vocals. You simply create a musical arrangement by positioning loops on a grid; your PC can then play these loops in the sequence you chose. Once you have started, ACID XPress also makes it easy to revise your composition by changing the order of the loops, as well as modifying the tempo. Before long, you'll be creating your own CDs featuring your own musical masterpieces!

> Download some sample projects from the ACID XPress website, so you can start creating music as soon as you have opened the program.

BEFORE YOU START

1 Go to www.sonycreativesoftware.com/download/freestuff.asp, and click on **ACID XPress**. In the next window, click on **Download** and then on **Save**. Choose to save the file on your Desktop, and click on **Save**. Once the file has downloaded, double-click on **acidxpress50a**, then follow the Installation Wizard instructions.

> The arrangement in this project was composed using Sony's ACID XPress. Whichever software you use, the basic principles of composition are the same. Consult your manual for specific guidance.

OTHER PROGRAMS

Register your Acid XPress software

When you first open ACID XPress, you will be asked to register. Make sure your PC is connected to the Internet, select **Register online** and click on **Next**. Fill in your details and then click on **Finish**. A box will appear confirming your registration is being processed. Finally, click on **OK** and the program will launch.

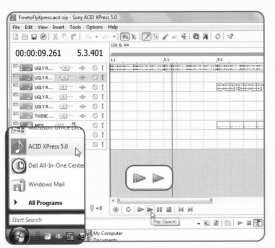

2 Go to the **Start** menu, click on **All Programs**, then **Sony** and then **ACID XPress 5.0**. Make sure your PC's speakers are turned on and click on the CD-style control that looks like a single arrow pointing to the right (these controls are just below the music track box). ACID XPress' preloaded song will start to play.

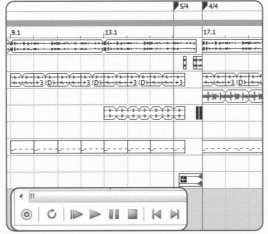

3 Experiment with the controls – the first button on the left is **Record**. The next buttons are **Loop** (lets you play part of your song over again), **Play from the start**, **Play** (from current position), **Pause** and **Stop**. The last two buttons move you to the start or finish of your song.

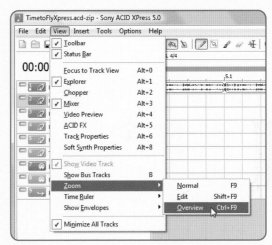

4 It can help to view the whole song. To do this, move the cursor to the top of the main window so it turns into a hand. Hold down the left mouse button and drag the contents of the main window to the left to see the rest of the song. Alternately, go to the **View** menu, choose **Zoom** and then **Overview** to see the whole song.

More instant music software

The eJay family of music programs (see example right) works in a similar way to ACID XPress, with variations available for many different types of music. Visit www.ejay.com for free demos and downloads.

If you enjoy unusual instrumental music, try Fruity Loops (www.fruityloops.com), which offers a free demonstration download. Or look at Music Maker music-composition software from Magix, (www.magix.com). The results from all these programs are of CD quality.

Keyword
Loops *These are small audio clips designed*
to create a repeating beat or pattern. Loops
are usually one to four measures long and are stored
in RAM for playback.

 Watch out
When experimenting with downloaded
samples, don't click on any files with a
green icon as they don't have any sound.

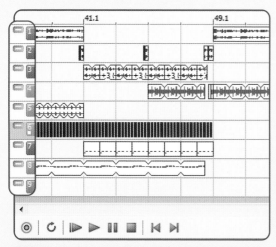

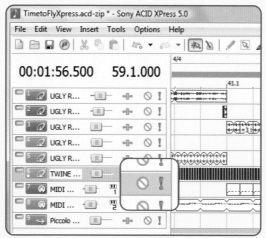

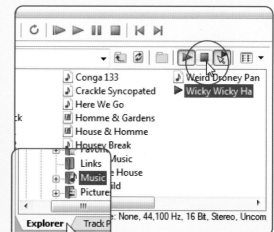

5 You create songs in ACID XPress by stringing
together "samples" – short clips of music
recorded in loops. These are arranged along tracks
that run horizontally across the screen. For example,
this song uses nine tracks. The blocks with squiggly
lines inside them in the middle of the screen are
the actual sampled sounds.

6 Now play the song again and try the Mute
and Solo functions. Go to the nine track
headings on the left – each one has two symbols.
Click on the circle with a line through it to "mute"
the track. Click on the exclamation mark to "solo"
the track – so that you can't hear anything else.
Experiment with these buttons on different tracks.

7 To create a new song, go to the **File** menu
and choose **New**. Click on **No** when asked if
you want to save changes. Give your song a title
and click on **OK**. Use the Explorer window to find
sample projects downloaded from the ACID
XPress website. Try the sounds by clicking on
them, and stop them with the **Stop** button.

Loops for free

Collections of loops are available on CD, but there are also
lots of sites on the Internet where you can download them for
nothing. Go to www.freeloops.com or www.looperman.com
for a good selection of modern dance-related sounds.
Elsewhere, the UK site www.samplenet.co.uk has interesting
orchestral samples, and www.platinumloops.com includes
mandolins, sitars and clarinets. Also, ACID's publisher, Sony,
makes a new pack of free samples available for download at
www.acidplanet.com/tools/8packs every week.

Bright idea
To produce a surprising effect, try reversing a sample. Also change the key of your song for the last chorus to add a "lift" at the end.

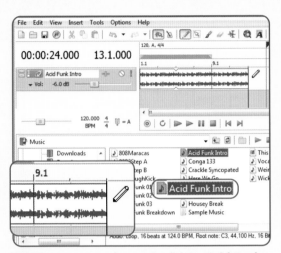

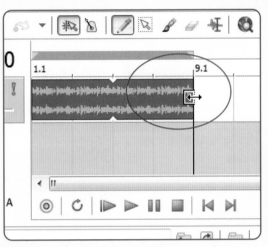

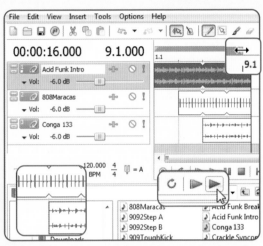

8 To create your first track, click on **Acid Funk Intro** in the Explorer window and, still holding down the button, drag it up into the main window. Let go of the mouse button. Now move the cursor into the main window and, holding down the left mouse button, drag along to your right so it looks like the screen above.

9 The scale above the track measures the number of bars in the composition – here "1.1" indicates the start of the first bar; "9.1" indicates the start of the 9th bar. Now make your song 8 bars long by clicking on the end so the cursor turns into a double arrow and dragging it back to the left until you reach the "9.1" mark.

10 Add two more tracks to the song by dragging them from the Explorer window onto the screen. To loop the whole song so it keeps playing over and over, click on the yellow corner at the right-hand end of the loop region bar above the main window and drag it to line up with the end of the song. Click on **Loop** and then on **Play**.

Getting the right results

Start by giving your song a time limit of, say, 3 minutes. If it's a song with lyrics, stick to the classic format of verse, chorus, verse, chorus, bridge, verse, chorus and chorus end. Modern music tends to be repetitive, so don't use more than ten samples in your first few songs. Instead, concentrate on being creative with what you have. To add lyrics, burn a copy of the background music onto a CD to play in the car and try singing over the top of it, so you experiment first. Your lyrics may be wonderfully poignant, but if they're too personal, nobody else will appreciate them, so always try to make what you write accessible to others. If you don't want to write another love song and are stuck for inspiration, look for ideas in a newspaper or magazine.

Learning to read music

Let your computer teach you the principles of musical notation

You don't have to be able to read music to compose it on your computer, nor is it necessary to know the names of individual notes to play them or compose a tune. However, as you become more confident and proficient at composition you may want to learn to read music. If so, a range of specialized software is available to help.

This project uses a program called Music Ace. Aimed at the complete novice, it teaches you notation through easy-to-follow lessons and related games. You will also be given the opportunity to test your knowledge by composing simple tunes. Much of the other educational music software available will follow these basic principles.

Check that your computer meets the minimum system requirements of the program before you install the software onto your hard disk.

BEFORE YOU START

1 Go to the **Start** menu, select **All Programs** then click on your music software. The opening screen of "Music Ace" contains musical notes playing a tune. Adjust the volume using the slide bar on the left of the screen. To begin, click on the **Start** button.

A wide range of music education programs – for all levels – can be sampled and downloaded from the Internet. A good starting place is the Hitsquad Musician Network website at www.hitsquad.com/smm.

OTHER PROGRAMS

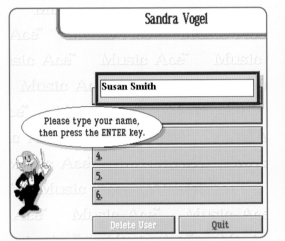

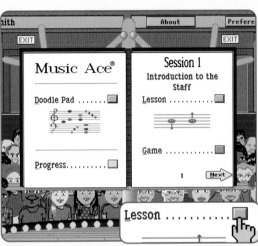

2 A music maestro will guide you through each stage of the program. Click in the first box, type your name then press the **Enter** key. Music Ace can accommodate several users, and it uses the names to keep track of each user's progress.

3 You are now presented with the Main Screen through which you choose whether to use the Doodle Pad (a music creation tool), follow a lesson or play a music game related to the lesson. To start a lesson click on the **Lesson** button.

4 Lesson 1 deals with basic music notation. An animated tutorial teaches you about the positioning of notes. After the tutorial you will be asked questions – click on the appropriate button to respond. Continue the exercises to the end of the lesson.

Set your preferences

The screen in which you elect to start a lesson or play a game also contains a Preferences button. Click on this to customize the way Music Ace works.

One set of choices, the Maestro Options, allows you to set the way in which onscreen help is delivered by the cartoon character, Maestro Max. If you wish, turn his voice or speech balloons off.

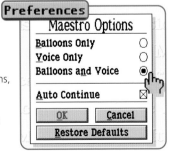

Use the Control Bar

Every lesson has a Control Bar running across the top of the screen. This provides access to basic options and settings.

To end the current lesson and return to the Main Screen click on the **Menu** button. The button to its right shows the name of the current lesson. To change the volume

click on the **Vol** button. To move forwards or backwards in each lesson click on the **Skip** buttons. Click on the **Pause** button to stop the lesson at the current point (the button then changes to **Resume**). To go straight to the game that relates to the lesson, click on the **Game** button.

| Menu | 1. Introduction to the Staff | Vol | ◀◀ Skip | Pause ‖ | Skip ▶▶ | Game |

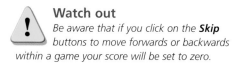

Watch out
*Be aware that if you click on the **Skip** buttons to move forwards or backwards within a game your score will be set to zero.*

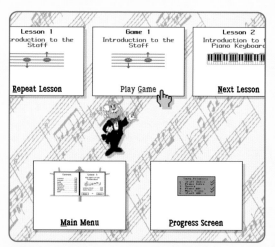

5 When a lesson ends you will be offered several options: to repeat the lesson, go to the main menu, check your progress, try the next lesson, or play the related game. To play the game, click on the **Play Game** button.

6 The game will encourage you to practise what you have learned in the lesson. To begin, click on the **Start** button and follow the onscreen instructions. As you complete sections of the game your score will be displayed in the top right-hand corner of the screen.

7 When the game has finished you can choose the next lesson, another game, repeat the previous lesson or game, or view your progress. Alternatively, go to the Doodle Pad to try out what you have learned so far. Click on the **Main Menu**, then on the **Doodle Pad** button.

Assessing your progress
The lessons in Music Ace are broken down into sections. An indicator in the top right-hand corner of the screen shows you how far you have progressed through your current lesson. Completed sections are shown in green; the section you are currently working on is in red.

Choosing lessons
You may not want to complete lessons or games in sequence – you may want to select specific ones to work on particular areas. You can do this from the Main Menu. Click on the **Next** arrow on the lesson page to leaf through the range of lessons available. When you find the one you want, click on the **Lesson** or **Game** button to access it.

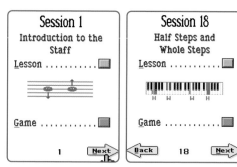

Keyword

Staff *This describes the group of five lines on which notes are placed. Depending on where they are placed, the pitch of the note will change.*

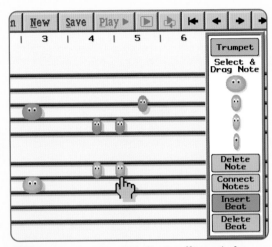

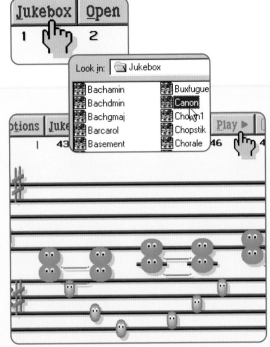

8 To move a note onto the "staff" ready for playing, select and drag it from the box on the right of the screen. Move notes on the staff by dragging them. Each note plays as you move it. To hear your tune, click on the **Play** button on the Control Bar.

9 Music Ace has a library of songs for you to listen to and edit. To open one in the Doodle Pad click on the Control Bar's **Jukebox** button, then double-click on a song. Click on **Play** to hear it. Edit it by moving its notes on the staff and adding new notes.

10 To end your session, click on the **Menu** button on the Control Bar, then on one of the **Exit** buttons in the Main Menu. The next time you run Music Ace, click on your name from the user list – Music Ace will remind you of your progress.

Using the Doodle Pad

To change the instrument you have chosen to compose with, click on the instrument name at the top of the box on the right of the screen. Each time you click, a different instrument name will appear – Oboe, Marimba, Trumpet, Jazz Guitar, Clarinet and Grand Piano. Stop on the instrument you want and all notes you create will then sound like that instrument, and will appear in a different colour.

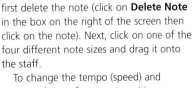

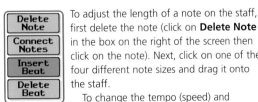

To adjust the length of a note on the staff, first delete the note (click on **Delete Note** in the box on the right of the screen then click on the note). Next, click on one of the four different note sizes and drag it onto the staff.

To change the tempo (speed) and volume of your composition, drag the markers along the slide bar in the bottom left-hand corner of the screen.

Profit from your

Make the most of your money by using your

Investment circle

Create a folder called "Investment circle." Add subfolders for each mini-project.

- Investment circle
  - Investors
  - Research
  - Accounts
  - Communications
  - Investments
  - Contacts

Investment circles have taken off around the globe, and the most successful have been known to outperform those of professional fund managers. These circles contain up to 15 people who enjoy making the most of their finances by selecting, purchasing and monitoring their own stocks and shares. They also save money by avoiding management charges.

All this has become possible in recent years because of the computerization of the world's stock exchanges. People outside the world's financial capitals can act as their own fund managers, using their computers to access and act upon a wealth of up-to-date financial information: stock prices are updated on the Internet as soon as they change.

So if you are thinking of playing the markets, make the Internet your first stop. There are many sites where you can gather data on companies your group is thinking of investing in. It's easy to find out how your stock has performed, current earnings-to-share ratios, liabilities, assets and profit forecasts. In fact, you can find virtually everything you need to make an informed assessment.

There are many financial news sites listing online share price data,

investment circle

PC as a window on the financial markets

enabling you to track shares you may be interested in or have already purchased. You can then paste downloaded data into your portfolio spreadsheet – and even use it to calculate projections for your share dividends.

Once you have decided on your investments, you have to choose an online broker and open an account. You can then trade shares on the world markets without getting up from your computer.

If you set up an online bank account for your group you can also access your current financial status in a matter of seconds.

With your portfolio in place you can use your PC to administer your investment circle. You could set up

an investors" database to hold relevant information. For example, some members may prefer not to invest in certain industries or countries on ethical grounds.

Create more spreadsheets to monitor members' individual holdings and produce a newsletter to keep everyone informed.

If your group wants to diversify into other areas such as antiques trading, the Internet holds a great deal of useful data. Sites that carry price guides, tips on authenticity, where to buy and what to look for, are easily accessible and will help you make informed choices. You could also participate in online bidding at some of the world's leading auction houses.

Prepare to invest

- Recruit members and set aims, level of investment and club rules
- Appoint club officers and outline their responsibilities
- Research and select an online broker
- Open a club bank account and set the signatories
- Set up online banking facilities
- Produce copies of initial research material for members

Ideas and inspirations

Adapt the following projects and exercises and then apply them to setting up your own investment circle. You may find that you don't need all of them to get things up and running, so include only the documents you need for your own requirements.

94 Searching the Internet
Use search engines to locate online brokers, share price and stock performance information.

268 Build a shares portfolio
Set up a spreadsheet for your investment circle to keep track of your portfolio's performance.

272 Keep your accounts
Use separate worksheets in a spreadsheet to keep track of individual and group holdings.

162 Create a newsletter
Produce performance updates for your group. If other members are online, e-mail it to them.

148 Write a formal letter
Keep it professional, if you need to send a formal letter to, say, request a prospectus.

Also worth considering...

If you've used most of the above to form your investment circle, you may want to refine it further.

318 Membership database
Create a record of members' details and notes on any investment preferences.

Close-up

*You may need to insert new rows of expenses. Click on the row below where you'd like the new row to appear and click on **Insert** in the "Cells" group.*

You can keep accounts for various aspects of the same project within one Excel document. Simply create a separate worksheet for each one (see below left).

ADD MORE WORKSHEETS

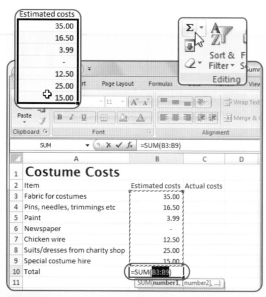

	A	B	C	D
1	**Costume Costs**			
2	Item	Estimated costs	Actual costs	
3	Fabric for costumes	35.00		
4	Pins, needles, trimmings etc	16.50		
5	Paint	3.99		
6	Newspaper	-		
7	Chicken wire	12.50		
8	Suits/dresses from charity shop	25.00		
9	Special costume hire	15.00		
10	Total	=SUM(B3:B9)		
11		SUM(number1, [number2], ...)		

	A	B	C	D
1	**Costume Costs**			
2	Item	Estimated costs	Actual costs	
3	Fabric for costumes	35.00	43.00	
4	Pins, needles, trimmings etc	16.50	12.85	
5	Paint	3.99		
6	Newspaper	-		
7	Chicken wire	12.50		
8	Suits/dresses from charity shop	25.00		
9	Special costume hire	15.00		
10	**Total**	**107.99**	**55.85**	

	A	B	C	D	E
1	**Ticket sales (estimated)**				
2	No.	Item	Ticket price	Estimated revenue	
3	500	Standard seats	3.00		
4	100	Privilege seats	4.00		
5	200	Children's seats	1.50		
6			Total		
7					
8					
9	**Ticket sales (actual)**				
10	No.	Item	Ticket price	Actual revenue	
11	389	Standard seats	3.00		
12	79	Privilege seats	4.00		
13	184	Children's seats	1.50		
14			Total		

5 Enter the individual estimates then add up your figures in the Estimated costs column. Click in the Total cell for column B (here, **B10**), then click on the **AutoSum** button in the "Editing" group. Press **Return** and the total will appear.

6 To copy the formula for Actual costs, click in the Total cell for Estimated costs (here, **B10**) then place the cursor in its lower right-hand corner. When the cursor turns into a cross, click and drag across to the Actual costs column. The sum will adjust as you enter each cost.

7 To create a second worksheet for, say, income from tickets, click on the **Sheet2** tab at the bottom of the screen. The spreadsheet above has sections for estimated and actual revenue from sales of different seats. Name the two worksheets Costumes and Ticket Sales (see below left).

Naming and adding worksheets

For easier navigation between worksheets, rename them. To rename Sheet1 double-click on the **Sheet1** tab at the bottom of the screen and type in a title (here, Costumes), then press the **Return** key.

To add more worksheets, click on the **Insert Worksheet** button to the right of the Sheet

names. To reorder the sequence of worksheets, click on the tab of the one you want to move and drag it to its new position.

Adding grids

To enclose your worksheet details in a grid, select the relevant cells, right-click and select **Format Cells**. In the dialogue box click on the **Border** tab. First, select a Line style and colour, then, in the Presets section, click on the **Outline** and **Inside** buttons, then click on **OK**.

To add a background colour, select the cells, right-click and select **Format Cells**. Click on the **Patterns** tab. In the "Cell shading" section click on your choice of colour, then click on **OK**.

Watch out
If you name your worksheets you must use the new names, rather than Sheet1, 2, etc., when referring to them in cell references. So, formulas should read "'Costumes'!B10" rather than "'Sheet1'!B10."

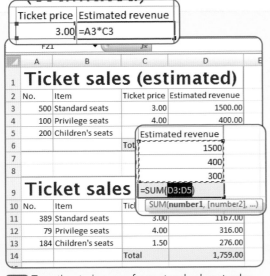

	Ticket price	Estimated revenue
	3.00	=A3*C3

Ticket sales (estimated)

	A	B	C	D
1				
2	No.	Item	Ticket price	Estimated revenue
3	500	Standard seats	3.00	1500.00
4	100	Privilege seats	4.00	400.00
5	200	Children's seats		

Estimated revenue

Tot	
	1500
	400
	300
	=SUM(D3:D5)
	SUM(**number1**, [number2], ...)

Ticket sales

	A	B	C
9			
10	No.	Item	Tic
11	389	Standard seats	3.00	1167.00
12	79	Privilege seats	4.00	316.00
13	184	Children's seats	1.50	276.00
14			Total	1,759.00

8 To estimate income from standard seat sales, click in the relevant cell (here, **D3**), type "=" then a formula for the total seats multiplied by the price (A3*C3). Repeat for other seats. Click in the Total cell (**D6**), go to the "Editing" group, click the **AutoSum** button and press **Return**. Repeat for actual sales.

	A	B	C
1	**Budget Summary**		
2	Item	Estimated costs	Actual costs
3	Costumes	='Costumes'!B10	
4	Refreshments		
5	Props	107.99	
6	Printing/publicity		
7	Total		
8			
9			
10	Item	Estimated revenue	Actual revenue
11	Refreshments		
12	Tickets		
13	Total		
14			
15	Balance		

9 Open a worksheet to add up costs and revenue of the individual parts of the project. Create columns as shown. In the costs and revenue columns enter the sheet and cell references of your totals for other worksheets. For example: "='Costumes'!B10".

	A	B	C
1	**Budget Summary**		
2	Item	Estimated costs	Actual costs
3	Costumes	107.99	
4	Refreshments	144.24	
5	Props	98.00	
6	Printing/publicity	50.00	
7	Total	400.23	
8			
9			
10	Item	Estimated revenue	Actual revenue
11	Refreshments	330.00	
12	Tickets	2,200.00	
13	Total	2,530.00	
14			
15	Balance	2,129.77	

10 Now calculate total costs and revenue. Click in the Total cell for Estimated costs (here, **B7**) click on the **AutoSum** button and press **Return**. Copy the formula into the Actual costs cell (see Step 6). Repeat for revenue. If you wish to work out balances, see below left.

Calculating balances

To calculate Estimated and Actual balances, click in the Estimated Balance cell (here, **B15**), type "=", then a formula that subtracts the total estimated costs from the total estimated revenue (B13-B7). Press **Return**. Copy and paste the formula into the Actual Balance cell (see Step 6).

7	Total	400..
8		
9		
10	Item	Estimated revenu
11	Refreshments	330.(
12	Tickets	2,200.(
13	Total	2,129.77	2,530.(
14		
15	Balance	=B13-B7

Printing out worksheets

To print a worksheet, first go to the **Microsoft Office** button and select **Print** then click on **Print Preview** to see how it looks. To make adjustments press the **Esc** key and edit accordingly. When you're happy with how it looks, click on **Print**, specify the pages you require then click on **OK**.

Form a Neighbourhood

Your PC can make it easier for friends and neighbours

Project planner

Create a folder called "Neighbourhood Watch." Add subfolders for mini-projects.

- 📁 Neighbourhood Watch
  - 📁 Membership
  - 📁 Contacts
  - 📁 Crime database
  - 📁 Holiday diary
  - 📁 Communications
  - 📁 Meetings & events

Any community-based project will benefit from some sound organization, effective communication and a high local profile. Your PC can help make each of these objectives achievable.

Neighbourhood Watch groups rely on volunteer members keeping an eye on each other's properties, particularly during working hours and holiday periods. Knowing who is available to patrol the area, and which houses are unoccupied, will make your Neighbourhood Watch project more efficient.

The ideal starting point is to create a tailored membership form using a database program. Distribute this to prospective members then, when you receive the completed forms, enter the details into a members' database.

Your database will then help in identifying who is at home and who is out, and at what times. By including work and holiday schedules, and using the program's "sort" facility, you can compile a day-to-day list of unoccupied properties – the ones most at risk. Then, using the information

Watch group
to guard against local crime

on members' availability, you can produce a list of neighbours who can keep an eye out for suspicious behaviour.

Once you have set up your group, your computer can help you to log incidents of crime. Use your database's Form Design feature to create an incident report form on which members can record the date, time, place and type of any incident.

If you set up a separate crime database you will soon be able to build up a profile of the types of crime that occur in your area, and when crime is most likely to take place. You can then review your activities and patrols accordingly.

To raise the profile of your group, use your PC's graphics capabilities to design a poster for members to display in their windows. You could also design a letterhead for correspondence, and produce a newsletter to keep members informed of any special events and new members, as well as raise awareness of crime trends and home security.

And if you're connected to the Internet, you can take a look at the wide range of Neighbourhood Watch information on the World Wide Web. You'll find messaging forums, details on training, useful contact numbers, home insurance information and lists of the type of items that most appeal to thieves. You can even join a weekly e-mailing list, giving tips on, among other things, home security.

Starting your watch

- Search the Internet for information on setting up a Neighbourhood Watch group
- Canvas interest and arrange first meeting
- Appoint a group chairperson and other officials
- Invite the local police to make a presentation
- Organize press coverage of launch and use it to recruit new members
- Arrange affiliation to a national/regional organization
- Compile a patrol schedule and holiday agenda, and set up a crime database

Ideas and inspirations

Below are project ideas to help you set up an effective Neighbourhood Watch group that the local community – and criminals – will take seriously. The projects can be adapted to your own requirements.

166 Membership database
Record members' details, including contact phone numbers and car license plate numbers.

162 Create a newsletter
Design an eye-catching publication to keep your neighbours informed of developments.

224 Design a poster
Attract attention to a forthcoming meeting, or publicize your group.

180 Create an agenda
Use this handy feature to keep track of members' travel plans, absences and availability.

144 Design a letterhead
Give your group's correspondence an official and businesslike appearance.

Also worth considering...

No matter how successful your group is, you may benefit from the experience of others.

94 Search the Internet
Find out more about established Neighbourhood Watch groups, and correspond by e-mail.

Record a family history

Explore **your** past **with a** database **of** relatives and ancestors

ompiling a family history can be hugely rewarding. It is amazing how soon knowledge about a family's past is lost if nobody writes it down, but the detail you can quickly and easily find out about your ancestors will fascinate every member of your family, young and old.

The database program in Microsoft Works is ideal for making systematic records of your family's history. Dates of birth, occupations, marriages and so on can all be noted – or left blank until your research bears fruit. You can also make space to record interesting facts about your forebears: the homes in which they lived, medals they won, famous people they met, the traces they left behind. Use your PC to explore your roots – your grandchildren will thank you for it one day.

> *You'll find the quickest way is to input all your information in one shot. Don't worry if you need to do more research though, as it's easy to add information at any time.*

▶ BEFORE YOU START

1 Go to the **Start** menu, select **All Programs** and click on **Microsoft Works**. Click on **Works Database** from the Quick Launch menu on the right. In the Microsoft Works Database window select **Blank Database** then click on **OK** to open a new blank database document.

> *You can also create a family database in Microsoft Excel. This will let you input and view your data in table form, ready for sorting and styling according to your needs.*

▶ OTHER PROGRAMS

Bright idea
Create a reference field, in which each record has its own reference number, and give it a "serialized" format. This way, record numbers will update automatically whenever a new record is added.

*To select more than one field at a time, press the **Ctrl** key and, keeping it pressed down, click on all the boxes you want to alter.*

Create Database

Add fields to create your database. To add a field, type a name and then select a format for the field.

Field name: Record No

Format
- ○ General
- ○ Number
- ○ Date
- ○ Time
- ○ Text
- ○ Fraction
- ● Serialized

Appearance
Next value: 00001
Increment: 1

Add
Exit

☐ Automatically enter a default value

Format

Alignment · Font · Border

Font: Times New Roman
Size: 40
Color: Dark Red

- Tr Tandelle
- Tr Teen
- Tr Teen Light
- ▣ Tekton Pro
- Tr Tempus Sans ITC
- Tr Times New Roman

20
24
30
32
36
40

Style
- ☑ Bold
- ☑ Italic
- ☐ Underline
- ☐ Strikethrough

Sample:
Family History

2 Now create fields, or categories, for your database. Type the name of your first field in the "Field name" box and select a format for it. When you have named and formatted a field, click on **Add**. When you have entered all your database fields, click on the **Done** button.

3 Your database appears in List form. Now name and save it. Then customize the look of it by clicking on the **Form Design** toolbar button. To move a text box, click on it and drag it. (To resize it, see below.) Rearrange your text boxes to leave space at the top of the page for a heading.

4 Click at the top of the page and type in your heading. To style it, highlight it, then go to the **Format** menu and click on **Font and Style**. Select a font, size, colour and style, then click **OK**. Style your field names using the same method.

Fields and formats
Consider using the following fields and formats. For an added sense of history, include a field for biographical facts.

Field	Format	Field	Format
Record No.	Serialized	Married to	Text
Surname	Text	Marriage date	Date
First names	Text	Children	Text
Date of birth	Date	Occupation	Text
Place of birth	Text	Date of death	Date
Mother	Text	Burial place	Text
Father	Text	Notes	Text

Resizing text boxes
To resize a text box, click on it. Place the mouse pointer over the side, bottom or bottom right-hand corner. When the pointer changes to a double-headed arrow, click the mouse and, keeping the button pressed down, drag it across the screen.

Different views
There are four ways to view your database:

List View is best for quick reference. It lets you view lots of entries at the same time.

Form View displays one entry at a time and is clearer for entering data.

Form Design lets you add and delete fields and alter their layout.

Report View allows you to compile selective reports from your database.

To move to the next field or record, press the **Tab** key. To move back, press the **Shift** and **Tab** keys.

Keyword

Report A report extracts designated information from a database. For example, from your family database you could make a report on relatives who emigrated, or who fought in wars.

Record No: 00001

Family History

Surname: Potts   First names: James Brian

Date of birth: 11/10/1957   Place of birth: Putney, London

Mother: Jane Potts (nee West)   Father: Jeffrey Potts

Married to: Gillian West   Marriage date: 08/02/1982

Children: Occupation:

Form View

List View — Microsoft Works Database

File Edit View Record Format Tools Help

Arial 10

"Grimley Moore Cemetery Leeds

✔		Date of death	Burial place	Not
	19	07/03/1954	Eversham Park Cresce	Arrested murde
	20	10/12/1971	Eversham Park Crescent	
	21	09/06/1962	Grimley Moore Cemete	Drove "The Flyi
	22	23/09/1962	Grimley Moore Cemete	Worked as don
	23	10/02/1943	Banbury Cemetery	Served under K
	24	14/07/1940	Du Pont Cemetery	
	25	23/05/1939	Leeds Municipal Cemetery	
	26	17/01/1957	Highgate Cemetery	
	27			
	28			
	29			
	30			

Family History - Microsoft Works Database

File Edit View Record Format Tools Help

Arial 10

"Bertram

✔		Record No	Surname	First names	Date of b
	11	00011	Bertram	Jim Bruce	29/11/195
	12	00012	Bertram	Sandra Kim	25/02/196
	14	00014	Bertram	Jamie Stuart	13/08/198
	15	00015	Bertram	Hayley Sonia	13/08/198
	27				

Find

Find what: Bertram   **OK**   Cancel

Match
○ Next record   ● All records

---

5 To enter information, first click on the **Form View** toolbar button. Click on the text boxes adjoining the field names and type in the relevant data. To move to the next field or record, press the **Tab** key. To move back to the previous field, press the **Shift** and **Tab** keys at the same time.

6 When you have entered all your data click on the **List View** toolbar button to view your complete database. To see all the data in a particular cell, click on it. Its contents appear in the Entry bar at the top of the form.

7 To find a record or piece of information – such as everyone who has the same surname – go to the **Edit** menu and click on **Find**. Type a keyword in the "Find what" box, select the "All records" option, then click **OK**. Works will display all the records containing the key word.

Sorting your records

You can "sort" or prioritize information within your database. For example, you may want to rank family members from the oldest to the youngest. In the ReportCreator dialogue box, click on the **Sorting** tab. Click on the arrow beside the first "Sort by" box, scroll through and select the field you want – in this case "Date of birth." Select the Ascending option, then click on **Done**.

ReportCreator - Family History

Title | Fields | Sorting | Grouping | Filter | Summary

Sort by
Date of birth   ● Ascending ○ Descending

Then by
(None)   ● Ascending ○ Descending

Next >
Previous
Done
Cancel

You may want to create a report – in other words, print out all or parts of your database – for the family to see or to help you in your research.

CREATING A REPORT

*If the report's contents are too close together, click on **Modify** and adjust the column widths. Place the mouse pointer on the right-hand edge of the column heading, then click and drag to the right.*

To print all records, select the "All records" option.

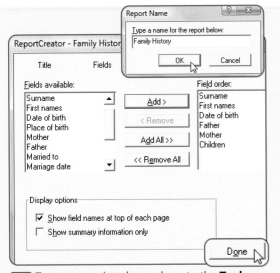

What to Print
- ⦿ All records
- ○ Current record only

OK

Record No: 00001

Family History

Surname: Potts	First names: James Brian
Date of birth: 11/10/1957	Place of birth: Putney, London
Mother: Jane Potts (nee West)	Father: Jeffrey Potts
Married to: Gillian West	Marriage date: 08/02/1982
Children: Robert and Emily	Occupation:

8 To create a printed record, go to the **Tools** menu and click on **ReportCreator**. Type in a name for your report and click on **OK**. Click on the **Fields** tab. Click each field you want to print in turn, clicking on **Add** as you do so. When you have finished click on **Done**.

9 A prompt box appears. Click on the **Preview** button to see how your report looks. If you are satisfied with it, click on **Print**. If you'd like to make some style changes, press the **Esc** key, highlight the text you'd like to change, go to the **Format** menu and click on **Font and Style**.

10 To print out a record in Form View, click on the **Print Preview** toolbar button. If you are happy with how it looks, click on **Cancel**, go to the **File** menu and select **Print**. Under "What to Print" select the "Current record only" option. Finally, click on **OK**.

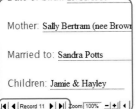

Scrolling
You can scroll through your records quickly by clicking on the arrows either side of the Record counter at the foot of the Form View window.

Create a family tree

Put faces to names with your own photo family tree

Researching your family's history can provide unexpected insights into the lives of your ancestors. You'll not only discover who they were, but where they lived, what they did, and the personal and historical events that shaped their lives. There's a wealth of research resources that you can take advantage of – much of this is online, including government files of family records.

When you've completed your research, this project will help you put together a comprehensive, illustrated family tree. Using Microsoft Excel, it is very straightforward to create a clear guide to your ancestry in which you can include photos if you have them available. Once you've finished, why not print it out and frame it for the rest of your family to learn about their personal history.

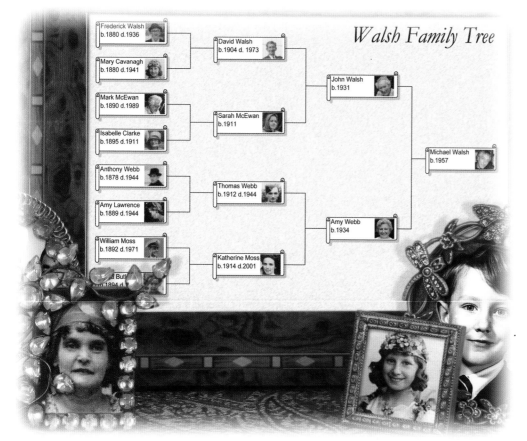

Try to gather together as many of your family photos as you can – don't worry if there are some missing as you can always add them later.

► BEFORE YOU START

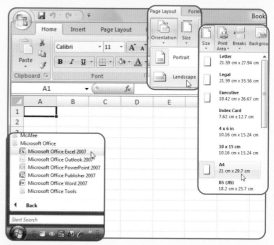

1 Go to the **Start** menu, select **All Programs** and click on **Microsoft Office** and then on **Microsoft Office Excel 2007**. A new blank workbook appears. To change it to landscape format, click on the **Page Layout** tab, then on **Orientation** and select **Landscape**. Next click on **Size** and choose **Letter** from the list.

There are a number of specialized packages for creating a family tree. Search on the Internet and choose one with a free trial download to check that you are happy with it.

► OTHER PROGRAMS

This should cover your whole page – there are dotted lines showing the page area. Make sure your coloured background covers the whole page even if you have to select more cells than stated here.

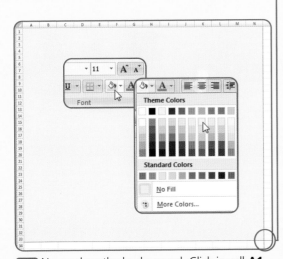

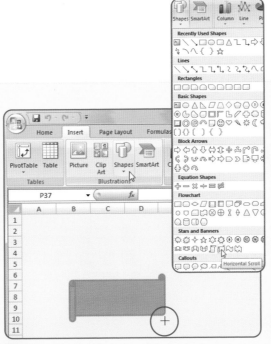

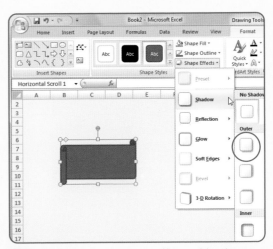

2 Now colour the background. Click in cell **A1** and then, holding down the **Shift** key, click in cell **N33**. Click on the **Home** tab and, in the "Font" group, click on the arrow next to the **Fill Color** button. Select a pale colour from the palette by clicking on it.

3 To add a scroll shape, click on the **Insert** tab and then on **Shapes**. Under "Stars and Banners" click on the **Horizontal Scroll** and then click and drag on your page to draw the shape. Don't worry about the size for now, but for a four-generation family tree you'll need to fit 15 of these on the page.

4 To give your scroll more effect, add a drop shadow. Click on the shape to select it and then click on the **Format** tab. In the "Shape Styles" group, click on **Shape Effects** and choose **Shadow** from the menu. Click on the first shadow under "Outer" to apply a drop shadow.

Research begins at home

It's best to start with what you already know: the names and dates of birth of your immediate family. You may already have copies of birth, marriage and death certificates that can tell you facts you might not be aware of. For example, your mother's birth certificate will tell you the maiden name of her mother and so your grandmother's surname. Also, talk to your older relatives about what they remember of their parents and grandparents.

Watch out
Make sure your text is aligned to the left to leave space for the family photo. Go to the "Alignment" group and click on the **Left Align** *button.*

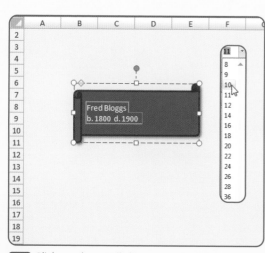

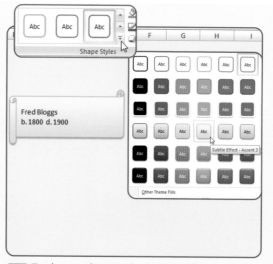

5 Click on the scroll shape to select it and then type a sample name in. It's fine to use dummy text at this stage. Double-click to select the typed name and then go to the "Font" group to choose a font and type size. Unless your family has particularly long names, try **10pt** text.

6 To change the standard colour of your scroll box click on it to select it, and then click on the **Format** tab. In the "Shape Styles" group, click on the **More** button to the right of the "Abc" images. In the dialogue box that opens, click on a colour that contrasts softly with your background.

7 Click outside the scroll box, and then click on the **Insert** tab. Click on **Picture** and browse your hard disk to find the first of your family photos. Click on **Insert**. If you need to resize the photo, see page 285. Position the photo inside the scroll shape to the right of the text. Use the **arrow keys** on your keyboard to nudge it into position.

Preparing your photos
Crystal-clear high-resolution images of relatives and ancestors aren't essential for your family tree, but it's worth adjusting colours and contrast so that the small images stand out clearly when you incorporate them. It can be worth opening the image in a photo editing program such as Photoshop Elements to adjust the brightness and contrast levels for the best result. Also, when you scan in old prints, set the scanner resolution to 600dpi (dots per inch) or greater, especially where the original is small. See pages 194 and 204 for more information on scanning and editing images.

Watch out

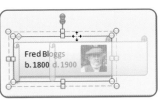

When selecting grouped items to be moved, make sure you click on the outer group frame. If you don't, you might select just one component and move that, leaving the other elements behind.

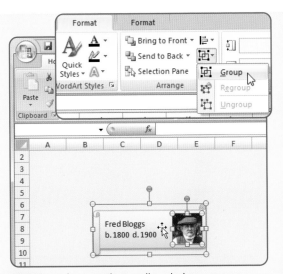

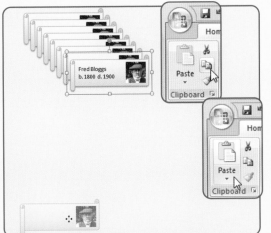

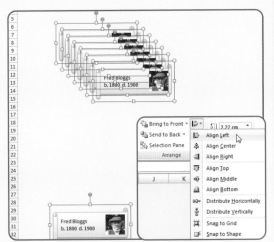

8 To make sure the scroll and photo stay together, hold down the **Shift** key and then click on both the photo and the scroll shape. Click on the **Format** tab and then, in the "Arrange" group, click on **Group**. Select **Group** from the menu. The photo and the scroll will now stay together, which makes it easier to move them.

9 Now add the rest of your family tree. Click on the scroll/photo group to select it and choose **Copy** from the "Clipboard" group. Now click on **Paste**. Click on **Paste** a further six times so that you have eight scroll boxes. Select the final scroll and drag it to the bottom left of the coloured background, roughly aligned with the top box.

10 Your scroll boxes are currently positioned on top of one another. To separate them neatly, first click on one of the scrolls and then hold the **Ctrl** key and press **A** to select them all. Click on the **Page Layout** tab and, in the "Arrange" group, click on **Align**. Choose **Align Left** from the menu.

Resize your images

As the images need to be quite small, you may need to resize your pictures. Right-click on an image and choose **Size and Properties** from the pop-up menu. Under the **Size** tab, the "Lock aspect ratio" box should be ticked – this means the image dimensions are kept if you make a change (i.e. if you adjust the height, the width will also change).

If you would like to crop an image, go to the "Size" group and click on **Crop**. Click and drag on the corners or on the bars – wait for the mouse to become a black bar – on the side of the image to crop out areas you don't need to show.

Bright idea
To position the "child" correctly between its two "parents," look at the vertical cell references and work out the midpoint.

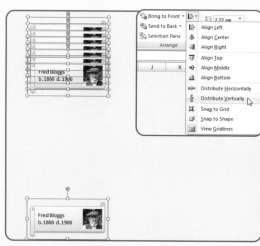

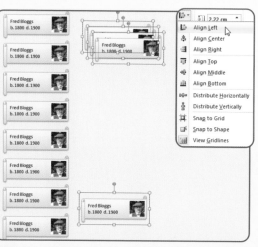

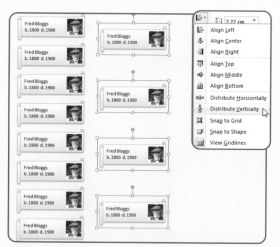

11 The scroll boxes are now aligned along their left edges, but still piled together. With all of the boxes still selected, click on **Align** again and choose **Distribute Vertically**. The eight scroll boxes will be distributed equally down the left-hand side of the page, forming the column that will hold the details of your great-grandparents.

12 Using the method in Step 9, copy and paste four more scroll boxes – these will hold the details of your grandparents. Click on the fourth box and drag it to the bottom to form a column to the right of the others, positioned vertically to sit between its "parent" boxes in the left-hand column.

13 Ensure the four boxes are still highlighted. If not, hold down the **Shift** key and click on each of the boxes to select them. To arrange them neatly, click on the **Page Layout** tab and, in the "Arrange" group, click on **Align** and **Align Left**. Then click on **Align** again, this time selecting **Distribute Vertically** as you did in Step 11.

Different tree types

The family tree in this project is an "ancestor tree." This means that the subject, usually you, appears at the top, or to one side, and preceding generations branch out from that point. Another popular format is a "descendant tree" (right), also known as "dropline" format, in which an ancestor appears at the top and descendants branch off, down to the present generation.

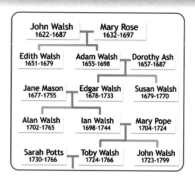

Shortcut

*To constrain an object so that it moves only horizontally or vertically, press and hold **SHIFT** while dragging it. To move an object in small increments, press and hold **CTRL** while pressing an arrow key.*

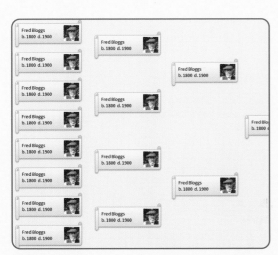

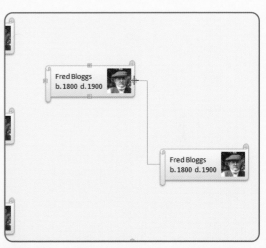

14 Repeat the process from Steps 12 and 13, pasting new scroll boxes and aligning them, to produce two more columns with two and one boxes respectively in each column. You now have 15 boxes (from left to right – eight, four, two and one) arranged over four columns, covering your great-grandparents through to yourself.

15 To start linking your scroll boxes, click on the **Insert** tab, then on **Shapes**. Choose the **Elbow Connector** shape under "Lines." Place the cursor over the first generation scroll/photo box on the far right – the cursor will change to a small cross and red dots will appear on the object showing where you can attach the line.

16 Click on the connection site on the left side of the first generation box and drag to one of the parent boxes to the left. The cursor will change to the small cross target again and red dots will appear on the parent box. Let go of the mouse when the cursor is over the connection site on the right-hand side of the parent box.

Online research

You can always start to create your family tree without having all the information in hand, and add details as you find them. Generally, where you look for information about relatives will focus on where they were born, lived and died, but online searches can produce great results. Good starting points are www.collectionscanada.gc.ca /genealogy/index-e.html or www.thatsmyfamily.ca; both are official Canadian government sources for family records. As well as information and advice on how to go about your research, these sites have links to public records and archive sources all over the world. The Canadian sources featured include birth, marriage and death certificates; census data and immigration and emigration records; and military records from the Imperial War Museum. Other useful research and advice websites include www.ancestry.ca and www.rootsweb.com.

Source: Library and Archives Canada's website (www.collectionscanada.com)

Bright idea
If you have a family coat of arms –
or would like to create one – scan
in an image and add it to your family tree for
a bit of extra colour.

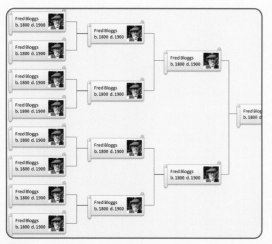

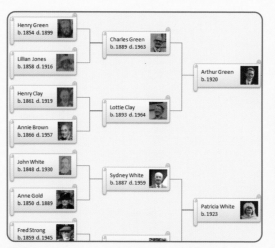

17 Repeat Steps 15 and 16, adding connectors between each child box and its two parent boxes. The lines may need some adjustment, see below. If you accidentally move a scroll box, hold down the **Ctrl** key and press **Z** to undo the action and return the box to its original position.

18 Now make your family real. Highlight the default "Name" text and type in the correct name. Then right-click on the photo and select **Change Picture**. Browse your hard disk to find the correct picture, and click on **Insert**. Repeat for all the other members of your family tree.

19 To add further interest, you could replace the plain background with a texture or picture. Click in cell **A1** then on the **Insert** tab and then on **Picture**. Search for a suitable image and then click on **Insert**. The image will initially appear on top of everything else.

Adjusting the connecting lines

It isn't always easy to put the connecting lines in exactly the right space. However, you can modify them afterwards by clicking on the line and then pulling the round handles that appear. You can also move them around by clicking on the line to select it and then pressing the arrow keys on your keyboard. To make sure the lines connect neatly to your boxes, go to the "View" group and click on **Zoom** to choose a higher magnification. You will then be able to have a really close look.

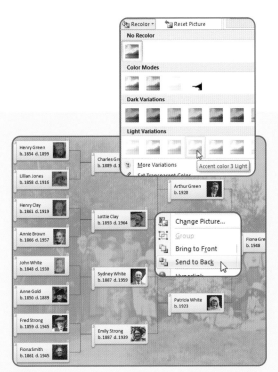

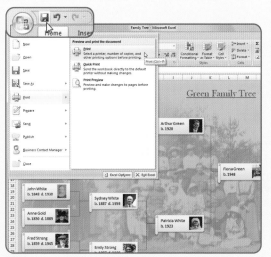

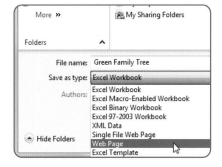

20 If necessary, resize the image to fit your page (see page 285). To place the image behind your family tree, right-click on the image and select **Send to Back**. Your family scroll boxes will now appear on top of the image. To soften the background click on **Recolor** in the "Adjust" group and select a light variation or washout.

21 Now add a title. Click on the **Insert** tab and click on **Text Box** in the "Text" group. Click and drag to create a text box, then type in your title. Highlight the text to select it and then click on the **Home** tab. Go to the "Font" group and choose a font, size and colour.

22 Make sure you save your finished family tree by clicking on **Save** on the Quick Access toolbar next to the Office button. If you are ready to print it out, click on the **Office** button and then on **Print**. You could then frame or laminate your printed history to show the rest of your family.

Share it on the Web

Having made your family tree in Excel, you can print it out and even frame it. But one way many people can get to see it and explore the information and pictures is to save it as a Web page. If you have Web space supplied by your Internet provider, save the file as a Web page to upload. Go to the **Office** button and choose **Save As**. In the "Save as type" drop-down menu, select **Web Page**. Excel creates a Web page document and a folder containing images for the Web page that you can upload.

Make a recipe collection

Keep all your family's favourites together in a database

Most people keep recipes in different places – in books, written down on bits of paper, or cut out from magazines. Tracking them all down can take time.

Save yourself the trouble by creating a recipe database. This allows you to keep all your recipes together, and lets you sort them to find the right recipe for the occasion. When you've found the recipe you want, you can print it out to use or make copies for friends. Once you've created your database, you can add new recipes as you discover them.

HOME RECIPE COLLECTION

Recipe type: Poultry & Game   Recipe Ref: 00001
ecipe name: Thai chicken curry
te of entry: 04/06/2007
ries: 520
r served: 6
ne: 15 + 30 mins (marinade)
g time: 30 mins
redients: 2 garlic cloves 1 medium onion 1 lemon grass stalk 2.5cm/1in piece root ginger 2 small chillies fresh coriander to taste 1 tsp ground coriander grated rind & juice 1 lime 2 tomatoes 6 chicken breast fillets 2 tbsp vegetable oil 2 tbsp fish sauce 1 pint coconut milk salt & pepper.
rnishes: Toasted coconut, coriander leaves
uctions: Peel garlic, peel and quarter onion, halve lemon grass, also peel and halve ginger. Put these ingredients in a food processor and blitz to a smooth paste. Marinate the chicken in a little of the paste for 30 mins, then add a little oil and the chicken to a hot saucepan or wok. Fry for 4 mins, then add the marinade. Stir in the coconut milk, bri for 8 mins until chicken is cooked. toasted coconut and coriander le rice.
Variations: 100g prawns defrosted

1 Go to the **Start** menu, select **All Programs** and click on **Microsoft Works**. Click on **Works Database** from the Quick Launch menu on the right. In the Microsoft Works Database window select **Blank Database** then click on **OK** to open a new blank database document.

Once you have chosen a format, select a style for it in the Appearance section.

Bright idea
Always include a serialized reference number field in your database so that each record will have a unique reference number. Works will automatically update the numbers.

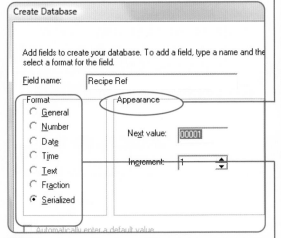

2 The Create Database dialogue box will open where you can input your field names and specify a format for each field. When you have typed in your field name click on **Add**. When you have entered all your fields, click on **Done**. Save your document by clicking on the **Save** toolbar button.

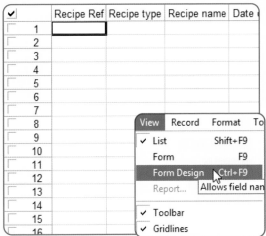

3 Your database appears in List form with the field names at the top of columns. To structure your database go to the **View** menu and select **Form Design**. You can now adjust the position and size of text boxes to make sure your recipe details are visible.

4 Click on the text box adjoining each field name. Keeping the mouse button pressed down, drag it into position. When positioning text boxes, rearrange them so that there is about 8 centimetres of space at the top of the page for your heading.

Fields might include:

Field	Format
Recipe ref	Serialized
Recipe type	Text
Recipe name	Text
Date of entry	Date
Calories	Number
Number served	Number
Cooking time	Time
Ingredients	Text
Instructions	Text

Field name:

Format
- General
- Number
- Date
- Time
- Text
- Fraction
- Serialized

Sizing field boxes

To increase the size of fields, click on the field box to highlight it then move the mouse pointer over the bottom right-hand corner. When the cursor changes to a double-headed arrow, click the mouse and, keeping the button pressed down, drag the box to the size you require.

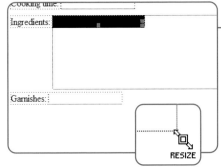

RESIZE

Design a baby book

Keep a special book of memories for all the family to enjoy

Watching children grow up is one of the greatest pleasures in life, and creating a record of their early years allows you to relive the experience time and again. By designing a baby book on your PC you can use as many photographs as you like, and you can also print copies of the book for your relatives instead of paying for expensive photographic reprints. It's very straightforward to add a few personal design touches that will make your unique baby book a delight for generations to come.

Decide which photographs you want to include in your book and download them from your digital camera (see page 200) or scan them in (see page 194).

BEFORE YOU START

1 Go to the **Start** menu, select **All Programs** then click on **Microsoft Office Word 2007**. Go to the **Page Layout** tab and click on the **Page Setup** dialogue box launcher. Click on the **Margins** tab to set your orientation and on the **Paper** tab to select your paper size. Click on **OK**. Now save and name your document.

You can create a baby book using Microsoft Works. To import scanned photographs or digital camera images, make sure the files have been saved in JPEG or TIFF formats.

OTHER PROGRAMS

Keyword

Styles *This describes the text attributes you set for particular sections of your document. Styles will add continuity to your book, and will make it quicker to style new text.*

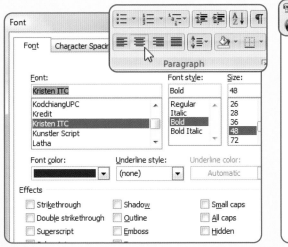

2 First, make a title page. Type in the title then highlight it and click on the **Font** dialogue box launcher. Click on the **Font** tab and select a font, style, size, effect and colour. Click on **OK** when you have finished. To position the title on the page, select it again and click on the **Center** button in the "Paragraph" group.

3 To insert a photo, go to the **Insert** tab and click on **Picture** in the "Illustrations" group. Locate your image – try looking in your "Pictures" folder – and click on a photo to select it, then click on **Insert**. To position photos, see below.

4 To add a new page, go to the **Insert** tab and click on **Page Break**. You might like to add text in a text box for easier positioning. From the **Insert** tab click on **Text Box**, then on **Simple Text Box** from the options given. Move and resize the box in the same way as pictures (see below left).

Placing your pictures

To ensure you can move and resize pictures with ease, click on your image, go to the **Format** tab and select **Text Wrapping** from the "Arrange" group. In the Advanced Layout dialogue box, click on the **Text Wrapping** tab. In the "Wrapping style" section, select **In front of text**, then click on **OK**.

Move a picture or text box by clicking on it and dragging it. Resize a picture by clicking on a corner handle and dragging it diagonally.

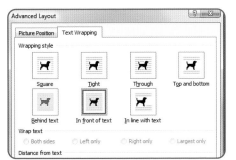

Page and picture borders

To add a border around a page, go to the **Page Layout** tab and click on **Page Borders** in the "Page Background" group. Click on the **Page Border** tab and choose the type of border you want. Click on the arrow beside the "Apply to" box and scroll down to "This section – First page only." Then click on **OK**.

To put a frame around a photo, double-click on it and then click on **Picture Border** in the "Picture Styles" group. Select a colour, weight and style. Click on **OK**.

Watch your health

Keep a detailed record of your family's medical history

Everyone values their health, and that of their family, above all things. Yet few people keep accurate records of their own illnesses and treatments.

This information can be useful in establishing patterns of illness, providing up-to-date records for health-care workers, and in keeping an account of medical and dental expenses.

With your PC, you can create a database that keeps detailed records of your family's health: what medications have been prescribed; dates of inoculations, checkups and operations; allergies suffered. You can extract specific data when someone gets ill (for example, the name of a medicine that helped last time), and you can print out lists of future appointments.

Gather all the information you have about your family's health records, such as dates of checkups, details of consultations, and so on.

BEFORE YOU START

1 Go to the **Start** menu, select **All Programs** and click on **Microsoft Works**. Click on **Works Database** in the Quick Launch menu on the right. In the Microsoft Works Database window select **Blank Database** then click on **OK** to open a new blank database document.

*You can create a family health database in Excel. Go to the **Start** menu, select **All Programs** and click on **Microsoft Office Excel 2007**. Enter your data into the empty grid.*

OTHER PROGRAMS

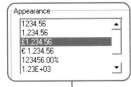

Some formats, such as Number and Date, give a choice of appearance. Click on your choice from the list displayed.

To resize a text box, click on it then place the mouse pointer over the bottom right-hand corner. When the cursor changes to a double-headed arrow, click the mouse and drag the corner until the box is the right size.

Bright idea
When styling your fields and text boxes, use different fonts for each one to make them stand out.

2 In the Create Database dialogue box input your field names. Type the name of your first field in the box, select a format for the field, then click on the **Add** button. Continue to add all the fields you want and then click on **Done**. Your document will appear in List form.

3 Name and save your document. To ensure your details are visible and appear as you wish, adjust the design of your file. Click on the **Form Design** toolbar button. Click and drag on the text boxes to move them. To adjust the size of text boxes, see above.

4 To add a general heading to appear on each record, click at the top of the form and type in your heading. Highlight it, go to the **Format** menu and select **Font and Style**. Select a font, size, colour and style. Click on **OK**. Use the same method to style all the field and text boxes.

Fields and formats

For a family health database, you might want to create these fields, together with these formats.

Field	Format
Record ref	Serialized
Name	Text
Date of birth	Date
Consult type	Text
Consult date	Date
Appoint time	Time
Appoint type	Text
Details	Text
Comments	Text
Treatment cost	Number

Using Works templates

Microsoft Works has several health records templates already set up.

Go to the **Start** menu, select **All Programs** then click on **Microsoft Works**. Click on the **Templates** icon and choose **Home & Money** from the categories on the left. Select **Medical records** from the list that appears, choose a style to preview it, then click on **Use this style** to start your database project.

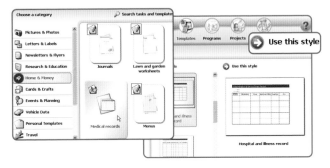

Plan a new kitchen

Try out a **variety** of room designs **to find the one** that suits you

Drawing up a plan for your new kitchen helps you decide how best to arrange all the elements for ease of use and optimum storage. You can create a two-dimensional plan on your PC using Microsoft Word. The plan can be easily adjusted as you make new additions, and you can create several alternative versions for comparison. When you are planning your kitchen think about how you will use it. If you do a lot of cooking, make sure you have plenty of work surfaces and that the three key elements (range, fridge and sink) are close to each other and easily accessible.

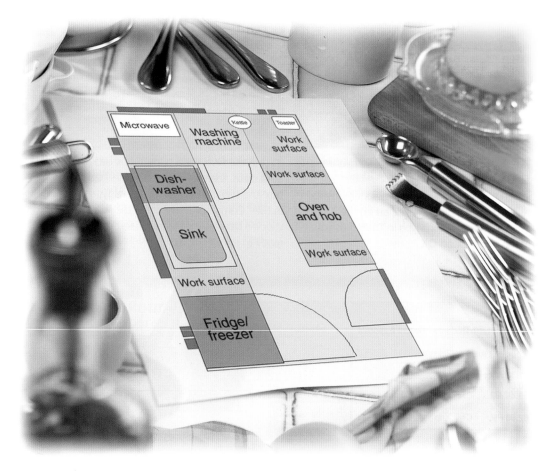

Measure the dimensions of your kitchen, including all doors, windows and appliances. Also note the position of electrical and plumbing outlets.

▶ BEFORE YOU START

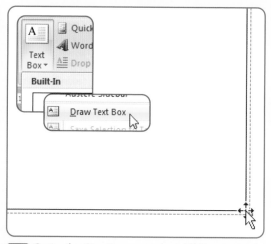

1 Go to the **Start** menu, select **All Programs** then click on **Microsoft Office Word 2007**. A document opens. Go to the **Insert** tab and click on **Text Box** in the "Text" group, and then on **Draw Text Box** at the bottom of the menu. Click and drag the mouse diagonally to create a text box that will act as the outline for your kitchen.

*It isn't possible to create a detailed plan to scale in Microsoft Works, but specialized interior design programs are available. IKEA offers a free planner on its website (http://www.ikea.com/ca/en). Go to "Kitchen" and click on **Ikea Planning Tools** for the download link.*

▶ OTHER PROGRAMS

In the Line section select a colour, style and width for your kitchen border.

*As soon as you have opened your new document, save and name it. Click on the **Save** button on the Quick Launch toolbar and save the document into a suitable folder.*

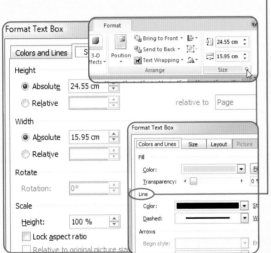

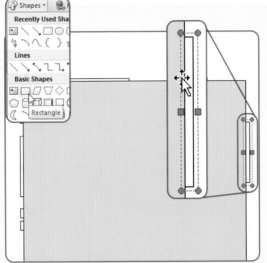

2 To make sure your text box is to scale (see below), go to the **Format** tab and click on the **Size** dialogue box launcher. Click on the **Size** tab. Specify the height and width of your box. Click on the **Colors and Lines** tab to select a colour for your box in the "Fill" section and then click on **OK**.

3 Now create boxes for all your fixed features, such as doors, windows and electrical outlets. Go to the **Insert** tab, click on **Shapes** and from "Basic Shapes" select **Rectangle**. Click and drag in your document to create the shape. To move a shape, click on the edge of the box and drag to the required position.

4 It's a good idea to colour all the fixed features in the same way. To select all the boxes at once, hold down the **Shift** key while clicking on each of them in turn. Click on the **Shape Styles** dialogue box launcher, then on the **Colors and Lines** tab, select a colour and click on **OK**.

Drawing to scale

Measure your kitchen, then scale it to fit onto a letter-sized page. If your kitchen measures 650 cm x 450 cm, divide each figure by the same number to calculate measurements that will fit on the page. Dividing the real measurements by 25, for example, would create a box of 26 cm x 18 cm. Design to real-world standards by scaling down 30, 60 and 90 cm kitchen units and appliances in the same way, and using the same number.

Avoid clashes

To indicate the space needed to open a door, draw an arc. Go to the **Insert** tab and select **Shapes**.

Click on the **Arc** icon in the "Basic Shapes" section, then click and drag on your document to draw the shape. Now add a straight line to form a complete segment. Adjust the arc's shape and size by clicking on a handle and dragging it.

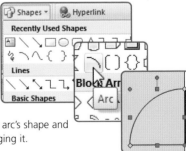

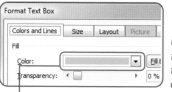

Use different colours for each appliance to make them distinguishable.

Bright idea
Write down some ground rules for planning your kitchen. For example: "Don't put the sink below electrical outlets" and "Appliances should be placed in positions where their doors can be opened safely."

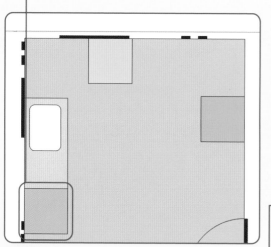

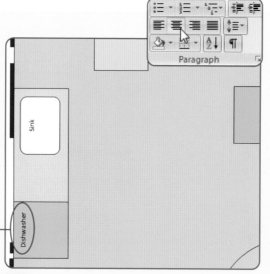

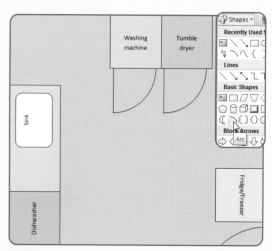

5 You now have the basic structure of your kitchen in place. Create more text boxes to represent your floor-standing appliances, such as a washing machine and range. Remember to scale them down in size in the same way that you scaled your kitchen dimensions.

6 To name an appliance, click in the box and type the name. To move the text down, click at the start of the word and press the **Return** key. To position it centrally within the text box, highlight it and click on the **Center** button in the "Paragraph" group.

7 Move your appliances into position by clicking on the edge of the boxes and dragging them. Remember to allow for the space needed to open appliance doors. If you wish, draw arcs to indicate how far they will extend.

Style changes
To change the size and font of your text, highlight it, click on the **Font** dialogue box launcher, then click on the **Font** tab. Select a font and size then click on **OK**. To rotate text, go to the **Format** tab and click on **Text Direction**. Each time you click, your text will rotate 90 degrees clockwise.

You may find it easier to position items on your plan by increasing the magnification of your page. Click on the current zoom value (here 100%) found to the left of the slider at the bottom right of your window and, in the Zoom panel that opens, select **Whole page** and then click on **OK**. Alternatively, click and drag on the slider to select a suitable viewing value.

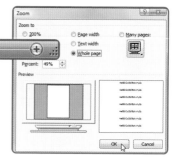

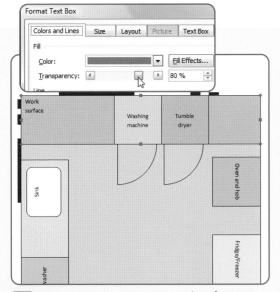

Watch out
Although you can "layer" items in Word, it can be tricky to select the bottom layer, so build your page as you would your kitchen, from the bottom up.

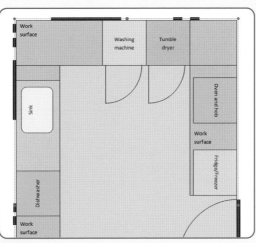

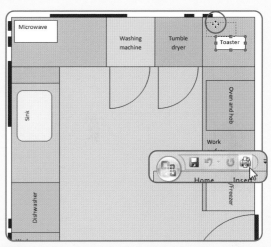

8 Create a semi-transparent text box for your work surface. This will allow you to see the floor-standing items below. Click on the **Text Box Styles** dialogue box launcher. In the "Fill" section, select a colour and then click and drag the slider on the **Transparency** bar to choose a transparency value of around 80%. Click on **OK**.

9 Continue to add and position as many elements as you need, working with spaces that match standard cupboard sizes. Take into account the space needed for doors and allow enough room to move around comfortably. Experiment with several alternative plans.

10 Finally, add smaller items such as the microwave and toaster. They need not be exactly to scale, as this is merely to show you whether your design is feasible in terms of your electric outlets. To print out a copy of your plan, click on the **Print** button from the Quick Launch toolbar.

Creating different plans

You don't need to start from scratch to create different versions of your plan – you just save them as you go along.

Whenever you want to save a version of what you have done, go to the **Office** button and click on **Save As**. Give the plan a different name from the original (e.g., Kitchen Plan 3) then click on **Save**.

Bright idea
Add wall units to your plan by creating semi-transparent boxes as described in Step 8.

Take the effort and stress out

Finding, buying and moving to a new property is hard work – make sure

Moving can be one of the most exciting events of your life, but also one of the most stressful. Big decisions and large amounts of money are involved, and you will need all the help you can get to make the process go smoothly.

You can get your PC involved as soon as you start looking for a new home. Use the Internet to look for property, gather information about mortgages, find a lawyer or notary (depending on your province), and investigate the local amenities in the place you would like to move to.

Before deciding which is the best mortgage for you, you could input the details of different packages into a spreadsheet program and compare the costs. All the various and confusing factors such as cash-back offers,

# of moving

your computer is the last thing you pack

varying interest rates and so on premiums can be built into the equation, so you can see the best deal at a glance. Keep another spreadsheet for additional costs and fees, deposits and realtor's commission.

When you find the right house for you, create folders for all the correspondence with lawyers, lenders, realtors and surveyors. You don't even need to print off a copy for yourself: the file on the PC is your record.

Once the deal is complete there is, of course, the whole matter of moving. The key to a successful move is sound budgeting and

effective planning – and here too you should make the most of your PC. Make a spreadsheet to track the cost of a moving truck and other moving expenses. You might also make a checklist of tasks to do – have you cancelled the milk delivery, transferred the cable and phone accounts, and arranged to have the utility meters read?

Before moving day, you can get ready by printing off labels for the packing boxes. Then, once you are safely installed in your new home, remember to send a card (which you have designed yourself) or an e-mail to all your friends, to let them know your new address.

Countdown to moving

- Book time off work for the move
- Inform friends, bank, work and schools of your move
- Re-catalogue and value home contents
- Set up a budget document for the move
- Source moving firms and insurance (request quotes)
- Buy packing boxes and materials
- Plan packing schedule
- Arrange final readings and closing accounts for utilities: gas, electricity, telephone and water
- Arrange house clearance for unwanted items
- Design invitations for new house-warming party

Ideas and inspirations

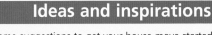

Below are some suggestions to get your house move started. The projects can be adapted to your particular circumstances. You may want to give various tasks to different family members. Plan early to avoid the last-minute rush that plagues most home moves.

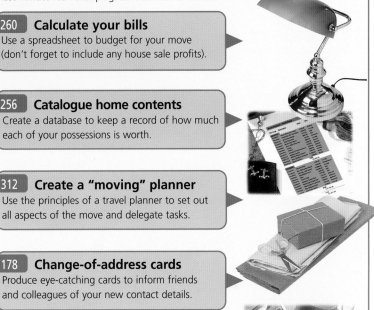

260 **Calculate your bills**
Use a spreadsheet to budget for your move (don't forget to include any house sale profits).

256 **Catalogue home contents**
Create a database to keep a record of how much each of your possessions is worth.

312 **Create a "moving" planner**
Use the principles of a travel planner to set out all aspects of the move and delegate tasks.

178 **Change-of-address cards**
Produce eye-catching cards to inform friends and colleagues of your new contact details.

170 **Packing labels**
If your boxes are clearly marked you'll be able to unpack items at your own pace, as you need them.

Also worth considering...

Once you've moved into your new house, put your own stamp on it by designing your dream kitchen.

302 **Plan a new kitchen**
Create a simple, overhead 2D plan of your new kitchen and organize your space effectively.

Devise a fitness plan

A simple spreadsheet can help you schedule regular exercise

Along with your running shoes, stopwatch and sheer determination, your computer can play an integral part in creating and maintaining an effective fitness plan. Using a spreadsheet program, such as the one in Microsoft Works, you can create a fitness log to keep track of your progress, using both figures and written comments. Getting in shape can involve many forms of exercise so, while these pages show you how to put together a jogging schedule, you can adapt the project to suit any fitness plan.

Keeping a log of your progress can help you to see how well you are doing, or how far you have to go to achieve your goals. It also allows you to make changes if you've miscalculated your time and abilities – and you can note down sessions missed due to illness or injury.

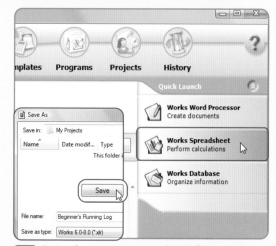

> It's important that the schedule you create is appropriate for your level of fitness. If you do not exercise regularly, consult your doctor first.

BEFORE YOU START

1 Go to the **Start** menu, select **All Programs** and click on **Microsoft Works**. Click on **Works Spreadsheet** in the Quick Launch menu on the right to start your spreadsheet project. From the **File** menu click on **Save**. Now name the document, choose an appropriate folder and click on **Save**.

> You can create a similar fitness schedule using Microsoft Excel, perhaps creating a new worksheet for each week.

OTHER PROGRAMS

Keyword

Formatting *This term describes the collection of style elements – including fonts, colours, effects and alignment – that determine how a cell looks.*

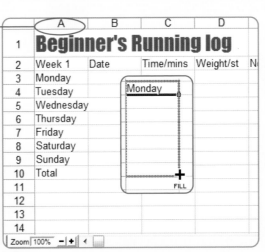

2 Cell A1 is automatically selected in your spreadsheet. Type a title for your plan into this cell. Highlight it, go to the **Format** menu and click on **Font**. Select a font, style, size and colour in the Format Cells dialogue box. The row height will automatically adjust to include your text.

3 Starting in cell **A2**, and continuing in the cells along the same row, type in headings as shown. In cell **A3** type in "Monday." Drag the bottom right-hand corner of the cell down so that the rest of the days of the week appear in the cells below. In cell **A10** type in "Total".

4 To change the position of text within cells, select a cell or block of cells with the mouse, then click on your choice of alignment toolbar button. Click on **OK**.

Adjusting column widths

Some of the text that you enter into cells may not be visible. To adjust the width of cells in a single column to accommodate your text, place the mouse pointer on the right-hand edge of the beige lettered column header. When the mouse pointer changes to a double-headed arrow, hold down the left mouse button and drag the column edge to the required width. Or double-click on the column header and it will resize automatically.

Your jogging schedule

When you start your schedule, concentrate on running continuously for a certain time, rather than covering a certain distance. Don't push yourself too hard. In the early sessions, alternate between brisk walking and running.

Before each jogging session warm up by walking briskly for 10 minutes. Cool down afterwards by walking for 5 minutes then stretching. Hamstring stretches are especially important.

Close-up
When you choose a large font size for text, the spreadsheet row automatically adjusts to accommodate it.

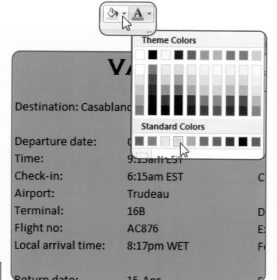

5 To style your heading, highlight it, then click on the **Font** dialogue box launcher. Choose a font, style, size and effect, then click on **OK**. Style the rest of your text in the same way. To select a number of adjacent cells at the same time, click on the top cell and then drag over the others.

6 To add a background colour, select the cells and click on the arrow beside the **Fill Color** button in the "Font" group. A drop-down colour palette appears. Choose a colour and click on it to apply it.

7 To colour all your text with the same colour, select the cells and click on the arrow beside the **Font Color** button in the "Font" group. As before, a colour palette appears. Click on a colour to apply it.

Centre your heading

To position the heading in the centre of your page, click on cell **A1** and drag your cursor along the top row of cells until the full width of your form is covered (here, to column F). Then click on the **Merge & Center** button in the "Alignment" group.

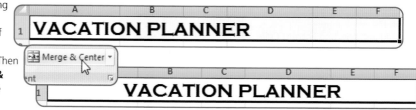

Bright idea
If you want to add another page to your spreadsheet, go to the **Insert** *menu and click on* **Worksheet***. Another sheet tab will appear at the bottom of your screen.*

Currency converter

Dollars:	5000
Exchange rate:	7.448
Foreign currency=	37240
Foreign currency:	785
Exchange rate:	0.134
Dollars value=	56.07143

Format Cells

Number | Alignment | Font | Border | Fill | Protection

Line
Style:
None

Presets
None | Outline | Inside

Border

Text   Text
Text

Color:

The selected border style can be applied by clicking above.

Currency converter
Dollars: 5000
Exchange rate: 7.448
Foreign currency= 37240
Foreign currency: 785
Exchange rate: 0.134
Dollars Value= 56.07143

New
Open
Save
Save As
Print

Preview and print the document

Print
Select a printer, number of copies, and other printing options before printing.

Quick Print
Send the workbook directly to the default printer without making changes.

Print Preview
Preview and make changes to pages before printing.

Print Preview (Ctrl+F

Close Print Preview

VACATION PLANN

Destination: Casablanca, Morocco

Departure date: 01-Apr
Time: 9:15am EST
Check-in: 6:15am EST
Airport: Trudeau
Terminal: 16B
Flight no: AC876
Local arrival time: 8:17pm WET

Return date: 15-Apr
Time: 6:15pm WET
Check-in: 3:15pm WET
Airport: Mohammad V
Terminal: 18
Flight no: AC976

Currency converter
Dollars: 5000
Exchange rate: 7.4
Foreign currency= 372

Foreign currency:
Exchange rate: 0.
Dollars value= 56.07

Home   Insert

ION PLA
PACKING LIST

Mom	Tick	Michael
Underwear (7)		Underwear
Socks (5)		Socks (5)
Tee shirts (6)		Tee shirts (
Shorts (4)		Shorts (4)
Pants (3)		Pants (3)
Tops (8)		Shirts (4)
Dresses (4)		Tie
Swimmsuit (2)		Shoes (3)
Sun Hat		Hat
Jackets (2)		Jacket
Blouses (3)		Sweater

8 To separate your currency converter from the rest of your travel details, place a border around it. Highlight the relevant cells, right-click with the mouse and select **Format Cells** from the menu. Click on the **Border** tab, select a line style, colour and outline for your border and then click on **OK**. Do the same for the page heading.

9 Before printing your planner, check the layout. Click on the **Microsoft Office** button and select **Print Preview** from the "Print" options. If it needs adjusting, click the **Close Print Preview** button and edit the layout accordingly. When you are happy with it, click on the **Print** button on the Quick Access toolbar.

10 Using the same process, it is possible to create a packing list and a list of tasks to complete before going on holiday. At the bottom of the window you will see a series of tabs. Click on the **Sheet 2** tab. A blank spreadsheet page appears, ready for your next list.

Currency converter

To make your headings really stand out, reverse your "fill" and "font" colours. In this case, the background has been coloured red, and the text yellow. Finally, click on the **Center** *button in the "Alignment" group.*

Setting up your page

You may need to adjust the page settings of your document. Click on **Page Setup** when in Print Preview mode (see step 9) and click on the **Page** tab to check that Orientation is set to **Landscape**. Also, ensure **Letter** is selected in the "Paper size" box. To centre the page, click on the **Margins** tab and, under "Center on page" options, tick both **Horizontally** and **Vertically**. Click on **OK**.

Page Setup

Page | Margins | Header/Footer | Sheet

Orientation
Portrait   Landscape
A

Print
Page Setup
Print

100   % normal size
1   page(s)

Center on page
☑ Horizontally
☑ Vertically

Paper size: A4

Plan a vacation you'll

Don't leave your vacation enjoyment to chance –

Project planner

Create a folder for the entire project, called "Vacation." Add subfolders as below.

- Vacation
  - Research
  - Preparation
  - Flights
  - Accommodation
  - Dining
  - Overall budget

Everyone dreams of escaping from their day-to-day routine. For some, the ideal escape is a beach and a book on a desert island; for others it is a hectic round of entertainment and shopping in a big, cosmopolitan city. Whatever your dream, your PC can help you make it a reality.

With your computer you can access websites on the Internet to check out national, regional and resort destinations. You can look up weather forecasts to help you decide which clothes to pack. You can even find out about wider weather patterns to ensure your visit doesn't coincide with monsoon or hurricane seasons. You may also be able to read

remember forever

your PC can help it go smoothly

about local event listings such as carnivals or exhibitions scheduled to happen during your stay.

Through the Internet you can order brochures, purchase travel guides and check whether any inoculations or other health precautions are needed. Once your destination has been chosen, you can book flights and accommodation, rent cars and organize excursions. You could even check train timetables, ferry services and bus routes for destinations on the other side of the world, and pick up tips from fellow travellers.

In short, every aspect of your vacation arrangements can be researched, sourced and paid for via your computer.

Once everything is booked, your computer is also the ideal tool for your vacation planning. You can create a database to organize all the tasks that need to be undertaken before your departure, and set up a spreadsheet to project costs and a budget. You can then create an agenda for your trip and take a printed copy with you.

On your return you'll be able to scan in or, if you have a digital camera, download your vacation pictures and produce your own photo album, which you can either display on a website for your friends to see or e-mail/post to them. You could even send a vacation newsletter to friends with stories and pictures from your trip!

The adventure starts here

- 6 months: book time off work
- 5 months: check whether inoculations are required
- 4 months: budget for your vacation
- 3 months: confirm booking/itinerary
- 1 month: organize travel insurance
- 2 weeks: buy currency/travellers' cheques

Ideas and inspirations

Below are project ideas to make your vacation run as smoothly, and be as memorable, as possible. All the projects can be adapted to your own circumstances and will give you further ideas of your own. Just alter the wording, layout or search details of each exercise as you work.

94 Find information on the Net
Research destinations and weather conditions, and book accommodation and tickets online.

252 Travel budget planner
Spreadsheet software on your PC helps you plan the finances for any purchase or project.

312 Make a vacation planner
Produce a document containing all the practical details of your trip, from time zones to car rental.

82 Use your PC as a fax
Confirm bookings and itineraries with hotels and tour operators by fax.

210 Create an online photo album
Make sure your trip is one you'll remember with a pictorial souvenir created on the Internet.

Also worth considering...

Once you've finished, don't let your research go to waste. You can use information again and again.

166 Create a contact database
You can produce address and contact lists specific to transport, accommodation and new friends.

A collector's database

Keep a detailed record on every addition to your collection

Whatever you collect, whether it's rare stamps, coins, wine or CDs, it can be useful to keep a log of each item you own. As your collection grows, it becomes necessary to keep track of its contents, its value and even the whereabouts of each item. You can use a database program on your PC to keep such records.

Creating a database is straightforward and, once you have entered all your details, you can find any information you need quickly and simply. Not only do you have all the information about your collection in one place, but a database is also a way of detecting "gaps" in your collection and can help you to plan future purchases.

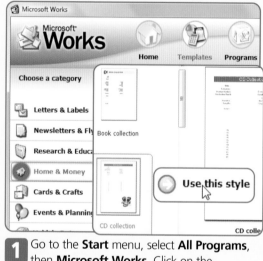

For a music database, gather together all your CDs, records and cassettes. If you have kept receipts for them, have these handy too.

BEFORE YOU START

1 Go to the **Start** menu, select **All Programs**, then **Microsoft Works**. Click on the **Templates** icon and select the **Home & Money** category from the left-hand list. Select **Home inventory worksheets** and choose **CD collection**, then click on **Use this style**.

You can also make a record of your collection using Microsoft Excel. Use the spreadsheet to type in your headings and data, then the Filter feature to create your reports.

OTHER PROGRAMS

Classical CDs

CD ref: 00003

Composer: Bach

Title: Preludes and Fugue

Musician(s): Academy of St. Martin-in-the-Fields

Venue: St Paul's Cathedral London

Conductor: Marriner

Date: 05/96

Label: Philips

Catalogue No: 745892971

Purchased: 02/97

Price: 14.45

Keyword

Fields *A field is a space allocated for a particular item of information. For example, in a database of contact details there might be different fields for names, addresses and telephone numbers. Fields appear as columns of data in a database. Several fields about a single subject make up a "record."*

2 The CD Collection database opens up. It is quite comprehensive, but you may want to change some fields to suit your needs. For instance, we are going to change "Producer" and "Copyright" to the purchase cost of the item, and its estimated collector's value now.

3 To delete fields and add new ones, go to the **View** menu and click on **List**. Click on the column header entitled "Producer," then right-click and select **Delete Field**, then **OK**. Right-click again and select **Insert Field**, then **Before**. Name your new field "Cost" and select **Number** in the "Format" section. Click on **Add**, then on **Done**.

4 Repeat the actions in Step 3 to delete the "Copyright" field and add a "Value" field. Go to the **View** menu and select **Form Design**. The new fields appear in the top left-hand corner of the window. Click on them and drag them into position. ("Copyright" may still appear in this view; click on it, then press the **Delete** key.)

Fields and formats

Before you build a database, take some time to familiarize yourself with the various field formats.

You can preset data fields to style numbers, dates and text, applying font characteristics, rounding decimal places and so on. It is a good idea to include a serialized reference number to automatically update each record with a new number.

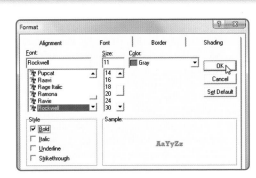

Styling fields

You can assign fonts, colours, effects and styles to your fields and their adjoining text boxes. Click on the **Form Design** toolbar button, then on a field name or adjoining text box. Go to the **Format** menu and click on **Font & Style**. Select a font, size, style and colour, then click **OK**. Click on the alignment toolbar buttons to position the text within the text boxes. To style several text boxes at once, press the **Ctrl** key and, keeping it pressed down, click on the boxes in turn and then style them.

Record your golf scores

Keep track **of your rounds and** calculate your handicap

A spreadsheet is a great way of keeping a full record of your sporting achievements. In this project, we create a golf scorecard but you could use the same method to design a spreadsheet for any sport. In this example, each time you input a scorecard, your playing handicap will be updated. There are two handicap calculators: one provides an overall handicap, based on every scorecard entered into the system; the second calculates your current handicap by taking an average of your last three rounds.

Collect at least three of your recent scorecards to provide scores and the course data you need to set up your spreadsheet.

BEFORE YOU START

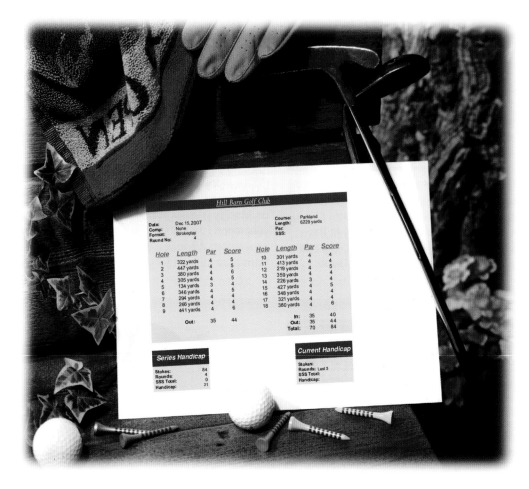

Hill Barn Golf Club							
Date:	Dec 15, 2007			Course:	Parkland		
Comp:	None			Length:	6229 yards		
Format:	Strokeplay			Par:			
Round No:	4			SSS:			

Hole	Length	Par	Score	Hole	Length	Par	Score
1	322 yards	4	5	10	301 yards	4	4
2	447 yards	4	5	11	413 yards	4	4
3	380 yards	4	6	12	219 yards	4	5
4	305 yards	4	4	13	359 yards	4	4
5	134 yards	3	5	14	226 yards	3	4
6	346 yards	4	5	15	427 yards	4	5
7	294 yards	4	4	16	348 yards	4	4
8	266 yards	4	4	17	321 yards	4	4
9	441 yards	4	6	18	380 yards	4	6
	Out:	35	44		In:	35	40
					Out:	35	44
					Total:	70	84

Series Handicap

Stokes:	84
Rounds:	4
SSS Total:	0
Handicap:	21

Current Handicap

Stokes:	
Rounds:	Last 3
SSS Total:	
Handicap:	

1 Go to the **Start** menu, select **All Programs** and click on **Microsoft Office Excel 2007**. To name and save your new document, click on the **Save** button from the Quick Access toolbar. Select a suitable folder in which to save it, type in a file name then click on **Save**.

*You can also record your golf scores in Microsoft Works. Open Works, then choose **Works Spreadsheet** from the Quick Launch menu on the right.*

OTHER PROGRAMS

Watch out
Make sure that you enter the headings and data into exactly the same cells as used below. If you do not, the cell references used later in the handicap calculation formulas will not be correct.

Close-up
Unless directed otherwise, AutoSum adds figures immediately above the selected AutoSum cell. To adjust the formula, include new cell references (simply click on the cells themselves to do this) and appropriate calculation symbols, such as "+", "-", "/" and "".*

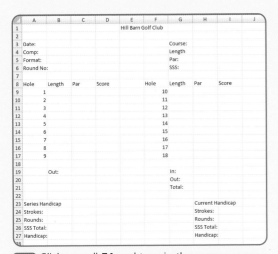

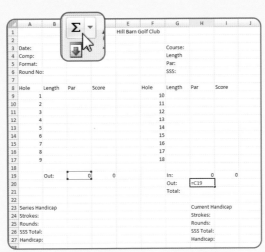

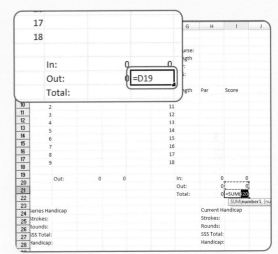

2 Click on cell **E1** and type in the course name. Type in the text for the rest of the spreadsheet as shown above. It is important that you use the same cells as here, otherwise your formulas won't work. Now you are ready to prepare for your Score and Par totals.

3 Click on cell **C19**, then on the **AutoSum** button. Select cells **C9** to **C17** and press **Return**. When course data is entered, AutoSum will add it up. Repeat for all Par and Score columns. Then click **H20**, type "=C19" and press **Return** to carry over par from the front nine.

4 Click on **I20** and type "=D19" to carry over the front nine score. To calculate total par for the round, click on **H21**, then on the **AutoSum** button. Highlight cells **H19** and **H20**. Press **Return**. For your total score, click on **I21**, then on **AutoSum**. Select cells **I19** and **I20** and press **Return**.

Working out handicaps

A handicap is the number of strokes a golfer takes, on average, to play a course, over and above Standard Scratch Score (SSS). SSS is the score a scratch golfer, with a handicap of "0," should take to play the course. SSS can differ from par for the course as it takes account of the difficulty of the course, while par for each hole is dictated by length.

The handicap calculators in this project are "Series" and "Current." Series is calculated by subtracting the SSS total for all rounds played from the total number of strokes for those rounds, and then dividing the remainder by the number of rounds played. The Current Handicap is calculated by taking the SSS total for the last three rounds only from the strokes played in the last three rounds, and then dividing the remainder by three.

Series Handicap = (B24 [total number of strokes played] minus B26 [SSS total for all rounds]) divided by B25 [number of rounds played].

`=(B24-B26)/B25`

*Format the cell to ensure your handicap is rounded to a whole number. Click on the cells showing your Current and Series handicaps, go to the **Format** menu and click on **Cells**. The Number tab is selected. Click on **Number** in the Category pane and set "Decimal places" to "0". Click on **OK**.*

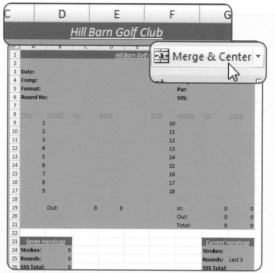

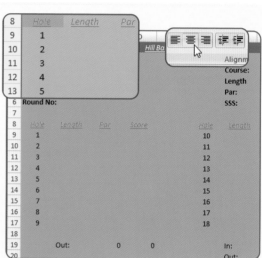

5 To set up the Series Handicap calculator, click on cell **B24** and type in "=I21". Click on **B25** and type "=B6". Click on **B26** and type "=H6". Then click **B27** and type in the formula "=(B24-B26)/B25". For the Current Handicap, click in **I25** and type "Last 3".

6 To centre your heading, select cells **A1** to **I1**. Click on the **Merge & Center** button in the "Alignment" group. Style your document (see below). To widen a column to fit all the text, place the mouse pointer on the right edge of the column heading and double-click.

7 To centre the hole numbers and other data at the same time, click and drag the cursor over the relevant cells then click on the **Center** button in the "Alignment" group. Now enter all the course, length, par and score data. Excel will automatically calculate your formulas.

Using buttons to add style
You can style text and colour using the buttons in the "Font" group. To change cells, select them and then use the drop-down lists for font and font size. Click on the **Bold**, **Underline** and **Italic** buttons to further enhance the text. To alter text colour, click on the arrow beside the Font Color button and select from the colour palette. To add a background colour click on the arrow beside the Fill Color button and choose a colour.

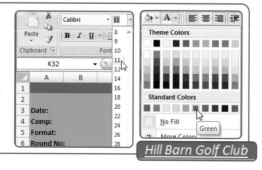

Adding worksheets
When you open an Excel document, the default settings give you three sheets to work with (tabs for each sheet appear at the bottom of each page). To add more sheets for new rounds, click on the **Insert Worksheet** button on the right of worksheet tabs.

Apply the same formulas each time, but don't forget to add in another value for each sheet, for example: =H6+Sheet1!B26 +Sheet2!B26.

Current Handicap = (I24 [total number of strokes played in last three rounds] minus I26 [SSS total for last three rounds]) divided by 3 [number of rounds played].

Handicap: =(I24-I26)/3

Sheet1 | **Sheet2** | Sheet3

	A	B	C	D	E	F
1						Hill Barn Golf Club
2						
3	Date:	25/06/2007				
4	Comp:	None				
5	Format:	Strokeplay				
6	Round No		4			
7						
8	Hole	Length	Par			ole
9	1	322 yards	4	5		10
10	2	447 yards	4	5		11
11	3	380 yards	4	6		12
12	4	305 yards	4	5		13
13	5	134 yards	3	4		14
14	6	346 yards	4	5		15
15	7	294 yards	4	4		16
16	8	266 yards	4	4		17
17	9	441 yards	4	6		18

Home — Paste — Clipboard

23	Series Handicap	
24	Strokes:	0
25	Rounds:	0
26	SSS Total:	0
27	Handicap:	

				10	30.
9				11	413
10					219
11	21				
12	4	305 yards			359
13	5	134 yards			226
14	6	346 yards			42?
15	7	294 yards			348
16	8	266 yards			321
17	9	441 yards	4	6	
18					
19	Out:	35	44		In:
20					Ou
21					Tot
22					
23	Series Handicap				
24	Strokes:	182			
25	Rounds:	5			
26	SSS Total:	140			
27	Handicap:	10.5			

21		
22		
23	Series Handicap	
24	Strokes:	=I21+Sheet1!B24
25	Rounds:	4
26	SSS Total:	0

18	380 yards	4	6
	In:	34	46
	Out:	35	44
	Total:	69	90

Current Handicap	
Strokes:	272
Rounds:	3
SSS Total:	210
Handicap:	=(I24-I26)/3

8 To create a second scorecard, copy and paste the document. Highlight cells **A1** to **I27** and click on the **Copy** toolbar button. Click on the **Sheet 2** tab and then the **Paste** button. Adjust column widths and fill in the new scorecard, overwriting data where it is different.

9 For each new scorecard, carry over total strokes and SSS from the previous card. On Sheet 2, click on **B24** then type "=I21+Sheet1!B24". Click on **B26** and type "=H6+Sheet1!B26". After three rounds, and three sheets, set the Current Handicap calculator.

10 Click on cell **I24** and type "=I21+Sheet1!I21+ Sheet2!I21". Click on **I26** and type "=H6+Sheet1!H6+Sheet2!H6". To work out the Current Handicap, click on **I27**, then type in '=(I24-I26)/3". To print, click on the **Print** button.

Current Handicap

For the Current Handicap calculation you must total up the strokes and SSS for the last three rounds:

● **Strokes:** to add the last two rounds to the current score, click on **I24** and type "=I21+Sheet1!I21+Sheet2!I21".

● **SSS:** to add SSS for the last two rounds to current SSS, click on **I26** and type "=H6+Sheet1!H6+Sheet2!IH6".

When you play a new round, adjust the sheet references in the formula. After 50 rounds, for example, the formula for the SSS for the last three rounds would be "=SUM(H6+Sheet48!H6+Sheet49!H6)".

fx =I21+Sheet1!I21+Sheet2!I21

Current sheet total score

Sheet 1 total score

Sheet 2 total score

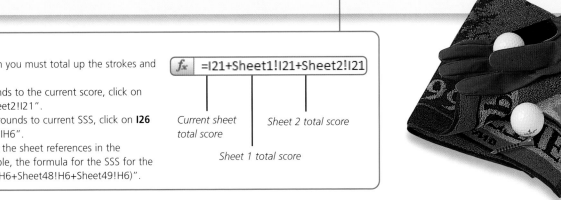

Organize a reunion and relive

Whether bringing distant family members together, or catching up with

Project planner

Create a folder called "Reunion." Then add sub-folders as below.

- 📁 Reunion
  - 📁 People
  - 📁 Communications
  - 📁 Event logistics
  - 📁 Finance
  - 📁 Suppliers
  - 📁 Design & logos

It is all too easy to lose touch with the people who used to be part of our lives. All of us have friends we would like to see more often. That is why a reunion is so special – and your PC can help bring together people separated by the years and even by continents.

Start by setting up an event planner database. Record what tasks need to be taken care of, by when and by whom. Add details of each guest, such as address, e-mail address and phone or fax numbers, as well as contact information for caterers and other professionals you may need to hire to make the reunion a success.

The increasing popularity of sites like www.classmates.com means old school friends can be easy to trace. There are also worldwide e-mail directories of people who are online.

Once you have compiled your initial guest list, try searching online for those you haven't yet

the good old days

old school friends, your PC can help you

been able to trace. Some people – as well as your old school or workplace – might be easier to contact by e-mail. For letters, e-mails and faxes, you could create an attention-grabbing "reunion" letterhead, then adapt it for subsequent gatherings.

Use your word processing program to produce a newsletter to keep everyone updated on the arrangements. This could be a "missing

persons bulletin," to encourage others to help you trace "lost" invitees.

When you have a rough idea of how many people will be attending the event, book the venue and arrange catering and entertainment, at the same time as keeping track of expenses through a spreadsheet.

One item you won't have to pay for is the invitations. Just design and print them on your PC – personalize the design and create a stir from the start.

Get old friends together

- Contact your old company or school for a list of previous employees or students
- Conduct research over the Internet
- Draw up a guest list
- Mail, e-mail or fax a proposal to potential guests
- Start to compile a reunion database
- Design and send final invitations
- Scan in photos or download digital images and e-mail photos of the event

Ideas and inspirations

Co-ordinating guests, possibly from all over the world, requires military-style planning. Make sure you dip into your arsenal of PC-based skills to cover as much of the hard work as possible. Adapt the following projects as required, then prepare for a truly memorable occasion.

94 Searching the Internet
Locate people anywhere in the world via e-mail address databases and make contact with them.

312 Event planner database
Set up a document to handle the logistics of your reunion, and delegate jobs to others.

166 Compile a guest list
Make a database to incorporate people's address, phone, fax and e-mail details.

162 Create a newsletter
If the timeline for planning your event is long, you may wish to update guests on progress.

218 Create an invitation
It may be the first or the last task you carry out, but it's sure to be distinctive with your PC's help.

TROUBLE

Frozen screens, printing errors, corrupt programs and malevolent computer **viruses** can happen to any PC user. But in most cases these and many other problems are **easy** to solve. Wherever the fault lies – in Windows, in any application or in the computer hardware – this section will help you to **identify** the symptoms, **diagnose** the problem and come up with a **remedy**.

SHOOTING

My computer won't start up

There are steps you can take when you can't get your PC to start up

A startup problem is the most serious and worrying of hardware hiccups. It is hard to cure the sickness if the patient cannot tell you what is wrong and it is difficult to assess how serious the problem might be. Thankfully, startup problems are rare with Windows Vista, but if you are unable to start up your computer there are a number of steps you can take to diagnose the problem. Then, even if you cannot solve the problem yourself, you can at least give some useful leads to a PC specialist.

Are you connected?

If your computer doesn't react at all when you turn it on, the first thing you should do is to check whether the power lights on the system unit and monitor are on. If not, check that both units are plugged into the wall, that the outlets are working and that the breaker hasn't tripped (or the fuse hasn't blown in an older home). Also, check that the brightness control on the monitor hasn't been turned down. Finally, you should also check the cable that connects the monitor to the PC.

Try resetting

If none of this helps, turn your computer off and then leave it for a minute before switching it back on again. If the screen remains blank, note down the number of beeps given out by the computer during the startup routine as this might be helpful for a PC specialist in diagnosing the problem.

Hard disk problems

If your computer won't start, it may be due to problems with the hard disk. This vital part of your PC stores Windows files and all of your documents. The hard disk consists of a "read/write" head which hovers over magnetized disks. If the read/write head touches the disk the result is a "head crash" – a damaging collision between the head and the fast-spinning platters. This can destroy large amounts of data on the hard disk, including the data needed to make Windows operate. A hard-disk failure of this type is difficult to solve and should be dealt with your PC's manufacturer (or your supplier if the computer is still under warranty).

Keyword

POST *The POST (Power On Self Test) routine checks that your most vital hardware components are working correctly. If the POST messages move up the screen too fast for you to read them, press the **Pause** key on the top right of your keyboard. Press **Return** to continue.*

Windows Vista repair tool

There are many different problems that might prevent your computer from starting up. Thankfully, Windows Vista has a recovery tool called Startup Repair that can diagnose and fix many problems for you. If it cannot fix a problem, it will give you the necessary details to pass on to a specialist.

Startup Repair

The Windows Vista recovery tool Startup Repair can fix many of the problems that might prevent Windows from starting up correctly, such as missing system files, drivers, boot configuration settings, or damaged registry settings and disk metadata (information about your hard disk). When you run Startup Repair, it scans your computer for the problem and then tries to fix it so your computer can start correctly. If a startup problem is detected, it automatically launches a troubleshooter that will attempt to resolve the issue with little or no intervention from the user. If successful, the computer will reboot and an "event" will be written to the "event log," providing information about the problem. If Startup Repair cannot repair the problem without user intervention, it will help you through the process to manually deal with the fault. If Startup Repair is unsuccessful in its attempt to identify or fix the problem, it will restart the computer, reverting to the settings and configuration used before the problems occurred.

Startup Repair cannot fix hardware failures, such as a faulty hard disk or incompatible memory, nor can it protect against virus attacks. Also, it is not designed to fix Windows installation problems. If repairs are unsuccessful, you will see a summary of the problem. You can view a log of this and any earlier problems by accessing the Event Viewer (see page 363). For further information on Startup Repair and how to use it, see page 356.

Start with your Vista disk

If all else fails, you may need to use your Windows Vista disk to start up the computer.

If you've checked the connections and power supply and Windows still won't start up, locate your Windows Vista installation DVD. Insert it into your CD/DVD drive and switch your PC off. Then switch it back on again to start your system from the Windows Vista disk. You can then go to the installation menu and select the "Repair Your Computer" option to try to correct the fault.

Some older PCs may not support startup from the CD/DVD, in which case you will not be able to use the Vista DVD as a rescue disk. If this is the case, you should consult an expert.

If Vista was pre-installed

If you are using a pre-installed edition of Windows Vista, you may not have an installation DVD. In this case, ask your PC supplier how to access the "Repair Your Computer" option.

Your supplier might have provided a special "boot disk" with the system, or supply instructions on how to make a boot disk that contains all the files necessary to repair your installation.

Watch out

Don't move your computer when it is switched on. This could cause the hard disk's read/write head to touch the disk platters, which would destroy a great deal of data. When the computer is turned off, the head moves away from the platters. However, you should still be careful when moving the unit in case any other components become loose.

My printer isn't working

Check your hardware and software to solve printing problems

Nothing is more frustrating than to put the finishing touches on a document, only to find that you can't print it out. But don't worry. While printing problems are the most common of hardware hiccups, they are also among the easiest to solve.

Nowadays printers are usually very good at telling you what went wrong. Sometimes it's simple: is there paper in the tray? Has the ink (or the toner) run out? Otherwise, there is a limited number of things that can go wrong: paper jams, loose connections, and mistaken setup commands cover most difficulties. The steps on this page should lead you to the root of any problem. After a while, you will develop a feel for what went wrong with your own printer. In the meantime you can use the excellent Help and Support files in Windows Vista.

In the hardware

If you send a document to print, and it fails to do so, the first thing you should check is that the printer is switched on – is the power light on? Check that it is plugged into an outlet as well.

Next, make sure there is paper in the printer paper tray, and that none of it has become jammed as it has been fed through. If the printer runs out of paper you should get an error message on your computer screen. If your printer is quite old and is jamming frequently, getting the rollers replaced may help. Otherwise, you may need to buy a new printer.

When your computer recognizes that you have a printing problem, Windows will alert you by bringing up an error message suggesting certain actions that you can take.

Is the printer connected?

Many modern printers connect to the PC through a USB connection. USB cables plug into a free USB port. Problems with USB printers can often be cleared simply by unplugging and reconnecting the cable from the the computer. Older printers use serial and parallel connections. With these types of cable, make sure all connections are secure and screwed in firmly. Wireless printing? Try restarting the router.

Dell Photo AIO Printer 966: USB003

Communication Not Available

The printer cannot communicate with the computer.

Try These Solutions:

- Ensure the printer is powered on
- Disconnect and reconnect the USB cable
- Disconnect and reconnect the printer's power cable
- Restart your computer

OK

Start again

One way of quickly solving a printer problem is to try resetting the printer. To do this, just turn it off, wait a few seconds, then turn it on again.

Getting ready to print

The first step to successful printing is making sure you have selected the correct settings.

Page Setup

Occasionally, a page will fail to print, or will print out incorrectly, if your page isn't "set up" correctly. Get into the habit of checking your Page Setup before you print. To do this, go to the **Page Layout** tab and click on the **Page Setup** dialogue box launcher.

Margins	Paper	Layout

Paper size:

Letter

Width: 8.5"

Height: 11"

Paper source

In the Page Setup dialogue box set the parameters for the way the document will print – its physical size and orientation. If you want letter size, click on the **Paper** tab and select **Letter** in the "Paper size" box. Check you have the correct orientation, too: with Portrait the page's width is the shorter dimension; with Landscape, the page's height is the shorter.

Print Preview

In many programs you can look at how the page will appear before you print it. To do this, click on the **Office** button, move your mouse down to **Print** in the left pane and then clicking on **Print Preview**. You will be able to see any setup problems,

such as if text runs over to other pages because the orientation is wrong.

Paper source

Your printer may have more than one feeder tray for paper, such as a manual feed tray needed to print envelopes. If so, make sure that you have selected the correct tray to print from. In the **Page Setup** dialogue box click on the **Paper** tab and select the tray under "Paper source."

Then check that the tray you want to print from has the right size paper.

Paper source

First page:
Default tray (Automatic)
Automatic
Tray1/Bypass
Tray 2

Other pages:
Default tray (Auto
Automatic
Tray1/Bypass
Tray 2

Troubleshooting

If none of the above solutions works, you may have a software problem. Windows Vista has an extensive set of help files that can help solve problems with your printer.

Go to the **Start** button, click on **Help and Support**, then **Troubleshooting**, and then type "printing" in the search box at the top of the window. Now choose from the options presented to you, here **Troubleshoot printer problems**. These help files can identify whether problems with printing are being caused by the printer itself or by a piece of software.

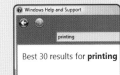

Windows Help and Support

printing

Best 30 results for **printing**

1. Getting started with printing
2. Demo: Printing
3. Print a document or file
4. Troubleshoot printer problems

Printer tools

Many printers come with a set of tools on a disk or CD-ROM that check for common printer faults and may even try to fix them. If you do not have the original CD-ROM, try downloading the utility from the manufacturer's Web site.

Reinstalling your printer

If all else fails, you could try reinstalling your printer. Go to the **Start** button, select **Control Panel** then **Printer** from the "Hardware & Sound" group. Click on **View installed printers or fax printers**. Click on your printer's icon and press the **Delete** key to uninstall the printer. Confirm your choice. Click on **Add a printer** and

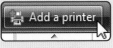

follow the onscreen instructions to identify the type of printer you are installing and install its driver.

Add Printer

Install the printer driver

Select the manufacturer and model of your printer. If your printer came with an installation disk, click Have Disk. If your printer is not listed, consult your printer documentation for compatible printer software.

Manufacturer	Printers
Gestetner	HP 2500C Series Printer
HP	hp business inkjet 1000
IBM	hp business inkjet 1200
infotec	HP Business Inkjet 2200/2250

This driver is digitally signed.
Tell me why driver signing is important

Windows Update | Have Disk...

Next | Cancel

Checking ink levels

If the printer is printing your work but the printed text is faint or invisible, check that the ink or toner has not run out. Most printers will have a light on the front that will indicate if either is running out, and may also have software that warns you when levels are getting low. Sometimes with colour inkjet printers, the cartridge for one colour gets blocked or runs out sooner than the others. This can lead to strange colours being printed. It may be possible to clear a temporary blockage – check the printer's manual for details. If this doesn't work out, you'll have to replace the cartridge.

My keyboard isn't working

Hardware or software may be at fault if your keyboard is acting up

Your keyboard is perhaps the most vulnerable part of your computer. It gets the heaviest wear and tear; it is more likely to be moved and dropped; it takes a physical pounding every single time you key in a letter; and it is also exposed to dust, dirt and the occasional spill. Fortunately, most modern keyboards are robust and can take a lot of punishment before they start to malfunction.

The best way to avoid problems in the first place is to look after your keyboard (see page 62). But even if you take good care of your equipment, you may find keys start to stick or fail to respond when you press them. The problem may be due to a faulty connection or (more rarely) to a software error. Check every possibility before you give up and buy a new keyboard: the fix could be as simple as giving the keys a quick clean.

If the whole keyboard fails

If none of the keys on your keyboard is responding, check whether your PC has crashed. Try using your mouse to move the pointer on screen. If it moves as usual and the PC responds, the problem must be with your keyboard.

First check the connections. All modern keyboards connect to the PC via a USB socket. Try unplugging and plugging the keyboard in again as this can sometimes restore a lost connection. On older keyboards which connect via a serial or parallel port, make sure the keyboard is plugged into the right socket on the system unit (it is possible to plug the keyboard into the mouse port by mistake). Also check the wire for signs of damage.

If a key won't respond

If one of the keys on your keyboard isn't working properly check whether dirt has built up between the keys. Use a dust spray, or work cleaning cards dipped in cleaning solution between the keys, to solve the problem. As a final measure, gently pry out the offending key and check for debris trapped underneath.

If this doesn't work, and you know the software isn't to blame (see opposite), it is often less expensive to buy a new keyboard than to have the existing one repaired.

Dealing with a spill

If you spill a drink on your keyboard, unplug the keyboard, wash it using a clean sponge and a bowl of soapy water and leave for a day or two to dry thoroughly. Modern keyboards can be washed without suffering ill effects.

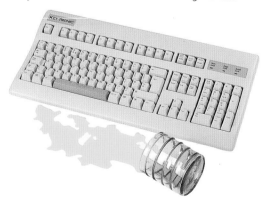

Solving keyboard software problems

Windows has several settings that can affect the use of your keyboard. Check these if you are having problems with the keyboard or if the settings don't suit your particular needs.

Select the correct language

Sometimes, a new PC will be set up for a different country, so that keyboard letters produce unexpected symbols onscreen. Also dates and numbers may appear with unfamiliar formats.

To check this, go to the **Start** button, click on **Control Panel**, then on **Change keyboards or other input methods** under "Clock, Language, and Region." In the Regional and Language Options dialogue box, click on the **Formats** tab. Ensure the correct country is selected in the drop-down box. Next, click on the

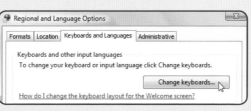

Keyboards and Languages tab and then on the **Change keyboards** button. If the correct language is not displayed in the pane – English (Canada) for Canada; English (United Kingdom) for the UK, etc. – click on the **Add** button. Click the arrow to the right of

the "Input language" box, scroll down and select the correct language, here German (Germany). Click on the "+" to the left of "German," then again on the "+" to the left of "Keyboard" to expand the available options. If you have changed any of the settings, click **Apply**, then on **OK**. Note that you will need to restart your computer before the settings

Make your keyboard easier to use

If you have difficulty using your keyboard because of a disability, Windows Vista has a special Accessibility function that will make it easier. You can set up your PC so that you don't have to press more than one key at a time (StickyKeys). You can also set it up to ignore multiple presses of the same key (FilterKeys), or to warn you when you have pressed an important key, such as the Caps Lock (ToggleKeys).

To customize the keyboard in this way, go to the **Start** button, click on **Control Panel**, then on **Ease of Access**. Click on **Change how your keyboard works** and choose options and settings for how you want your keyboard to work.

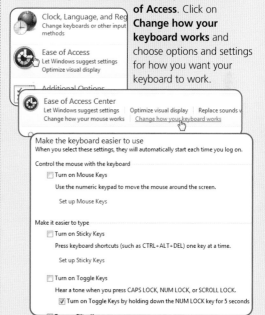

! **Watch out**
If you press a key and an unexpected character appears, it may not necessarily mean the language your PC is using is incorrect. You may simply be using the wrong font. Some fonts, such as Zapf Dingbats and Wingdings, are entirely composed of unusual characters. Highlight the character then look at the font box on the toolbar to view the font used.

My mouse isn't working

If your mouse stops responding, it isn't necessarily broken

Don't be alarmed if something goes wrong with your mouse. There are many ways of determining where the problem lies.

If your cursor starts to move in a jerky way, or stops moving altogether, there are a few likely causes. Most modern mice use an infrared light to track the mouse's movements. They may be wired or wireless. They are less likely to malfunction as they have no ball and rollers to get dusty or sticky. If this type of mouse *does* malfunction, check the surface you are using it on – it should be smooth and clean – and that the infrared transmitter is clean (see page 63). If the mouse is wired, check the connection (see opposite). If all else fails, the problem is likely to be the software and will require professional attention.

If you have an older mouse with a ball and rollers, check if the inside of the mouse needs to be cleaned (see page 63) and whether it is properly connected (see opposite).

Different types of mouse

The traditional type of mouse connects directly to the system unit via a wire. However, many other styles of mouse are available today.

● Infrared mice track your hand's movement using infrared light. They may be wired or wireless. The only maintenance they need is gentle cleaning of the lenses and the small pads underneath them.

● Trackballs contain a ball and rollers on top of the mouse and need maintenance and cleaning just like conventional mice.

● Touchpads and tiny joysticks used on laptop computers cannot be cleaned easily. If you experience problems, take your laptop back to the shop you bought it from (if it's still under guarantee), or an authorized repair shop.

Trackball

Touchpad

Bright idea

If you want to shut down your computer but your mouse isn't working, press one of the **Windows** *keys on your keyboard (to either side of the space bar). This will bring up the Start menu. Now press the* **U** *key twice to shut down.*

Watch out

If your mouse isn't plugged in properly when you turn on your computer, Windows will give you a warning message and you will find that the mouse will not respond to your hand movements.

Pointing you in the right direction

If you are having problems with your mouse, first check that the hardware is connected and in working order, then check for software trouble.

Check your connection

If your mouse stops responding while you are working, first check that the cable (or receiver, if cordless) is plugged in properly to the system unit, and that it is in the correct port. The different types of mouse connections are explained below:

USB

All modern input devices connect to a computer using a USB port. Such devices include tablets – touch sensitive pads that you write or draw on with a pen-like tool – and a wide variety of joysticks. Often, problems with input devices which are connected via USB ports can be solved by simply unplugging and then reconnecting the device in the socket.

PS/2 and serial ports

Older computers used PS/2 ports or serial ports for the mouse and keyboard. If you are using these connections and your mouse stops responding while you are working, check that the cable is plugged in properly to the correct port. Mice are connected to PS/2 ports using a round 5 or 6-pin plug and to serial ports using a large 9-pin "D" type plug. Switch off the PC then disconnect and reconnect the mouse in the correct port. Then switch the PC back on.

Infrared

This type of connection uses an infrared light to transmit mouse movements from the mouse to your PC. Infrared mice can be wired or wireless. A wireless infrared mouse transmits mouse movements to a receiver attached to your PC. Both the mouse and its receiver need to be in "line of sight" in order to work properly. Check this and that the infrared lasers are clean (see page 63). If the mouse is wired, check the connections. You should also try restarting the PC.

Bluetooth

Typically a cordless device, which requires a receiver (attached to the PC) and a transmitter (the mouse). Bluetooth uses similar technology to infrared except that mouse movements are transmitted via radio signals from the mouse to the receiver. This technology offers freedom of use, but may suffer interference from microwave ovens or cordless phones. If you are encountering problems with a Bluetooth mouse, check the connection for the receiver and try restarting the PC. If this doesn't solve the problem, the software may be at fault and will need to be looked at by a specialist.

If all else fails…

If none of the solutions offered above work, try borrowing a mouse that definitely works from another computer. Make sure the mouse has the same connector as yours. If the borrowed mouse works on your computer, there must be something wrong with the mechanics of your mouse. If you are sure your mouse is broken and it is not under guarantee, then you will have to buy a new one.

Check your mouse properties

Strange mouse behaviour may be caused by settings in the Mouse Properties dialogue box. To open this dialogue box, go to the **Start** menu, click on **Control Panel**, then on **Mouse** under "Hardware and Sound."

The Buttons tab lets you switch the functions of the left and right buttons (to suit a left-handed user, for example). You can also set the interval between the two clicks of a double-click.

If you have a scroll wheel you can change the way it works under the Wheel tab. To investigate other mouse problems, click on the **Hardware** tab, and then on **Troubleshoot**. Follow the steps to discover where the trouble lies.

My speakers don't work

What to do if the only sound coming from your PC is silence

Computer speakers will generally give many years of use without any need for maintenance, apart from regular cleaning. Over time – years, in fact – the sound computer speakers generate may become increasingly crackly. This is merely a sign of wear and tear, and the most economical solution is to replace them. So seldom do computer speakers malfunction that,

if you're using your computer and no sound comes out of them, the likelihood is that the problem lies not with the speakers but with the way they have been connected to the PC, or with the software you are using.

A little knowledge of how speakers connect to your computer and interact with your software should help you get to the bottom of the problem fast.

Some sound advice

It may seem obvious, but first check that the volume control is turned up. Next, check that the speakers are plugged into a wall outlet and switched on – is there a power light? Also check that they're plugged into the correct socket on your sound card in the system unit. There are usually a number of connectors, for microphones as well as speakers. Sometimes these are colour-coded – the speaker port is often green. Swap the speaker plug around until you hear the speakers. If you have stereo speakers, you need to make sure they are connected to each other.

Software options

Another user may have disabled the sound facility on the piece of software you are using. Many games allow you to turn off the sound, out of consideration to those who share your space. If you can find no reference to sound in the program, check that sound is actually supposed to come from the software you are using (look in the manual).

Watch out

The ports on a sound card can be very difficult to tell apart so it's easy to plug your speakers into the wrong one. This could be the cause if your speakers don't appear to be working but make sure the volume is turned down when you connect them to the correct socket.

Checking your volume control

If none of the checks of your connections and external controls reveals the fault, then you probably have a software problem. First of all check that the system's volume is not turned off.

Locate the small speaker icon that appears on the right-hand side of the

Volume: 95
Speakers
SigmaTel High Definition Audio CODEC

Windows Taskbar. (If you cannot see it, click on the white **Show hidden icons** arrow.) Hover your mouse pointer over the speaker icon to reveal a pop-up message identifying your speaker volume and type. Click on the message to display the Volume Control settings. Check that the "Mute" box underneath the volume slider doesn't have an icon (red circle with a diagonal line) next to it and that the volume slider is near the top of its

scale. Click on "Mixer" to display an additional volume control setting for your system sounds under "Applications." These are sounds which your computer plays when certain events happen, for example, when you log on to your computer or when a new e-mail arrives in your

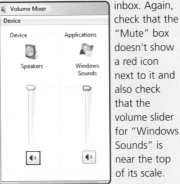

inbox. Again, check that the "Mute" box doesn't show a red icon next to it and also check that the volume slider for "Windows Sounds" is near the top of its scale.

Extra help

Remember that Windows has its own built-in help and support pages which explain how it works and what to do when things go wrong. Go to the **Start** button and click on **Help and Support**. In the "Find an

answer" panel click on **Troubleshooting** then in the "Hardware and drivers" panel click **Troubleshoot sound problems**. Now click on either of the links showing the most common types of sound problems and their possible solutions.

Types of speakers

Most PCs emit sound through their own separate, free-standing speakers. However, it's possible that your PC's speakers are built into the monitor, one on either side of the screen. These speakers also connect by cables to the main system unit.

Ensure your speakers are part of your regular cleaning routine (see page 62), and that their cables are kept clear of any obstruction.

If all else fails...

Borrow a pair of speakers from a friend and connect them to your PC. If these work (keep the volume low to avoid damage), then you need to get your own speakers repaired or replaced.

Bright idea

If you can't borrow a pair of speakers to check the connection, you may be able to use your stereo speakers. Use a cable to connect between the speakers port on your system unit and the auxiliary jack socket of your amplifier (you may need to get a special cable). Do not place your stereo speakers too close to your PC as they are magnetic and may corrupt your hard disk and affect the picture quality on your monitor. Proper computer speakers are magnetically shielded to avoid these problems.

My modem isn't working

How to solve problems connecting to the Internet or sending e-mail

On some occasions, a piece of software or hardware that has been functioning well for months can suddenly go wrong or stop working altogether. If something like that happens with your modem, don't panic. There are a number of reasons why your modem might not be working, and most of the problems are easily resolved.

Problems with your ISP

You should first check whether the problem is at your end. Try to connect to your Internet Service Provider (ISP). If you have a dialup modem and you hear a series of loud, high-pitched tones (the sort you hear when you connect to a fax machine) then you know your modem is trying to make a connection. If the connection process does not complete, the cause could well be with the service provider's equipment rather than yours. If you have a broadband modem it is more tricky to find out where the problem lies. In either case, call your ISP to find out if other customers are having problems and, if so, when the fault will be fixed.

Modem checks

If you are still having problems connecting and the problem does not lie with your ISP, the problem may be with the modem setup on your computer – the modem might not be properly installed, for example. Sometimes, if you add a new piece of hardware or software to your computer, it can affect the way your modem is set up. Run through the setup procedure in the modem manual to check that everything is arranged correctly. Alternatively, Windows Vista has a number of helpful tools which will diagnose and repair problems, including an interactive Modem Troubleshooter (see opposite).

Plugs and switches

Although it may seem obvious, check that the modem is properly connected. If you have an internal modem, check that the cable that connects it to the phone socket is plugged in at both ends. If you have an external modem, check that all its cables are firmly plugged in, and that the right cables are plugged into both the PC and the power line. Check that the modem is switched on.

If you are sure that your modem is set up correctly, that your phone line is working and that all your cables are correctly fitted, but you still can't make a connection, it's possible that the delicate head of the modem cable that connects the modem to the phone line is damaged. This is a standard cable, so simply buy a new one from a computer store and reconnect your modem (see opposite).

Keywords

Modem On Hold *(MOH) is a feature that allows a dialup modem to work with call waiting. If you have Modem On Hold running and receive a call on the line that the modem is using, the modem can go into a hold state and pick up where you left off after you have finished with the call.*

To use this feature you need your modem as well as your Internet Service Provider (ISP), to support it. Contact your ISP and check your modem settings to determine if you can use Modem On Hold.

Watch out

*Never leave your wireless network unsecure – don't be tempted to let your router work without wireless security – someone **will** hack into it before long!*

Modem Troubleshooting

If your ISP and your connections seem OK, try using the help facility available in Windows Vista.

Before troubleshooting

Establish what type of modem you have. Most modems built into computers are dialup modems and connect to the Internet through a telephone line.

Go to the **Start** button and click on **Control Panel**. Select **Hardware and Sound**, then **Phone and Modem Options**. Click on the **Modems** tab and check that your modem is listed (this means your computer recognizes it as installed).

If your modem is not listed, it may have been accidentally removed by another installation. Reinstall it by clicking on **Add** to bring up the Add Hardware Wizard dialogue box. Work through the simple steps suggested by the Wizard to reinstall your modem.

Broadband modems

If you have broadband Internet access through an Internet Service Provider (ISP), then you will have a broadband modem. This is usually connected to a cable or DSL line, which in turn is connected to your computer through an ethernet cable and network adapter.

If you are unable to connect to broadband look at the lights on your modem.

1. Power light is on and the ADSL light is flashing. Shut down your computer and after 1 minute, restart. Once the computer has completely rebooted check the lights again – as well as the cabling.

2. Power light is on and the ADSL light is off. More than likely caused because the modem cable (RJ11) is not plugged in properly. Check cable at both ends and that the cable is plugged into an ADSL filter and not directly into a main telephone jack.

3. Power light and ADSL light is off. Shut down your computer and recheck all connections. Remove all USB devices, wait 1 minute and restart. Reconnect modem, and if still no lights on, try uninstalling and then reinstalling your modem software.

4. Power light and ADSL light is on. Possibly you are mistyping your username and password. Check this, and if the problem persists consult a computer expert.

Networks

Broadband routers (wired or wireless) enable computers to communicate with each other and also the Internet. If you have multiple computers, a router is an ideal way for them to access the Internet via one modem. They also typically provide built-in "firewall" security.

Wired

A wired router has numbered lights corresponding to each computer connected to it, so if a connection is "down" the router light for that connection will be off. This probably means that there is a fault with that computer's ethernet cable.

If none of your computers are able to access the Internet, you will need to unplug the ethernet cables from the router, disconnect the router from the phone jack and remove the router's power supply cable. Wait for a minute, then reconnect the router, then each of your computers in turn.

Wireless

Make sure the router is positioned away from anything else electrical. Wireless routers ideally should be placed on a high shelf in a midpoint of the house, say the hallway. Do not place them on the floor or behind a TV. Choose the best wireless channel and do not use the same channel as a neighbour. Finally, make sure your drivers and adapter are up to date.

Using Windows Help and Support

Go to the **Start** menu and click on **Help and Support**. In the Windows Help and Support dialogue box click **Troubleshooting** then in the next box type "modems" into the search bar at the top of the screen. Scroll through the list of options and click on one of the links – here we have chosen "Troubleshoot network and Internet connection problems." In the next box scroll down through the list of options and click on a question to reveal the answer. If this does not help you, choose another possible answer, or click on the back arrow button at the top left of the window, and choose another option.

Upgrading your hardware

Improve the capabilities of your PC by adding or replacing a component

As your computer gets older you may find that it does not run as quickly as you would like, particularly when you add new software applications. The easiest way to resolve this problem is often to add more RAM (Random Access Memory). RAM is the place where your PC stores the program you have open and the data you are currently working on.

Installing more RAM will help your computer to function better, but it will not get the best performance from newer programs. If, for example, you load the latest computer game onto an old machine, you may find that the quality of graphics and sound effects is not what you were hoping for.

While it is possible to upgrade individual components you may find that if there are several items requiring replacement it might be more cost-effective to buy a new PC. As time passes it will become more expensive to "match" upgrades to the capabilities of your old PC.

Before installing new components, create a System Restore Point (see page 350) and back up your hard disk (see page 357), so you can revert to a properly functioning system should something go wrong.

Watch out

As with all electrical devices, treat your PC with caution. Unplug the machine before doing any work on it. If your PC is an "all-in-one," take care – components in your monitor can give you a painful shock, even if the machine is unplugged.

Bright idea

Computer developments come thick and fast. It's hard to know whether this month's hot new item will be next month's white elephant. Wait for new products to establish themselves before you buy; successful devices will improve in quality and fall in price.

The basics of upgrading

Upgrading your PC will often involve opening up the computer's case. Here we show you how to install a graphics card – use the instructions as a guide to fitting a sound card or internal modem.

Installing a new graphics card

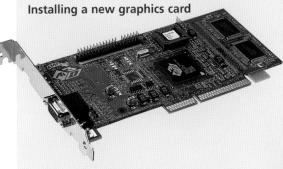

A graphics card generates the picture signal and sends it to the computer monitor. The latest graphics cards generate faster and smoother 3D graphics, and many support DVD and television playback. These cards will be designed to fit into a PCI or AGP slot at the rear of your system unit. To make sure you buy the appropriate card for your PC, consult your PC's manual or contact the manufacturer.

Switch off the PC, remove the power cables from the back of the system unit, then take the cover off (consult your PC's manual to find out how to do this). Locate your existing graphics card – this is the card your monitor cable will be attached to at the rear of the unit.

Unplug the monitor cable and then remove the screw that holds the card in place and put it to one side. Carefully but firmly ease the card out of the slot, then gently insert the new card in its place, making sure the socket for the monitor cable is facing outward from the

back of the unit. Secure the card by replacing the screw, then replace the system unit's cover.

Replace all the cables and turn on your PC. Windows will automatically detect the change to your components and, if it can, will install drivers for the device and configure it for use.

If Windows does not have the required drivers it will run the Add Hardware Wizard so you can tell Windows where to find them (see below). If you have an Internet connection Windows Vista will automatically search the Windows Update Internet site for an up-to-date driver. If all else fails you may find a suitable driver on the manufacturer's Web site.

Remove the existing graphics card to make space for the new one

Gently insert the new card, pushing it firmly if necessary to make sure it is in place

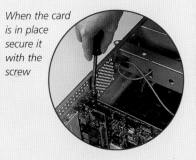

When the card is in place secure it with the screw

The Add Hardware Wizard

All modern hardware devices are "Plug and Play," which means they will work immediately, without requiring you to manually install a device driver. A driver is the piece of software that Windows uses to run or access the device, and these days many drivers come pre-installed. When you add older hardware devices, Windows will usually detect the new hardware when you start your PC and automatically run the Add Hardware Wizard to help you install a driver. If Windows does not, you will

need to start the Add Hardware Wizard yourself. To do this, go to the **Start** menu and click on **Control Panel**. In the task panel on the left, click on **Classic View**. Double-click on **Add Hardware** (note that you will need Administrator rights to run the Wizard). Click on **Next** and follow the prompts. The Wizard will look for new hardware. If it finds any it will check to see whether it already has a driver available. If it cannot find an appropriate driver it will prompt you to insert the hardware.

Add Hardware

Welcome to the Add Hardware Wizard

This wizard helps you install driver software to support older devices that do not support Plug-and-Play and which are not automatically recognized by Windows.

You should only use this wizard if you are an advanced user or you have been directed here by technical support.

⚠ **If your hardware came with an installation CD, it is recommended that you click Cancel to close this wizard and use the manufacturer's CD to install this hardware.**

Watch out

Modern PCs use RIMMs or DIMMs (dual inline memory modules), older ones use SIMMs (single inline memory modules). They each have different size and pin configurations and SIMMs often need to be fitted in pairs of the same capacity.

What to get and why

Think carefully before you upgrade. Be sure the new hardware will make a real difference.

Upgrading memory

Installing extra RAM in your PC is one of the most cost-effective upgrades you can make. Windows Vista (Home Premium) needs at least 512Mb of RAM, but will perform much better with 1Gb. If you find that your PC operates very slowly, or that your hard disk light flickers constantly as you use your PC, you will almost certainly benefit from additional RAM.

Installing memory is easy. Remove the cover from the system unit and "clip" the chip into the appropriate slot (your PC's manual will show you the exact location). Make sure you fit the correct type of memory for your machine (see above). If in doubt, take your PC to a dealer to have your RAM installed correctly.

Sound cards

Although PCs have come equipped with perfectly adequate stereo sound cards for some time, the higher-quality devices now available provide a richer audio experience. High definition digital sound cards can provide a surround sound environment for the latest computer games or for setting up a digital home cinema. Some cards also create realistic instrument sounds and "acoustic environments" that make it seem as though sounds are coming from some distance away. They may also allow recording from several sources to enable mixing, which is useful for video editing, as well as for musicians.

Fitting a sound card is almost the same procedure as replacing your graphics card (see page 343). The sound card is easy to identify – it's the card your speakers are attached to at the rear of the system unit.

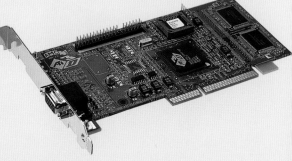

Graphics cards

Modern computers are sold with a graphics card that will handle most programs with ease. But if you work on very large scanned images, or if you want to run 3D games at top speed and high resolution, you might find that you need to upgrade to a faster graphics card.

Some graphics cards will also improve the picture when viewing DVD movies on your computer screen (see below), and may allow the use of a second monitor.

DVDs

Digital Versatile Disks (DVDs) store video as well as audio and computer data. A DVD can store over 2 hours of high-quality film footage whereas a CD-ROM can only accommodate just over 1 hour of low-quality video. As well as the ability to play DVD films and software, a DVD-ROM drive will also play existing audio CDs and CD-ROMs. There are a number of competing formats of writeable DVD that will allow the recording of between 4 and 17GB of data, much more than a recordable CD.

If you want to fit a DVD-ROM drive to an older system you should consider buying an "all-in-one" kit. This adds an MPEG-2 decoder which is required for DVD movies, unless you already have a suitable card. Check the manufacturer's specifications for your graphics card if you are unsure.

Adding a DVD-ROM player will expose any weaknesses in your current graphics and sound cards and you may need to make further upgrades to get the most out of the system.

Bright idea
Software manufacturers have a vested interest in encouraging you to buy products that might mean having to upgrade hardware. So, if in doubt, read product reviews in computer magazines for impartial advice on whether such an item is worth buying.

CD-RW Drive

Virtually all software supplied by computer manufacturers and software vendors comes on a CD or DVD. If you work with graphics or video on your Desktop you're going to want a device capable of holding hundreds of megabytes of data. A CD-RW (Re-Writeable) disk can be used over and over again and can hold up to 750MB of data. If you are upgrading your PC, get your dealer to install and configure the new drive for you.

Monitors

Buying a bigger or better-quality monitor won't make your PC run any faster, but in conjunction with a modern graphics card it will improve the quality of images you see on the screen. Most PCs are sold with 17 or 20-inch monitors. Buying a 24-inch monitor will make using your PC more fun, especially for games and DVD movies.

Hard disks

Modern programs take up a lot of hard disk space, especially if they use graphics, sound or videos. If your hard disk is nearly full, your PC will run more slowly (for guidance on how to check its capacity and available space, see page 52). Adding a new hard disk, and keeping your current one for extra storage, is one solution. Installing a new hard disk and making the necessary adjustments to the old hard disk is a job for a PC dealer.

New processors

You can even upgrade the central processing unit (CPU) of your PC. This is the main chip on the motherboard, through which signals between all the other circuit boards are routed. The latest Intel chips are very fast: A 1.86 GHz Core 2 Duo processor "thinks" up to 3,700 million times a second, and the latest chips work at 3.2 GHz or more. A faster processor will improve the speed of computer games and other processor-intensive activities such as video editing as well as making your computer simply "feel" faster. Buying a new processor can be expensive, and there may be a variety of options to consider. Your motherboard may also need upgrading to maintain compatibility. Your PC dealer will advise you

on the best match with your current setup and will be able to install it for you. If your PC is old, you may well be better off buying a whole new system.

Speakers

The standard speakers supplied with most PCs are adequate for normal use. However, if you want the loudest, Hi-Fi quality sounds, and you have a new sound card, you may want to upgrade your speakers. Changing speakers is easy – simply plug the new speakers into the sound card at the rear of the system unit.

Only buy speakers intended for a PC – they are specially shielded to stop their magnetic components from damaging your computer.

Problems after upgrading

Here's how to solve glitches encountered with new hardware

Upgrading your system with new hardware will rarely present you with a problem. Usually, after you connect additional hardware to your computer, Windows will automatically detect it and install the relevant software files for operating it. The process is designed to be straightforward and you should be able to complete it yourself. However, if you are concerned, you can ask a dealer to carry out the upgrade for you. If problems do arise, these may often stem from using an incorrect or outdated driver, and Windows Vista can resolve them with very little fuss. Faulty connections or incorrectly fitted cards also cause difficulties – don't be brutal, but fit all components and cables firmly, and ensure they are plugged into the correct jack or slot.

Troubleshooting new hardware

Take some precautions to help things run smoothly when you tackle problems with new hardware.

Before you begin
In most cases installing new hardware is a relatively straightforward process. But there are some important preparations you can make.
- Make a System Restore Point (see page 350 for details).
- Always check the requirements of your new hardware. For example, are you running the correct version of Windows? Do you have enough RAM? Do you need any other components – if you want to use a new widescreen monitor, for instance, can your graphics card drive it? If you want to add a new surround-sound speaker set, does your sound card actually support them?

- Always check the manufacturer's website to see if there are any updated drivers you should download. New software may have been tweaked soon after its release to improve compatibility.

Why upgrades can be a problem
Hardware and software upgrades can cause difficulties. With hardware you may have been supplied with an incorrect part – for instance, the wrong kind of RAM. Software glitches are more common and fall into two categories. The first is simply that the software you are adding is incompatible with your existing setup and therefore won't work – an example might be installing a program that's not compatible with Windows Vista. The second category is that the new software conflicts with existing programs and causes a system crash.

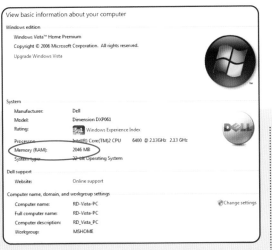

View basic information about your computer

Windows edition

Windows Vista™ Home Premium

Copyright © 2006 Microsoft Corporation. All rights reserved.

Upgrade Windows Vista

System

Manufacturer: Dell

Model: Dimension DXP061

Rating: Windows Experience Index

Processor: Intel(R) Core(TM)2 CPU   6400 @ 2.13GHz   2.13 GHz

Memory (RAM): 2046 MB

System type: 32-bit Operating System

Dell support

Website: Online support

Computer name, domain, and workgroup settings

Computer name: RD-Vista-PC   Change settings

Full computer name: RD-Vista-PC

Computer description: RD_Vista_PC

Workgroup: MSHOME

Memory problems

If your computer is unable to locate a new memory chip, it may be because it is not plugged in properly. To check the memory, go to the **Start** menu, right-click on **Computer** and click on **Properties** in the pop-up menu. The dialogue box will tell you how much memory your PC thinks it has. If your RAM memory has increased, your memory card is installed correctly.

If a series of error messages mentioning memory problems and "parity errors" are displayed, your memory may be of the wrong type. In that case, check with your PC manufacturer to learn the correct specification.

Hard drives

Your PC may not recognize a new hard drive. If so, take the computer back to your dealer. There are several possible solutions, but they require specialized knowledge.

External drives

If a new external drive – such as a hard disk, CD or DVD writer – is not recognized by your PC, first check that the cables are properly connected. Then ensure that any new driver card, such as a SCSI card, is correctly seated in its slot. If the problem persists, you may be using the wrong driver or have a hardware conflict (see page 348).

Sound cards

If you cannot get any sound from your computer after fitting a new sound card, first check that the card has been fitted properly, that your speakers are plugged in, and that all the connections have been made, including the cable from the CD-ROM to the sound card. If this doesn't solve the problem, or the sound from the speakers is very poor, you may have a driver problem.

Monitor problems

If your new monitor does not work, first check that it is properly plugged into the power supply and the graphics card. Check the settings by turning up the brightness and contrast controls. If it still doesn't work, connect another monitor that you know works (this may be your old one). If this one works, then the new monitor is defective and should be taken back to your dealer. If the other monitor doesn't work either, the fault lies with the graphics card.

Keywords

Expansion card This is a circuit board that adds certain functions to a computer. Expansion cards can be installed for improved or additional features. For example, a sound card gives a PC the ability to record and play sound.

Graphics cards

If the graphics card is not working at all, you won't see anything on your screen, but you should still hear your hard disk "whirring" when you turn on your PC. The most likely explanation is that the card is not connected properly. Switch the PC off and unplug it. Open the case and make sure the card is seated along its full length.

If your screen is "snowy" or your Windows display looks strange, you have a graphic driver problem. Make sure you use the latest driver – you can visit the card manufacturer's website to obtain the latest version.

A driver problem may also be the cause if the standard 640 x 480 with 16 colours is the only screen resolution available. To view the resolution settings, go to the **Start** button, click on **Control Panel**, then on **Personalization**, and select **Display Settings**. The current resolution and colour depth is displayed in the **Monitor** tab.

1. Generic PnP Monitor on NVIDIA GeForce 7900 GS

☑ This is my main monitor
☑ Extend the desktop onto this monitor

Resolution: Colors:

Low ——————High   Highest (32 bit)

1680 by 1050 pixels

How do I get the best display?   Advanced Settings...

'Plug and Play' upgrades

Most new hardware is described as "Plug and Play" and installs automatically, or with minimum involvement from you. Most Plug and Play devices are external and have a USB-type connector: you just plug them in and let Windows do the rest.

USB connection has replaced most earlier peripheral connections, and appears to be immune to the kind of hardware conflicts that plagued older systems. However, to ensure future Plug and Play compatibility it is essential that you keep your system up to date.

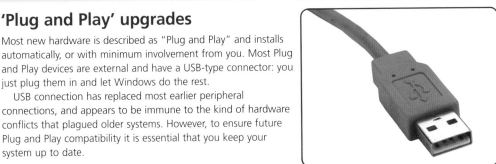

Bright idea

Always install the software supplied with your new device. Vista will probably find functioning drivers, either after a restart or by using the Add Hardware Wizard. However, the manufacturer's software may have better features and compatibility than the basic drivers supplied by Windows.

Troubleshoot using System Restore

If an upgrade results in a problem, here's one way of solving it

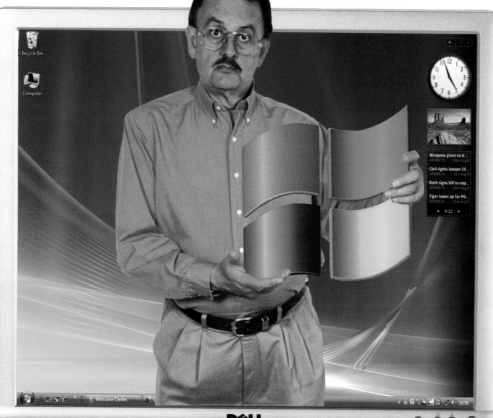

Windows Vista is designed to be user-friendly, versatile and robust. Even professional users making complex videos or animations find crashes are rare. However, Vista does not leave you on your own even if a crash does occur. Indeed, it has one of the most reliable and comprehensive recovery and diagnosis tools available: System Restore.

Use 'time travel' to fix problems

System Restore is a clever utility that lets you take "snapshots" of the state of your system at regular intervals. If something goes wrong when you install new software or hardware, you can use System Restore to quickly put your machine back into working condition – effectively stepping back in time to a point before your PC became unstable.

In addition, System Restore can be used for much more. With a little logical thought you can diagnose and track down the source of any problems so you can repair them.

The process involves trial and error – you start from a point where you know your PC works, add in suspect software and devices, making "System Restore Points" as you go, until your PC crashes again. You then roll back to your last "Restore Point." The chances are that the last piece of software or hardware you added caused the crash. Often problems are caused by a conflict between two programs. If this is the case, an additional Windows system tool called "Conflicts/Sharing" can help.

Using System Restore to diagnose a conflict

Your computer might crash for a variety of reasons, such as a power surge or failure. System Restore gets you up and running again very quickly. Persistent failures, however, may have deeper roots.

System Protection

Create a restore point

Type a description to help you identify the restore point. The current date and time are added automatically.

Pre-digital projector software installation

Create   Cancel

First steps

Before you install new hardware, use System Protection to create a Restore Point. Click on the **Start** button, then on **Control Panel**, then double-click on **System**. In the left pane click on **System Protection** (you may be asked for an administrator password or confirmation). In the System Properties dialogue box, ensure the System Protection tab is selected, then scroll down and click on **Create** next to "You can create a restore point right now for the disks selected above." In the System Protection dialogue box, give your Restore Point a name and click on **Create**. A progress bar displays. Click on **OK** when it has finished. Next install your new items. A subsequent crash indicates that one or more items, or their drivers, are causing problems.

Reverting to an earlier state

After a crash you can jump back to your Restore Point where the PC worked well. Open the System

Properties dialogue box as before, then click on **System Restore**, then on **Next**, and then choose which Restore Point you want to revert to. Continue selecting options and clicking on **Next** until you finally click on **Finish**. Windows Vista will automatically create Restore Points whenever you install files or hardware so, even if you haven't set many manual Restore Points yourself, you may have a long list to choose from.

Use the System Restore Wizard to move through subsequent Restore Points, restarting the PC each time, to locate the point at which problems develop.

System Restore

Choose a restore point
System Restore will not change or delete any of your documents and the process is reve

Click the restore point that you want to use and then click Next. How do I choose a restore p

Current time zone: GMT Daylight Time

Date and Time	Description
10/08/2007 13:34:46	Manual: Pre-digital projector software installation
10/08/2007 00:11:01	System: Scheduled Checkpoint
09/08/2007 00:00:02	System: Scheduled Checkpoint
08/08/2007 08:29:47	System: Scheduled Checkpoint
07/08/2007 08:13:54	System: Scheduled Checkpoint
06/08/2007 00:00:06	System: Scheduled Checkpoint

System Restore

Confirm your restore point

Time: 10/08/2007 13:34:46 (GMT Daylight Time)

Description: Manual: Pre-digital projector software installation

< Back   Finish

System Information

File   Edit   View   Help

System Summary	Resource	Device
Hardware Resources	I/O Port 0x00000000-0x00000CF7	PCI bus
Conflicts/Sharing	I/O Port 0x00000000-0x00000CF7	Direct memory access controller
DMA		
Forced Hardware	I/O Port 0x000003C0-0x000003DF	Intel(R) P965/G965 PCI Express F
I/O	I/O Port 0x000003C0-0x000003DF	NVIDIA GeForce 7900 GS
IRQs	I/O Port 0x000003C0-0x000003DF	Motherboard resources
Memory		

Focusing on the suspects

Once you have established the point at which your system became unstable, you can find out why. For hardware, check that all cards are firmly seated in their slots and that cables are securely attached. Then check that you have the latest drivers – either by visiting the manufacturer's website or by using the Add Hardware Wizard.

Go to the **Start** menu, click on **Control Panel**, then double-click on **Device Manager**, (you may be prompted for an administrator password or confirmation). Click on the plus sign next to the category matching your new device. Right-click on your device and choose **Update Driver Software** from the drop-down list. In the Update Driver Software window, select from the options presented. Follow the steps to search for an up-to-date driver for your device (you may need to connect to the Internet during the process). If these measures fail to remove the instability then go to **All Programs**, **Accessories**, **System Tools**, **System Information** then click on the plus sign next to **Hardware Resources**, then **Conflicts/Sharing** to see if your suspect device is clashing with any others. If it is clashing with a device you can do without, remove that item. If it is clashing with a built-in system component, contact the device's manufacturer for advice.

What System Restore doesn't do

System Restore is a clever piece of software. If you tried to do manually what it manages automatically you would spend long hours undertaking detailed work.

However, it gets better. A basic piece of software would simply take a snapshot of your system and, when a failure occurred, would revert to exactly that. System Restore doesn't. It recognizes that there will be many files that you *don't* want to dispense with – such as your recent Outlook e-mails and Word documents.

System Restore will not affect items like documents, e-mail messages, your Web browsing history, and passwords. All these are saved when you revert to an earlier state.

Furthermore, you can ensure that System Restore protects all your personal files, no matter what type they might be, by keeping them in the Documents folder. By default, System Restore leaves that untouched. Also, it does not overwrite or remove any files created with everyday programs such as Microsoft Word or Excel.

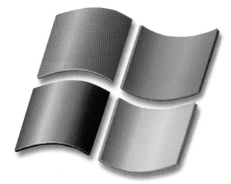

351

Windows won't shut down

This is what to do when your operating system freezes

Occasionally, Windows Vista will appear to freeze on screen – a condition known as "hanging." You will realize this may have happened when the cursor doesn't respond to your mouse movements, and you can't issue any keyboard commands.

If your computer has these symptoms but you're still not sure whether Windows has hung, press the **Num Lock** key (found above the numeric keypad on the right of the keyboard) on your keyboard a few times. If the Num Lock light above the key doesn't go on and off, then you know the system is definitely frozen.

The remedy for dealing with a hung program is fairly straightforward as you can still access Windows' help facilities. If Windows itself hangs however, it is a little more difficult to deal with. This is because Windows controls everything you do on your PC – including accessing help facilities. So if it seizes up, you will find you cannot carry out any of your normal actions.

First steps to closing Windows

When Windows hangs, you won't be able to restart by going to the Start menu as usual. Instead, press the **Ctrl + Alt + Del** keys together. You will then have several choices presented to you – either click on **Shut Down** immediately or, if you had programs running when Windows hung, shut them down and save any changes you made by selecting each in turn in the **Applications** panel and then clicking on **End Task**. A dialogue box will appear asking if you want to save changes. Click on **Save**. If you had Internet Explorer open, close this last as it doesn't have active documents.

Sometimes, closing programs in this manner can unfreeze Windows. If it doesn't, then restarting Windows usually does the trick. If the problem persists, however, run through the "Startup and Shutdown Troubleshooter" to diagnose and solve your problem.

Bright idea
If you cannot solve the problem using Windows troubleshooters you should consider reinstalling Windows. This is not as daunting a process as it sounds. See page 354 for more details.

Close-up
Whenever possible, make sure you restart or shut down your computer through the Start menu. This will mean that all current information is saved and that each program closes before Windows.

Use Troubleshooting to diagnose problems

If you often experience problems when you try to close Windows down, its own step-by-step Help facility will be able to give you guidance.

Use the Troubleshooter

Windows Vista is at the heart of your computer, underlying all the other programs you use. Because of this, the Startup and Shutdown options found under Troubleshooting may need to shut down your PC in order to examine and correct the files that govern your system's operation.

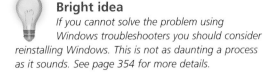

It is good practice to familiarize yourself with the troubleshooting options in advance, before beginning the real process. You will probably find that you want to print out the troubleshooting steps for later reference when the PC is restarting. If you have another PC available, also running Windows Vista, you could follow the instructions on that system as you examine your problem computer.

Don't panic

As with many Vista troubleshooters, this process covers quite complex areas and may at first appear too technical. Don't be put off; the Troubleshooters and related utilities are designed to give even a novice the help needed to repair their system, step by step. It is vitally important that you follow the Troubleshooter's instructions accurately, and also complete fully any process you begin.

What the Troubleshooter does

The path taken by the Troubleshooter will depend on your particular problem but, generally speaking, it will use the System Configuration Utility to launch Vista in different ways, aiming to detect damaged or conflicting software as it does. It is a "trial and error" process that will involve several restarts, each time loading or unloading particular batches of system

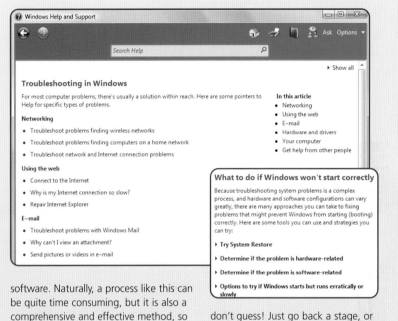

software. Naturally, a process like this can be quite time consuming, but it is also a comprehensive and effective method, so don't try to rush things. If you find yourself confused at any stage, or realize you have not printed out the necessary troubleshooting guidance in advance, don't guess! Just go back a stage, or even begin the process again – a stab in the dark at this level could cripple your machine and might force a complete system reinstall.

If all else fails

*If you cannot shut down Windows by pressing the **Ctrl** + **Alt** + **Del** keys, use the **Power on** button. Switch the PC off, wait 30 seconds and switch on again.*

Reinstalling Windows

If you can't repair a fault with the operating system, reload it

Reinstallation is the last resort for solving problems with Windows. The process leaves almost all your work unaffected, and returns Windows to its original state.

Complete reinstallation may be necessary if, for example, you keep experiencing serious crashes. All you need to begin reinstallation is your Windows Vista disk. For safety, back up your work before you start (see page 357).

If you do need to reinstall Windows, there are risks. It should only be tackled after you have tried all other remedies, and when you are sure that the problems relate to the Windows operating system, rather than an individual application. Windows Vista should reinstall without losing critical system data, such as Internet settings, but make a note of these first, just in case.

Generally you will be able to reinstall from the Vista disk as shown here. However, if Windows won't start up, you must restart with the disk in the drive (see page 356).

◄ IF REINSTALLATION FAILS

1 Put your Windows Vista disk into the drive. The disk will run automatically and begin leading you through the installation process. You will be asked to choose an option – either "Check compatibility online" or "Install now." Select **Install now** to completely replace your copy of Windows Vista.

Getting expert help

If you are worried about the reinstallation process, consider getting expert advice. For extra help during reinstallation, call the Microsoft technical support line or, if Windows came pre-installed, your PC's manufacturer.

Bright idea
*Making screen grabs is a good way to note system settings. Open the relevent panels, for instance, ISP settings. On your keyboard press **Print Screen**, then open a graphics program such as Paint and paste the grab into it. Print it out as a permanent record.*

Watch out
During the setup procedure you will be asked to enter your Windows Vista product key or serial number (you'll find this on your Windows installation disk sleeve or manual cover). Be careful to input the number correctly and not to lose it.

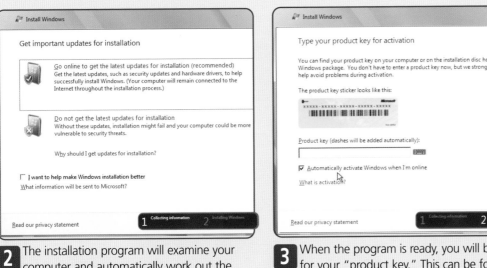

2 The installation program will examine your computer and automatically work out the best configuration for it. If you have an Internet connection, it will be used to check for Microsoft updates to Windows Vista – this means that you may get a newer system than that on your disk.

3 When the program is ready, you will be asked for your "product key." This can be found on the sleeve of your Windows Vista installation disk. If your PC came preloaded with Vista, your PC supplier should have given you this information. Check the box next to "Automatically activate Windows when I'm online." Then click on **Next**.

4 Much of the reinstallation time is taken up copying the vital Windows files to your PC. The time this takes will depend on the speed of your CD/DVD drive and hard drives, and on the speed of the computer. When finished you should see a "Thank you" message screen with a Start button. Click on **Start** to reboot your PC.

Explorer favourites

Internet Explorer is tightly integrated with Windows Vista – so much so that it is reinstalled at the same time as the operating system. Losing your Explorer favourites can be frustrating, so don't be caught out, and preserve your data first. In Explorer go to **File** and click on **Import and Export** to open the Import/Export Wizard. Follow the onscreen instructions to export your favourites. For added safety, export them to a file and save it on a CD. After your system reinstall simply insert the disk, open Internet Explorer and go to the Import/Export Wizard again and this time import the file. Your favourites will appear as before.

Watch out
To restart your computer from the Windows Vista installation disk, your computer must be configured to do so. Check with your manufacturer if you are unsure.

How to reinstall when Windows won't load

If Windows won't start up, you need to start from your Windows Vista installation disk and deal with any problems from there. Here's how.

If you bought a copy of Windows Vista and installed it on a PC yourself, the disk you used will contain all the files required to start Windows again. In addition, a new feature called Startup Repair is accessible from the disk. This can fix some problems, such as missing or damaged system files that might prevent Windows from starting correctly. There are also some other tools stored under the System Recovery Options menu, that can help in repairing or restoring data.

If you bought your computer with Windows Vista pre-installed, the Startup Repair option may have been saved to your hard disk. In some cases, manufacturers do not then also add it to the reinstallation disk they provide. If this is the case, follow the "Pre-installed method" outlined on the right of this panel.

If you have a hardware failure, Startup Repair will not be able to fix it. However, it will give a summary of the problem and links to contact information for support. Your computer manufacturer might also offer additional assistance and information.

If you upgraded to Windows Vista from XP, you should have a boot disk (sometimes called a startup disk). This "boot disk" – generally a CD – will have been provided with your PC and holds copies of the Windows startup files that were installed on your PC. If the files on your hard disk become corrupt, you should use this boot disk to get Windows started again.

Starting up from your installation disk

If Windows doesn't load normally when you switch on your PC you should be able to start your system from the original Windows Vista installation disk by placing it in your disk drive before starting the computer. Your PC will automatically detect that a disk is present in the disk drive and attempt to use the files held on it, allowing you to access the Startup Repair recovery tool.

To start the process, place the disk in the drive and then click on the **Start** button, then on the arrow next to the "Padlock" button, then on **Restart**. If prompted, press any key to start Windows from the installation disk. Choose your language settings and then click on **Next**. Click on **Repair your computer**. Select the operating system you want to repair – you can check this on your installation disk box – and then click on **Next**. Finally, on the System Recovery Options menu, click on **Startup Repair**. During this process you may be prompted to make choices as the program tries to fix the problem. You may also find that it is necessary to restart your computer during or at the end of Startup Repair.

Finally, it is important to keep your Windows Vista installation disk in a safe place as reinstalling the system can often solve PC problems.

Using the pre-installed method

If Startup Repair is already on your hard disk, try this method. Restart the computer and, as soon as the power comes on, press and hold the **F8** key until the Windows Advanced Options menu appears. This must happen before the Windows logo appears. If it doesn't appear, restart the computer and try again.

When you see the menu, press the "down arrow" to highlight "Repair Your Computer" then press **Return**. Select your language and click on **Next**. Log in as a user with administrative rights and click on **OK**. From the Choose a recovery tool menu click on **Startup Repair**. Once completed, click on **Finish** and then on **Restart**.

Give your hard disk a checkup

If your computer is having difficulty in loading Windows, you might have a hard disk problem. Use Windows Vista's built-in disk utility to examine and repair any flaws.

Go to the **Start** button, click on **Computer** and then right-click on your hard-disk drive – normally **C:**. Click on **Properties** and then on the **Tools** tab. In the Error-checking panel, click on **Check Now**. In the next panel, click in the boxes next to "Automatically fix file system errors" and "Scan for and attempt recovery of bad sectors," then click on **Start**. The utility will ask if you wish to schedule the disk examination for the next time you start your computer – click on **Yes**. Then restart your machine and let the utility check your disk.

A full check will take some time – do not cancel the examination half way through. If it does find errors, follow the onscreen instructions and you should be able to make repairs.

Close-up
For the earliest PCs, floppy disks were suitable for backing up data; later, Zip disks were used. Today, recordable CDs, DVDs and external hard disks have taken on the role of backup devices. For larger networks, fast tape drives or banks of hard disks are used to store data.

Making and storing backups

Windows Vista Backup and Restore Center is automatically installed, but you need to tell it where to place your copied files and schedule it to do its work automatically.

Initiating Backup

Click on the **Start** button, then on **Control Panel**. Now double-click on **Backup and Restore Center**.

The Backup or Restore files options window will open – click on the **Back up files** button. If a "User Account Control" permissions message appears, click on **Continue**. In the "Back Up Files" window, select where you want to save your backup from the drop-down menu under "On a hard disk, CD or DVD." If your hard disk has been partitioned, then that will be the first option in the list, here "RECOVERY (D:)". Make your

selection and click on **Next**. You will then be presented with a checklist of options covering the types of files you might want to back up. Click in the box to the left of an option to add a tick and select it. Click in a ticked box, to deselect. When you have finished, click on **Next**.

Set a schedule

Backing up can be a slow process – many people leave their PC on and set it to back up during the night or at the weekend. In the final window, select the frequency

of automating your backups, using the drop-down options next to "How often," "What day" and "What time." Click on **Save settings and start backup** to start the process. If this is the first time you have backed up, Windows will create a new full backup. For later backups, updated or new files will simply be added on.

Choose a backup medium

Before you back up you need to decide what you want to save and how often. It's worth planning in advance because you might need to buy new hardware or storage media. Your circumstances will probably govern your choices; for instance, how critical is your data? If you're running a small business it is vital to protect accounts on a day-by-day basis. If, on the other hand, you use your PC for creating a quarterly newsletter, then a weekly backup might be adequate. Also, how much time do you wish to devote to this?

Use a CD for data under 700MB or DVD disk if the amount of data to be backed up is less than 4.7GB. However, these options are still not large enough to be able to back up even the basic files installed by Windows, so if you want to back up your entire system you will need to invest in an external hard disk of at least equal capacity to your existing one. Click on **Computer** in the **Start** menu to check on the size of your hard disk and how much space you have used. External hard disks are available with capacities of more than 80GB – large enough to store multiple backups.

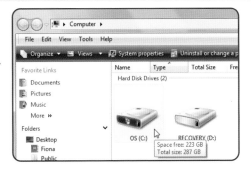

My program has crashed

If an application stops responding to your commands, here's what to do

When a program crashes, your mouse pointer will appear as an hourglass and you will not be able to type or access menus. It may seem that your PC has stopped working – but if the hourglass pointer changes back to an arrow when you move it onto your Desktop, this means Windows is still working. Windows runs each program in its own protected memory space, so problems with one active program do not usually affect the others.

It is possible to exit the crashed program using keyboard commands, and then to open it again. If you have not saved changes in the document you were working on before the crash, you will lose some of your work when you exit the program. This is why it is vital to make a habit of saving your work regularly, and why it's also worth remembering to save work in other programs that are running.

Closing a crashed program

When a program crashes you won't be able to close it in the usual way. In this case, you should press the **Ctrl + Alt + Del** keys simultaneously.

This brings up a list of options, the last one of which is "Windows Task Manager." Click on it and, under the "Applications" tab, you will see a list of all the programs currently running on your PC. Under the "Processes" tab you'll also see system programs that run invisibly on your computer. Under the Applications tab, scroll down the list until you see the name of the program that's crashed – it will be labelled "Not Responding." Click on it to highlight it and then click on the **End Task** button.

The crashed program window should then close. If it doesn't, another dialogue box will open, giving you the option of either waiting for the program to close by itself or terminating it immediately by clicking on the **End Task** button. Windows Vista will not usually ask you to restart your machine but, if more than one program has crashed, you should probably start up again.

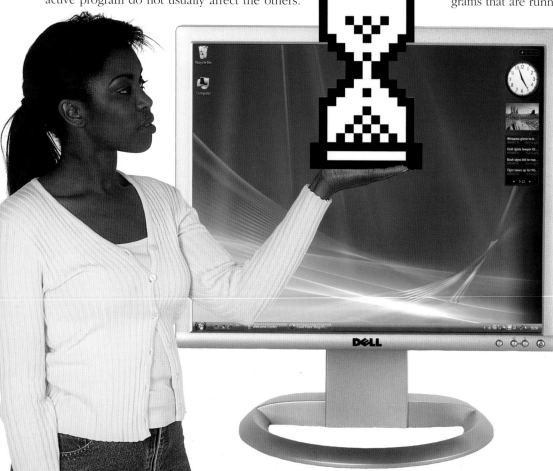

Close-up
*If you cannot exit from the crashed program by pressing the **Ctrl** + **Alt** + **Del** keys, you must press, and hold down, the **Power on** button on your system unit until it shuts down. Wait a minute and then press the **Power on** button again.*

Bright idea
*Some programs allow you to save data automatically at set intervals. In Word, for example, click on the **Office** button and select **Word Options**. In the left pane, click on **Save**. In the right pane under "Save documents," click in the box by "Save AutoRecover information every." Now set a time – say, 15 minutes – from the drop-down box and click on **OK**.*

What to do when a program crashes

Vista records and reports the problem and searches online for a solution. When you restart, check your PC and reinstall any troublesome programs.

How to check for problem solutions

When problems occur and a program stops working or responding, Windows creates a problem report so you can check for a solution.

Go to the **Start** button and click on **Control Panel**, then double-click on **Problem Reports and Solutions**. In the first window, any solutions already found are listed under "Solutions to install." Click on **See problems to check** from the left panel to display all problems recorded but not yet reported, the reason

why the software stopped working, and the date and time it occurred. Click on **View details** in the last column for more information.

Click in the tick box next to a recorded incident, then on **Check for solutions**. A progress window appears as an online solution to the problem is sought.

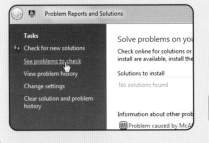

Reinstalling a problem program

If a program persistently crashes, the easiest remedy is to reinstall it. To do this, place the program's installation disk in the drive, click on **Computer**, then double-click on the CD/DVD drive icon. A warning message will appear asking if you will allow an unidentified program to access your computer. Click on **Allow** to confirm. Click on "Setup" or a similar start icon or link. Most programs will install over an older version of themselves without losing any alterations.

If this doesn't solve the problem, uninstall the program first. To do this, go to the **Start** button, click on **Control Panel**, then under "Programs" click on **Uninstall a program**. Select the relevant program from the list and follow the onscreen instructions. Restart your PC and install the program from scratch.

Automatic cleanup

When a program crashes it can leave behind temporary files (with filenames ending in ".TMP") that are usually deleted when you exit the program normally. Windows Vista comes with a tool called Disk Cleanup that is designed to remove these unwanted files.

Go to the **Start** button and select **All Programs**, **Accessories**, **System Tools** and then **Disk Cleanup**. In the dialogue box that appears, select either "My files only" or "Files from all users on this computer," depending on whether you wish to tidy up your files only or all those on the PC. In the next box, select the drive you want to clean (C: is usually your hard disk) from the drop-down menu and click on **OK**. A progress bar shows how much space can be gained. Select your options from the "Files to delete" panel (make sure only the items you want to delete are checked) then click on **OK**.

I can't read a document

Find out how to open and read seemingly impenetrable files

As a rule, if you receive a file from another source, such as the Internet, and you don't have the program in which it was created, you will not be able to open the file.

However, there are ways around this problem. Sometimes your software may recognize the type of document and be able to convert it. If not, you can ask the sender to supply it in a "neutral format." For example, a text document saved as "Text Only" can be read by any word-processing program (though this "no-frills" format strips all text formatting). Here we show you some other ways you can access "unreadable" files.

Find out what type of file it is (word processor, spreadsheet, etc.), which program created it, and if it can be sent to you in a different format.

▶ BEFORE YOU START

1 If Windows doesn't know how to open a particular file, it displays it as a plain icon. Double-click on the icon and in the Open With dialogue box that appears, select a program to open your file from the list offered to you and then click on **OK**.

A quick guide to file extensions

File extensions are letter combinations (usually three) that indicate which program created a file. To display the extensions on your files, go to the **Start** menu, then **Documents**. In the **Tools** menu select **Folder Options**. In the **View** tab, untick the "Hide extensions for known file types" box. Some common extensions are:

● **Text file** .asc .doc .htm .html .msg .txt .wpd
● **Image file** .bmp .eps .gif .jpg .pict .png .tif
● **Sound file** .au .mid .ra .snd .wav

Just as Windows sometimes cannot open a document created on another operating system, other systems can have difficulty reading files created in Windows. To reduce the risk of this happening, save documents in a "Plain Text" or "Rich Text" format. To do this, scroll down the "Save as type" menu in the Save As dialogue box and select one of these formats. Note that this will mean you will lose any complex formatting.

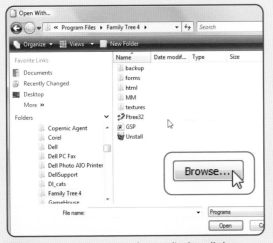

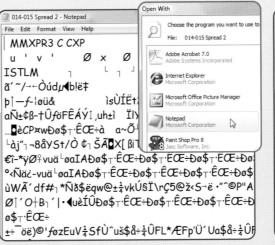

2 Windows does not always display all the programs installed on your PC in the Open With dialogue box. If you would like to choose a program that isn't shown, click on **Browse** to see all those in your "Program Files" folder. Scroll through and select from the list, then click on **Open**.

3 If the file won't open with the program you have selected, try another one – Notepad is able to open many types of file. However, you may still see an unreadable mass of code and symbols. If this happens, close the file without saving.

4 Another option is to launch a program such as Microsoft Office Word and try to open the file by going to the **Office** button and clicking on **Open**. Navigate to the folder containing the file, then choose **All Files** from the file type list. Select the file and click on **Open**. If this works, go to **Save As** to save the file in the appropriate format.

Opening compressed documents

To reduce the amount of space a file takes up on a hard disk or as an e-mail attachment, many people "compress" files. If you receive a compressed file (with the file extension ".zip") you will need the same compression program in order to decompress it and then open it. WinZip is a common compression program. You can download it from the Internet at www.winzip.com free of charge.

If you don't have the relevant program to decompress a file, ask the sender to mail it again in an uncompressed version.

I'm getting error messages

What to do when **your computer** warns you there's a problem

When your PC has difficulty carrying out one of your commands it will display an error message. Generally, error messages include a description of the error, a possible reason for it and, if appropriate, a way to resolve the problem. Some error messages are easier to understand than others.

Do not ignore error messages. If you do, you may lose your work or, at worst, make your computer unusable. Follow the onscreen advice, which may mean exiting from the program you are using or restarting your computer. There are many error messages – the ones described here are the most common.

Storage problems

One of the most common error messages appears when Windows detects that your hard disk is getting full and storage space is becoming limited. This can seriously affect the performance of your PC and may prevent you saving files. It will also limit the amount of space System Restore can use to back up critical data and will disable Virtual Memory.

If "Not enough disk space" messages appear, use Disk Cleanup to delete unnecessary files and create more space. Click on the **Start** button and select **All Programs**, **Accessories**, then **System Tools** and **Disk Cleanup**. In the Disk Cleanup Options dialogue box select from "My files only" or "Files from all users on this computer." Then in the Drive selection dialogue box select the drive to clean and click on **OK**. Disk Cleanup will then calculate how much space can be regained. Click in the tick box next to the items you want to delete and click on **OK**. Finally, click on **Delete Files** to confirm your choice.

Understanding error messages

Although the wording may vary, most error messages will fall into one of these categories.

Error messages caused by hardware

● Hardware conflicts

With the stability and improvement of Windows Vista over older versions of Windows, and the advent of "Plug and Play" devices, hardware conflicts should now be limited. However, if your hardware seems to be working properly but you still get error messages, a defective or conflicting driver may be the cause. (See page 351 for possible solutions.)

If your computer freezes – or "hangs" – when you try to use a particular device, or if a device refuses to work, this, too, could be the result of a hardware conflict which a new driver might remedy.

● Problems with your memory?

Memory problems can cause your computer to lose information or stop working. If you get an error message, Windows will ask you if you want to run the "Memory Diagnostics Tool" immediately or the next time you start your computer.

Make your selection and follow the prompts. You will need to press **F10** to start the test; it's best to keep the tool's default settings. If the Memory Diagnostics Tool detects problems, contact your computer or memory manufacturer for information on how to resolve them.

You can start the Memory Diagnostics Tool manually, if you wish. To do this, go to the **Start** button and click on **Control Panel**, then on **Administrative Tools** then double-click on **Memory Diagnostics Tool**.

Error messages caused by software

● This file is being used by another user

This occurs when you try to open the same document in different programs at the same time. You can either close down the document before opening it in a second program, let Windows tell you when the file is available for editing, or open a Read-only copy.

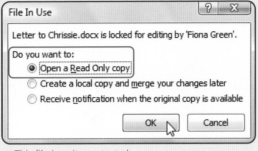

● This file is write protected

You cannot delete, rename or sometimes even copy write-protected files. To remove the protection, right-click on the file's icon, go to **Properties** and uncheck the box next to **Read-only** in the General tab.

● Error Deleting File

This happens when you try to delete a file that is open. Close the file and then try to delete it again.

● Sharing Violation/You don't have permission to open this file

This can be caused by having a file open in two programs at the same time, or by a program trying to open a file that is either corrupted or missing.

● File Corruption

Sometimes, a file gets "mangled" by Windows. The best solution is to replace it from your backup copy.

● Missing or Out-of-Date Files

This message appears if somebody deletes a file by mistake, or if a program overwrites, deletes or renames a file as it is installed or uninstalled. If the problem is with a program, you need to reinstall it.

What to do if you cannot understand messages

● Windows Vista's Help and Support Center will explain most error messages and suggest solutions. Click on the **Start** button and select **Help and Support** from the right-hand menu.

● Save any opened files. Shut down the program that prompted the message, then restart it.

● If the message reappears, shut down the program (and any others running) and restart your computer (go to the **Start** button, select **Restart**).

● If the message occurs again, make a note of what it says and seek expert advice. If the error is prompted by Windows rather than a program, contact your PC dealer. If a program is causing the problem, contact the software manufacturer.

Use Event Viewer

Event Viewer is an important diagnostic tool that runs in the background and logs information about any hardware and software problems. While the tool cannot remedy the problems, the information can be useful when discussing the issues with a PC engineer or the manufacturer.

Go to the **Start** button, click on **Control Panel**, then double-click on **Administrative Tools**. Finally, double-click on **Event Viewer**.

Under the "Level" column, log entries for serious problems are displayed with an "!" in a red circle, warnings appear with an "!" in a yellow triangle, and information entries have an "i" in a blue circle.

Using antivirus software

Run specialized packages to preserve or restore your PC's health

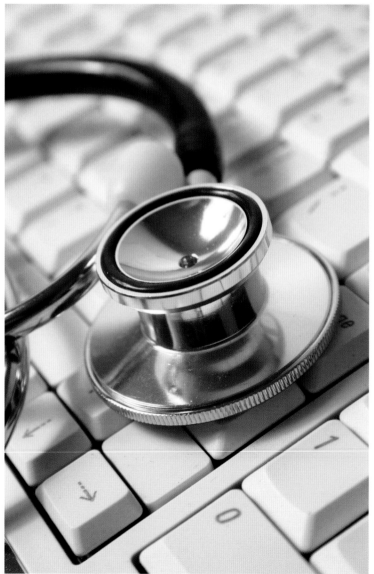

Although the spread of computer viruses is often reported in the media, the problem is not as widespread or difficult to deal with as most people think. Simple preventative steps (see page 56) will help you reduce the risk of getting a virus and put you in a better position to eradicate any that you do get.

Antivirus software

There are many packages available. In general, they detect viruses on storage disks, such as CDs, and files that have been downloaded from the Internet. Such programs stop viruses from infecting your PC in the first place.

Most antivirus packages can be set up to scan every item downloaded to your system, but it's also a good idea to run the program every week or so to examine your whole system.

If a virus does make its way onto your computer, the software will alert you by bringing up a warning onscreen. At this point you must use the disinfecting function in the antivirus program, which will attempt to repair the infected file. This is normally a straightforward process, performed by following the onscreen instructions given by the program. Sometimes, the infected item cannot be repaired. In this case you should delete the file or, in the case of a program, uninstall and then replace it.

Keeping up to date

It is vital to keep your software defences up to date. This doesn't mean having to buy new software. The best antivirus packages let you stay up to date by downloading new information from their websites. Check your software for details on how to do this. It is best to set the software to do this automatically.

> *A good antivirus package such as McAfee VirusScan or Norton AntiVirus is essential. Ask at a computer store for advice on which package is best for your needs.*
>
> ▶ **BEFORE YOU START**

Bright idea
There are several useful websites that offer information about viruses. Some also provide software updates to help you defend your PC. Try www.symantec.com/security_response/index.jsp and click on **information for home users**.

Keyword
Virus A virus is a computer program whose sole purpose is to get into your PC and cause unwanted and unexpected behaviour, such as erasing files, displaying messages and attacking your PC's setup.

Make the software do the work

Without the right software you might not know your PC is infected until it's too late.

The main types of viruses that are likely to infect your computer are "file viruses," "macro viruses" and "boot and partition sector viruses." Each one attacks different parts of your computer, including your hard disk, programs and document files. Some web-sites may also place small applets (mini-programs) on your system that can have similar highly destructive effects.

Stopping viruses at source

McAfee VirusScan, part of McAfee Security Center, is typical of the effective antivirus programs now available. You can configure VirusScan to examine every file downloaded or read from all forms of recordable media, such as CDs and DVDs. It continually checks for known viruses and other harmful software on your system and will alert you to any it finds.

You can also set the software to regularly check on the Internet for software updates, so you will always be protected against new viruses. If an infected file is located it is "quarantined" on your system and you will be notified of the best steps to take.

Disinfecting your system once a virus is found

If your software detects a virus you should use the disinfecting or cleaning function in the software to remove or isolate it. If it is a new virus, some antivirus programs may even send the file to their laboratory for examination.

If an infected file cannot be repaired then it will generally be renamed to prevent it being used again. You will then have the option of deleting it. Files that you delete may need to be replaced. If these are system files (the files that make up Windows) then you will definitely need to do so.

To reinstall program software, see page 359; or to reinstall Windows, see page 354.

Viruses affect computers in different ways. Some contain messages that appear automatically on screen.

Worst-case scenario

With proper use of an antivirus program, you should be able to detect and remove any viruses before they cause really serious damage. Without taking such precautions it is possible, although not likely, that a virus could destroy the contents of your hard disk.

In such a case you will have to restore the hard disk from your original system disks. This is like restoring your computer to its original state, as it was on the day you bought it. The original settings for it will therefore be restored, but you will probably have lost all your documents, pictures, e-mails, Internet favourites and data files.

Hit back at hackers

Top-level security packages like Norton's and McAfee's also protect your computer against the threat of hacking – unauthorized entry to your machine using the Internet. With the spread of "always on" broadband connections, hacking has become much easier and more widespread. Setting up a "firewall" – a barrier to hackers – is simple with these two products. Persistent attackers can also be tracked, providing evidence for possible prosecution.

Windows security

Windows Vista provides its own firewall to help protect your computer against malevolent attacks from others on the Internet. To check it is activated, click on the **Start** button, select **Control Panel**, then double-click on **Security Center** and make sure "Firewall" is marked "On." There is an automatic updating facility to ensure that you receive all critical updates and "Malware protection" guards against malicious attacks from spyware and viruses.

My text doesn't look right

If your fonts look odd on screen or when printed, the solution is easy

Font problems are rare nowadays, largely because the leading software developers have come together to create new user-friendly technologies such as TrueType and OpenType. Windows Vista's default fonts should display and print faultlessly.

Difficulties only arise when additional fonts are installed either by other software programs, or manually, from a free CD for instance. You may find that a font that looks fine on screen prints badly, or not at all. Alternatively your screen display could be terrible, but a document might print superbly.

Don't worry – by using Windows Vista's troubleshooters and utilities you can solve most typographical problems with ease.

Do you have a problem?

If a font looks strange on screen or when printed, first check whether there really is a problem. Some fonts are specifically designed to look unusual. Wingdings and Zapf Dingbats are made up entirely of quirky characters.

To check how a font should look, click on the **Start** button, select **Control Panel**, then double-click on **Fonts**. All the fonts installed on your PC will be listed. Double-click on the font in question to bring up a sample of what it should look like. If the sample text shown looks the same as the text in your document, you have simply chosen an unusual-looking font.

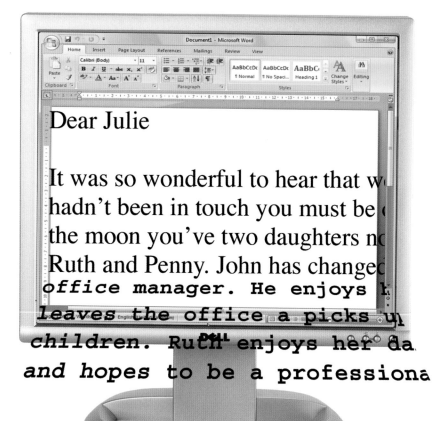

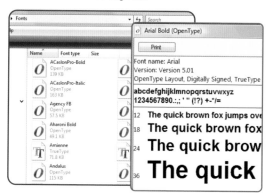

The fonts folder icon view indicates what kind of fonts you have; OpenType and TrueType should predominate, but you may also have some PostScript fonts. PostScript fonts need special software – Adobe Type Manager (ATM) – to display correctly. If a PostScript font's screen appearance is irregular or jagged, check the website at www.adobe.com/downloads/ for the latest version of ATM.

Bright idea
*Windows Vista has a great Printing Troubleshooter. Click on the **Start** button and select **Help and Support**. Then type "printing" into the search bar at the top and press **Return**. In the results list click on **Troubleshoot printer problems**.*

Solving font software problems

Understanding what different font files do and where they are located is the first stage of problem-solving.

Types of font

The type of font you are using may affect the way it appears on screen or when printed. TrueType fonts are designed to print as they look on screen. This is also the case with OpenType fonts, which are in fact a newer kind of TrueType file.

| OpenType | TrueType | PostScript |

PostScript fonts and printer-only fonts can look slightly different onscreen to how they appear when printed. PostScript fonts used on a PC that does not have Adobe Type Manager installed will often display jagged edges, particularly at larger point sizes, (see left).

Some printers (notably laser printers) use printer fonts, which are stored on the printer itself. Problems can develop when the font you are using onscreen, and its equivalent on the printer, don't match. To fix this, most printer driver options will allow you to override the printer fonts. Click on the **Start** button, then **Control Panel**, and double-click on **Printers**. Right-click on your printer driver icon and select **Printing Preferences**. All printers are different but you should find an option marked **Download as softfont**. Select that, or check the box next to it, and from that point on your printer will use the same fonts as in your documents.

Common difficulties

You have been e-mailed a Word document that prints badly

Look in the font box on the Ribbon to note the name of the font that prints incorrectly. Then click in a section of text that doesn't use that font, or add a few words in a system font such as "Arial." Return to the font box, click in it and scroll down to check whether the name of the problem font appears. If it doesn't, then the font is not installed on your system. Either install the font on your system (see right) or highlight the text and select a new font from the font box.

You can't print the Euro symbol

Planning a trip? Doing business across the pond? If so, you will at some point need to use the Euro symbol. On a standard keyboard hold down the **Alt** key and type **0128** on the numeric keypad. Older font groups may not have the sign, but you can go to adobe's Euro Font page at www.adobe.com/type/eurofont.html to get fonts with only the Euro symbol.

Managing fonts

Removing fonts

Fonts may become damaged, or non-standard fonts may have been generated. If all documents using a particular typeface have problems, remove the font. Click on the **Start** button, select **Control Panel**, then double-click on **Fonts**. Right-click on the suspect font and select **Delete**. Your system will ask "Are you sure you want to permanently delete this file?" Click on **Yes**.

Installing fonts

To install or reinstall a font, first insert the disk or CD-ROM containing it. Click on the **Start** button and select **Control Panel**, then double-click on **Fonts**. On the **File** menu click **Install New Font**. In the Add Fonts dialogue box click on the arrow beside the "Drives" box and select the drive containing new fonts. In the "Folders" section, scroll through and double-click on the folder that contains the font. Click on your chosen font, then on **Install**.

Viewing foreign text

Multilingual users will probably want to view foreign websites – in the past any language using unusual characters or pictograms, such as Russian or Japanese, could cause problems. Nowadays, Internet Explorer, used in conjunction with Windows Vista, will breeze through any linguistic complexities, even in reading "right-to-left" languages.

In most cases Windows Vista will automatically set up your system to view international texts such as Japanese, Russian or Hebrew. If it hasn't, when you load a Web page with unusual characters in Internet Explorer you will see the Language pack installation dialogue box. This will ask you to install the required files. If the files are not available on your installation disk, Explorer may suggest downloading them from the Microsoft website.

Problems with passwords

You can unlock your computer even if you forget your password

In Windows Vista it's easy to let several people use the same PC, each with their own set of files and folders, and preferences for Windows' appearance. You can set a password to protect your files, but the level of security is not so great that forgetting a password becomes a disaster. As long as a user with administration rights knows their password, they can get you back in. You can also create a special password

reset disk that gives you access. Even if you have not created the reset disk, technical support helplines can talk you through relatively simple ways to get back into your PC.

If you need real security for your work, there are plenty of reasonably priced programs you can buy that offer much stronger password protection. However, they are not as forgiving if you forget your password!

Create a password reset disk
Use Windows Vista's utilities to create this handy backup device.

Getting started
Once you have started a new user account, and chosen a password, you can create a password reset disk. This disk can be used at a later stage if your forget your log-in password.

Click on the **Start** button, select **Control Panel**, then double-click on **User Accounts**. In the panel on the left you will see **Create a password reset disk** – you can only create a disk for the user currently logged in. If you don't see it, shut down your PC and log in again.

Clicking on **Create a password reset disk** brings up the Forgotten Password Wizard. Insert a blank CD or DVD or use a Flash drive to store the file that will be created. Now follow the Wizard's instructions to create a disk that you can use as a "key" to unlock your PC.

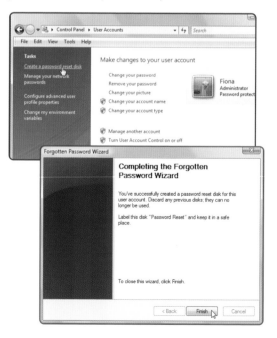

Bright idea
If you need tighter security check out the utilities at www.tucows.com/software.html?t2=1899. However, take care. If you forget a password for a high-security program you risk being locked out of your PC.

Watch out
Using one password for many applications is convenient, but it means that a single breach of security could render all your protection useless.

What to do if you forget your password
There is no need to panic if you forget your password. Load your password reset disk and you'll be up and running in no time.

If you have a reset disk
Simply start your PC as usual and when asked for your password type in a few random letters, then click on the blue circled **white arrow**. When you see the message "The user name or password is incorrect," click on **OK**. Your login window will open again displaying your "Password Hint" and the "Reset password..." link. If your hint does not remind you of your password, click on the link **Reset password...** and follow the instructions onscreen. At this point you will be asked to insert the reset disk that you have previously created.

If you don't have a reset disk
There are other ways to enter a password-protected system. If another user has an account set up on the machine you use, ask them to log on then go to **Start**, **All Programs**, **Accessories**, then **Run**, and enter "control userpasswords2," then click on **OK**. Click on your User Name, and then click on **Reset Password** and choose a new password. The user that does this, however, must have administrator rights to be able to change passwords.

Forget your passwords safely
Even a relatively light user of a computer and the Internet soon finds that they build up a long list of passwords and usernames for banking, shopping and logging on to websites. However, there are shareware programs (ones you can download and try before you buy) that can help out. The programs store all your passwords for you, and are activated by one single password – the only one that you will have to remember.

Two of the best-known utilities are Password Tracker, available from www.clrpc.com, and Password Agent from www.moonsoftware.com. Both programs are modestly priced and each is approved by Microsoft.

Shortcut	User ID	Password
http://www.chicagot... C:\Program Files\In...	lindasman	cubs&sox
http://www.irnet.co... C:\Program Files\M... C:\Program Files\M...	david87	Gv4z?%W
http://edit.my.yaho... C:\QUICKENW\QW...	dave	linda457 mYfinancE
http://www.digits.co... C:\WINNT\Profiles...	dave@t... davidsp	gFtCwo4l dave-linda

Beef up security
If you want to hide your files and applications from prying eyes, at home or in the office, there are a number of programs which give differing levels of protection.

User management systems replicate Windows Vista's own password-protected log-in system, but add much tougher controls. Passwords are non-recoverable and different levels of access can be permitted for different users. System use can also be monitored and recorded.

File and folder encryption systems do not block users out – they simply allow you to encrypt specific parts of your disk so that no one can read your personal files and folders. Different levels of encryption are available – the strongest is practically unbreakable, so be sure to remember your password. Travellers please note: the possession and use of strong encryption software is lawful throughout North America and the EU, but is strictly controlled in much of the Middle East, the former USSR, China and other countries.

Password Reset Wizard

Welcome to the Password Reset Wizard

If you forget the password for this user account and are unable to log on, this wizard helps you reset the password.

Note: To use this wizard, you must have first created a password reset disk.

Password for Fiona
To change the password for Fiona, click Reset Password.

[Reset Password...]

To continue, click Next.

< Back   Next >   Cancel

Tips for effective passwords
An effective password is one that cannot be easily guessed. For this reason make sure your password adheres to several of the following:
● It is at least six characters long.
● It contains a mix of capital letters and lowercase letters.
● It contains at least one digit or special character such as a punctuation mark.
● It cannot easily be guessed (for example, do not use your child's, spouse's or pet's name).
● It is changed frequently.

A

Accessories Mini-programs, such as Calculator, Notepad or Wordpad, built into Windows to perform simple tasks.

Active window The window you are working in. To activate a window, click on it and it will jump to the front of your screen, in front of any other open windows. See *Window*.

ADSL Asymmetric Digital Subscriber Line. A way of getting broadband Internet access through a normal telephone line. See *Broadband*.

Aero New ways of viewing open documents in Vista, with a 3D display and "thumbnails" above the filename shown on the Taskbar.

All-in-one (AIO) A single hardware device which does the job of a photocopier, scanner, printer and fax machine.

Alt key A key on the keyboard that gives commands when pressed in combination with other keys.

Application program A piece of software that performs specific kinds of tasks. For example, Microsoft Word is a word processing application program. See *Program*, *Software*.

Archive To transfer files to a separate storage system, such as a CD-R.

Attachment A file such as a picture or spreadsheet that is sent with an e-mail message.

Audio file A file containing a digital recording of sound. In Windows, audio files usually have ".wma" after their filename. See *Digital*.

B

Backup A duplicate copy of a file, made in case of accidental loss or damage to the original. Backups can be made onto a second hard drive connected to the computer, or on removable media like CD-Rs.

BIOS Basic Input/Output System. Instructions that control the computer's hardware at the most basic level. The BIOS tells the operating system which hardware to expect to come into operation and how it is arranged.

Bit The smallest unit of computer memory, Bit is a contraction of "binary digit." Its value can be only 0 or 1. All computers use the binary system to process data.

Bitmap An onscreen image made up of tiny dots, or pixels. See *Pixel*.

Blog A diary or log that you store on a website and update regularly. Blogs can include photos as well as links to other blogs or websites, and are usually free to set up.

Boot or **boot up** To turn on the computer.

Broadband High-speed Internet access via either an ADSL, cable or satellite connection.

Bug An accidental error or fault in a computer program. Bugs may cause programs to crash, which can lead to data loss.

Button An onscreen image that can be clicked on using the mouse. Clicking on a button performs a function, such as opening a dialogue box or confirming an action.

C

Byte A unit of computer memory, made up of eight bits. It takes one byte of memory to store a single character, such as a letter of the alphabet.

C: The hard drive of a PC, where programs and documents are stored. In speech it is referred to as the "C drive."

Cable Broadband Internet access that is delivered via a cable television network.

Cache A section of high-speed memory that stores data recently used by the PC's processor, thereby increasing the speed at which that data can be accessed again.

CD-ROM Compact Disc Read Only Memory. A storage device, identical in appearance to a normal CD, containing up to 650 MB of data. Most software programs come on CD-ROM. CD-ROMs are usually inserted into and accessed from the "D drive" on the PC.

CD-R/CD-RW Compact Disc Recordable/Rewritable. CDs that can be written to in a special type of disc drive (sometimes called a "burner"). CD-Rs can only be written to once, CD-RWs can be rewritten many times over.

Cell A small rectangular section of a spreadsheet or database, into which text or figures are entered. Click on a cell to make it active, ready for entering or editing data.

Chip A device that processes information at the most basic level within a computer. A processor chip carries out calculations and a memory chip stores data.

Click To press and release the left mouse button once. Used to select menu and dialogue box options and toolbar buttons. See also *Right-click*.

Clip Art Graphic images that can be inserted into text-based documents from the Clip Art gallery and then resized and manipulated.

Clipboard When text is cut or copied from a document it is stored on the Clipboard. The Clipboard has a viewer option that enables you to store several items of cut or copied data. You can put the current Clipboard material back into as many documents as you like using the paste command. See *Copy*, *Cut* and *Paste*.

Close An option that shuts the active document, but not the program. A document can be closed by clicking the close button in its top right-hand corner, or through a File menu or the Office button.

CMOS Complementary Metal Oxide Semiconductor. A type of memory chip that stores the computer's configuration settings and the date and time. To protect its data, this memory is maintained by battery. See *Configuration*.

Compressed files Files that have been temporarily condensed so they use less memory and can be copied or downloaded in a fraction of the time it would take for the full-sized version.

Computer An option found in the Start menu of a PC running Windows Vista. Select it to access everything stored in the system on the hard drive and CD/DVD drive.

Configuration The settings used to ensure hardware or software runs as the user requires.

Control Panel Adjustments made to your system or its settings are made through the Control Panel. You can change the look of your Desktop, add new hardware or alter your PC's sound output via the Control Panel's functions.

Control Panel

Copy To make a duplicate of a file, folder, image or section of text.

CPU Central Processing Unit. The brain of your PC, which carries out millions of arithmetic and control functions every second.

Crash Your PC has crashed if it has stopped working, the screen has "frozen" and there is no response to keyboard or mouse commands. A crash usually requires you to restart the computer.

Cursor A marker, usually a flashing vertical line, that indicates where the next letter or digit typed in will appear in the document.

Cut To remove selected text and/or images to the Clipboard, where they are stored for later use.

D

D: The CD/DVD drive on a PC. In speech it is referred to as the "D drive." See *CD-ROM* and *DVD*.

Database A program used for storing, organizing and sorting information. Each entry is called a record and each category of information held in a record is called a field.

Default Settings and preferences automatically adopted by your PC for any program when none are specified by the user.

Defragmenter A program which "tidies" files on the hard disk. When a file is saved to the hard disk, Windows may split it up into fragments which are stored in different locations on the hard disk. This makes the retrieval of the file much slower. The "defrag" program solves this problem by regrouping all related data in the same place.

Delete To remove a file, folder, image or piece of text completely. If you accidentally delete something from a document you can undelete it using the Undo button on the Quick Access toolbar in Office 2007 programs or the Edit/Undo function in Windows Explorer or Works.

Desktop The screen displayed when Windows has finished starting up. Any icon onscreen, together with the Taskbar and Start button, are known collectively as the Desktop. See *Icon* and *Taskbar*.

Dialogue box A window that appears onscreen displaying a message from the program currently in use. This usually asks for preferences or information to be input by the user.

Dialogue box launcher A small arrow to the bottom right of a group on the Ribbon in Office 2007

programs that you click on to launch a dialogue box providing more options related to the group.

dialup connection The process of accessing another computer via a telephone line.

Digital Data that exists in binary number form as 0's and 1's. Computers process digital data.

Digital camera A camera that can store many high-quality digital images on a memory card, removing the need for film. Images can then be downloaded onto a computer and edited, e-mailed or printed.

Digital image An image stored in number format, that can be transferred to hard disks or removable storage disks, displayed onscreen or printed.

Disk cleanup A program that will find and remove unwanted files from your hard disk, freeing up memory.

Disk tools Programs that manage and maintain the hard disk, ensuring data is stored efficiently and that the hard disk runs at optimum speed.

Document A single piece of work created in a program. Also referred to as a file. See *File*.

Documents A folder option found in the Start menu. Each user has a Documents folder for their files.

Dots per inch (dpi) The number of dots that a printer can print on one square inch of paper. The more dots, the greater the detail and the better quality the printout.

Double-click To press and release the left mouse button twice in quick succession.

Download To copy a file or program from another computer to your own. For example, when you collect e-mail from an Internet Service Provider, you are downloading it.

Drag A mouse action used to highlight text, reshape objects or move an object or file. To move an object with the mouse pointer, for instance, click on it and, keeping the left mouse button held down, move the mouse pointer.

Drive A device that holds a disk. The drive has a motor that spins the disk, and a head that reads it – like the stylus on a record player.

Driver Software that translates instructions from Windows into a form that can be understood by a hardware device such as a printer.

DVD Digital Versatile Disc. A CD-like disc that can store 4.7GB or more of information – several times more data than a CD-ROM. Often used for storing film or video footage. Rewritable DVDs are also available.

E

E-mail Electronic mail. Messages sent from one computer to another through the Internet.

Error message A small window that appears onscreen warning the user that an error has occurred and, where appropriate, suggesting action to fix it.

Point size Measurement used to describe the size of fonts. For example, this page is in 9 point; newspaper headlines are usually between 36 and 72 point.

Port A socket at the rear of the system unit that allows users to connect a peripheral device to the PC.

Portrait See *Orientation*.

Printer driver A piece of software that helps Windows to communicate with the printer. See *Driver*.

Print Preview onscreen display that shows how the active document will look when printed. Accessed from the Office button in Office 2007 programs and the File menu in Works.

Processor The central processing unit (CPU) of a PC. See *Chip, CPU*.

Program A product that allows the user to interact with the computer's hardware to perform a specific type of task. For instance, a word processing program allows the user to direct the computer in all aspects of handling and presenting text. See *Application program*, *Software*.

Prompt A window that appears onscreen to remind users that additional information is required before an action can proceed.

Properties The attributes of a file or folder, such as its creation date and format.

R

RAM Random Access Memory. The memory used for the temporary storage of information on active documents and programs.

Record An individual entry in a database comprising several categories of information. For example, an address book database comprises "records," each with a name, address and telephone number.

Recycle Bin A Desktop feature that allows you to delete files. To rescue or "recycle" a file, drag it back out of the bin. To delete a file completely, right-click on it and select Empty Recycle Bin.

Resolution The degree of detail on a screen or a printed document. It is measured in dots per inch (dpi). The more dots per square inch, the greater the detail.

Ribbon A new toolbar-focused way of working in Office 2007 and later. Clicking on the tabs at the top of the Ribbon gives easy access to a number of associated tasks, collected into "groups."

Right-click To press and release the right mouse button once. Right-clicking often calls up a pop-up menu and is often a shortcut to various actions. See also *Click*.

ROM Read Only Memory. Memory chips used by the computer for storing basic details about the PC, such as *BIOS*.

Router Device that links a network of computers to a remote network, such as the Internet. See *Internet*.

S

Save To commit a document to the computer's hard drive. To do so, press the Ctrl + "S" keys, or click on the Save button on the Quick Access Toolbar in Office 2007.

Save As A way of saving a file under a different name or format. If the file was previously saved under a different name or format, that version will remain unchanged. This is useful for saving an edited file, while still keeping the original.

Scanner A device for converting images on paper into electronic images that can then be manipulated and reproduced by a PC. See *Digital, Digital image*.

Screensaver A picture that appears onscreen when the PC is left idle for a specified time. You can choose to use one of your own images as a screensaver.

Scroll To move through the contents of a window or menu, using the arrows on the scrollbars at the top and/or foot of the item.

Search A program that searches a PC for a file. Searches can be carried out on various information, such as the filename, author or the date on which it was last modified.

Search engines Huge databases on the World Wide Web that are used to locate information on the Internet. They can look for key words or phrases, or for categories, then subcategories.

Select To choose a file, folder, image, piece of text or any other item, by clicking on it or highlighting it, before manipulating it in some way.

For example, selecting some text before styling it.

Shareware Programs, or reduced versions of programs, that can be sampled for free for a limited period. Users must then purchase the program to continue to use it.

Shortcut An icon on the Desktop that links to a file, folder or program stored on the hard disk. It provides quicker access to the file, and features the icon of the linked item, with a small arrow in the bottom left-hand corner, and its name below.

Sidebar A new feature in Vista that allows you to put "gadgets" in a bar on the Desktop, such as a weather report or currency converter.

Software Programs that allow users to perform specific functions. Microsoft Excel and Microsoft Outlook are examples of software. See *Application program*, *Program*.

Software suite A collection of programs that come in a single package. For example, Microsoft Works is a software suite that includes word processing, database and spreadsheet programs.

Sound card A device that lets users record, play and edit sound files. Fits into an expansion slot within the system unit. See *Sound file*.

Sound file A file containing audio data. To hear the sound, double-click on the file (you will need speakers and a sound card).

Spreadsheet A document for storing and calculating numerical data. Spreadsheets are used mainly for financial planning and accounting.

Start button The button on the left of the Taskbar through which users can access the Start menu and its options, including programs.

Status bar A bar that appears in some program windows, giving users information about the document being worked on.

Styling Altering the appearance of the content of a file. For example, by making text bold (heavier-looking and more distinct) or italic (slanting to the right), or by changing its colour and size. See *Format*.

System software The software that operates the PC, managing its hardware and programs. Windows is the system software for PCs.

System unit The rectangular box-shaped part of the PC that contains the hard disk, the CPU, memory and sockets for connections to peripheral devices.

T

Tab A function used for setting and presetting the position of text.

Tab key A key on the keyboard used to tabulate text, to move between cells in spreadsheets, or to move from one database field to the next.

Taskbar A bar usually situated along the bottom of the screen in Windows that displays the Start button and buttons for all the programs and documents that are currently open. The Taskbar can be moved to other sides of the screen by clicking on it and dragging it to a new location.

Template A format for saving a document, the basic elements of which you regularly want to use. When you open a template, a copy of it appears for you to work on, while the template itself remains unaltered for further use.

Terabyte A unit of memory capacity. A single terabyte is 1000 (or 1024) gigabytes.

Tile To reduce in size a group of open windows and then arrange them so that they can all be seen onscreen at once.

Toolbar A bar or window containing clickable buttons used to issue commands or access functions. For example, spreadsheet programs have a toolbar that contains buttons that are clicked on to perform calculations or add decimal places. See *Taskbar*.

U

Undo A function in some programs that allows you to reverse tasks. Word, for example, also has a Redo option.

Uninstall To remove programs from the PC's hard disk. Software is available for uninstalling programs that do not have an included uninstall option.

Upgrade To improve the performance or specification of a PC by adding new hardware, such as a higher capacity disk drive, or software. See *Hardware, Software*.

URL Uniform Resource Locator. A standard style used for all Internet addresses on the World Wide Web. The first part of the URL, such as www.yahoo.com, indicates the location of a computer on the Internet. Anything that follows, such as /myhome/mypage.htm, gives a location of a particular file on that computer.

USB Universal Serial Bus. A hardware connector that allows users to plug a wide range of USB devices into a computer without having to restart. The latest range is referred to as USB 2.0. See *Hardware*.

Utilities Software that assists in certain computer functions, such as uninstalling and virus-scanning.

V

View A menu through which users can change the way a file is displayed onscreen. For example, in a Works database users can choose to see a document in List, Form or Form Design View.

Virus A program designed to damage a computer system. Viruses can be "caught" through portable storage devices or through programs downloaded from the Internet.

W

WiFi Popular name for IEEE 802.11b, a standard for wireless networks suitable for use in the home.

Window Each program or individual file on your PC can be viewed and worked on in its own self-contained area of screen called a Window. Each window has its own menu bar. Several windows can be open at once on the Desktop.

Windows The most popular operating system for PCs, which allows users to run many programs at once and open files onscreen. The latest version is Windows Vista. See *Operating system*.

Windows Explorer A program that allows users to view the contents of a PC in a single window.

Windows Live Messenger A Microsoft program that enables you to "chat" online, and share folders and files with others logged onto Live Messenger.

Wizard A tool that guides users step by step through processes such as installing software and adding new hardware.

WordArt A graphic text image that can be customized and imported into a document.

Word processing Text-based tasks on the PC, such as writing letters.

World Wide Web The part of the Internet, composed of millions of linked Web pages, that can be viewed using web browsing software. Internet functions like e-mail do not count as part of the World Wide Web. See *Internet*.

Z

Zip file A file that has been compressed with the WinZip compression program. ■

*(Numbers shown in **bold** type are for pages dedicated to the subject listed)*

▶

ACKNOWLEDGMENTS

We would like to thank the following individuals and organizations for their assistance in producing this book.

Photography: Steven Bartholomew, Steve Tanner, Karl Adamson, Tim Course.

Styling: Mary Wadsworth.

Picture agencies: **56** iStockphoto.com. **80** iStockphoto.com/Daniel Halvorson, **T**; iStockphoto.com/Dan Wilton, **B**. **98** Lucas Racasse/PhotoAlto Agency. **152-3** ImageState/Carl Yarbrough. **162** iStockphoto.com/Jason Stitt, **C**; iStockphoto.com/Gregg Cerenzio, **BL**; **164** iStockphoto.com/Jason Stitt, **R**; **165** iStockphoto.com/Gregg Cerenzio, **C**. **174** Corbis/Jim Erickson. **184-5** Getty Images Ltd/Frans Lanting. **194** www.sports-photos.co.uk/George Herringshaw, **BL**; Colorsport/Andrew Cowie, **BC**; www.sports-photos.co.uk/Nigel French, **BR**. **199** www.sports-photos.co.uk/Ed Lacey. **218** iStockphoto.com/Jaroslaw Wojcik. **221** iStockphoto.com/Jaroslaw Wojcik **222-3** Jupiter Images/ Michael Stuckey. **228-9** Getty Images Ltd. **229** Getty Images Ltd. **250-1** Getty Images Ltd/Mark Harwood. **276-7** Corbis/Al Francekevich. **306-7** Corbis/Gary D Landsman. **316-17** ImageState/Ethel Davies. **326-7** Getty Images Ltd/Lonny Kalfus. **364** iStockphoto.com/Duck Do

Equipment and Photographs Courtesy of:
Microsoft Corporation, Epson Corporation, Fujifilm, Dell Computer Corporation, Canon (UK) Ltd, D-Link Systems Inc., Apple Inc. Alcatel, Nokia, Carrera Technology Ltd, Logitech, Iomega, Yamaha Kemble Music Ltd, Bite, KYE Systems UK Ltd, PMC Electronics Ltd.

Software: Microsoft Corporation, Steinberg Media Technologies AG, Guildsoft Ltd, Focus.

Logos: Microsoft Corporation, Bell Canada, TELUS Corporation, Rogers Communications, Inc., AOL Canada, Inc., Vidéotron Ltée, Shaw Communications.

PROJECT STAFF

For Reader's Digest Canada

Consulting Editor Jesse Corbeil

Proofreaders John David Gravenor,
  Peter Deslauriers

Designers Andrée Payette, Cécile Germain

Photo Editor Rachel Irwin

Manager, Book Editorial Pamela Johnson

Production Manager Gordon Howlett

Production Coordinator Gillian Sylvain

**The Reader's Digest Association
(Canada) ULC**

**Vice President,
Book Editorial** Robert Goyette

UK Project team

Editors Caroline Boucher, Kerensa Leith

Art Editor Conorde Clarke

Technical Consultant Tony Rilett

Proofreader Barry Gage

Indexer Marie Lorimer

The Reader's Digest Association, Inc.

President and Chief Executive Officer
Mary Berner

HOW TO DO just about ANYTHING ON A COMPUTER
Microsoft® Windows® Vista™ Edition

Library and Archives Canada Cataloguing in Publication

How to do just about anything on a computer : hundreds of ways to get more out of your PC / the editors of Reader's Digest. -- 1st Canadian ed.

Includes index.

ISBN 978-0-88850-968-0 (bound). --ISBN 978-1-55475-005-4 (pbk.)

1. Microsoft Windows (Computer file). 2. Microsoft Office (Computer file). 3. Microsoft Works (Computer file). 4. Adobe Photoshop (Computer file). 5. Operating systems (Computers). I. Reader's Digest Association (Canada)

QA76.5.H69 2009   005.4'46   C2008-906395-3

We are committed to both the quality of our products and the service we provide to our customers. If you have any comments about the content of this book, please write to The Editor, The Reader's Digest Association (Canada) ULC, 1100 René-Lévesque Blvd. W., Montreal, QC H3B 5H5.
To order copies of this or any other Reader's Digest product, call 1-800-465-0780 or visit our website at **rd.ca**

Printed in China

09 10 11 12 / 5 4 3 2